THE PARIS

of

HENRY OF NAVARRE

THE PARIS
of
HENRY OF NAVARRE

as seen by Pierre de l'Estoile
Selections from his *Mémoires-Journaux*
translated and edited by
Nancy Lyman Roelker

HARVARD UNIVERSITY PRESS · CAMBRIDGE

1958

To the Memory of my Father
WILLIAM GREENE ROELKER
who gave me my love of Paris
and to those who fostered it
Members of the History Department
of Harvard University

PREFACE

This translation of the *Mémoires-Journaux* of Pierre de l'Estoile is based on the edition of Messieurs Brunet, Champollion, Halphen, Paul Lacroix, Charles Read, Tamizey de Larroque, Tricotel, published in twelve volumes, in Paris, 1875–1896.

The whole would not warrant publication, aside from its great bulk, due to repetitiousness and the indiscriminate nature of the entries, especially after 1600. A selection has therefore been made, with a view to presenting the rich tapestry of social history from May 1574 to January 1599. The greatest amount of space is given to the years of the League Rebellion, 1588–1594, which was the most important event of the period in France. L'Estoile's diary provides the fullest grass-roots account of this movement in its purely Parisian aspects, and has been used as a reliable source by scholars. It is to be hoped that these excerpts will whet the appetite of the reader and lead him to explore the period further.

Headings to certain entries in the text are Pierre's, as are all remarks in parentheses. Insertions in brackets required to make the meaning clear are my own. The standard procedure of triple dots is used to indicate omissions. The reader will understand that only a small proportion of the total number of entries is included, although no page references are made to the Brunet edition. This method is adopted to avoid clumsy scholarly apparatus. A reader desiring to find what is omitted in a given month can do so quite easily by comparing these excerpts with the Brunet edition.

In certain cases L'Estoile relates an event with an interpretation requiring hindsight; for example, he comments on the reconciliation of Henry III and Henry of Navarre in April 1589, that it was his enemies — of the League — who brought Henry IV triumphant to his throne, which did not take place until years later. Such entries were obviously written long after the event, probably after 1601 when L'Estoile sold his office of *audiencier* to devote full time to his reading, collections, and *Journaux*. They constitute, nevertheless, the *original* as far as posterity is concerned, for Messieurs Brunet *et al*. have reproduced the *Mémoires-Journaux* precisely as they are found in the various manuscripts described by them in volume XII, most of which are in the Bibliotheque Nationale in Paris.

Because of the complexity of the period of religious wars in France, a Chronological Outline of Events, and a Glossary of Terms, follow the text.

The list of friends who have helped generously in a variety of ways is much too long to itemize, but special gratitude is due to Mrs. Hermine Isaacs Popper and Mrs. Dorothea MacMillan Hanna for endless time and thought in working out problems of style and presentation and to Mr. Peter Wick of the Print Department of the Museum of Fine Arts, Boston and Mr. Philip Hofer of the Department of Graphic Arts at Harvard University for their interest, time, and generosity in permitting the reproduction of some of their treasures for the illustrations. I am deeply indebted to Radcliffe College for a generous grant from its Publications Fund. Without the help of Professor Myron P. Gilmore of Harvard, in countless ways above and beyond the call of duty, Pierre would still be without an audience, as he has been for four hundred years.

NANCY LYMAN ROELKER
Cambridge, Massachusetts
1958

CONTENTS

INTRODUCTION: THE BACKGROUND

The Drama of the Sixteenth Century 3
Summary of the League Rebellion 7
The *Mémoires-Journaux* 12
The Observer: Pierre de l'Estoile 14
Character and Philosophy of Life 20

THE YEARS LEADING TO THE LEAGUE REBELLION

(MAY 1574–MAY 1588)

1574 The Last Valois King 31
1575 Unpopularity of Italians 40
1576 Origin of the League 47
1577 Scandal of the Italian Players 56
1578 Feuds of the Valois 62
1579 Death of Bussy d'Amboise 69
1580 Civil War and Plague 73
1581 Wedding Pomp Increases Discord 78
1582 Funeral of an Homme de Bien 84
1583 Religious Excesses in Paris 91
1584 Death of Alençon 99
1585 Henry of Navarre Defies the Pope 107
1586 Strike at the Palais 118
1587 The Clerical Offensive 126
1588 Guise's Triumph and Henry III's Revenge 138

THE LEAGUE REBELLION IN PARIS

(MAY 1588–APRIL 1594)

1589 League Murders Henry III and Defies Henry IV 167
1590 The Great Siege of Paris 186
1591 L'Affaire Brisson 198
1592 The Crumbling of the League 216
1593 Conversion of Henry IV 224
1594 The Reduction of Paris 250

PARIS UNDER HENRY IV
(MAY 1594–JANUARY 1599)

1595 Jesuits and Huguenots 272
1596 Capitulation of Mayenne 278
1597 The Siege of Amiens 282
1598 End of the League and Peace with Spain 287
1599 The Edict of Nantes 295

APPENDIX

Chronological Outline of Events 301
Glossary of Terms 306

Index 313

ILLUSTRATIONS

End papers. MAP OF PARIS. Drawn by an anonymous Italian, published in Venice, 1567. Reproduced from A. Franklin, *Las Anciens Plans de Paris* (Paris, 1872)

Title page. COAT OF ARMS OF HENRY OF NAVARRE. Nicholas de Thou, Bishop of Chartres, *Ceremonies Observées au sacre et couronnement du Très-Chretien et Très-Valeureux Henri IIII, Roy de France et de Navarre* (Paris: I. Mettayer et P. L'Huillier, 1594)*

Following page 28. HENRY III, King of France and Poland. Portrait engraving by Thomas de Leu (Museum of Fine Arts, Boston)

CATHERINE DE MEDICI. Portrait engraving by Granthomme (Museum of Fine Arts, Boston)

BALLET CELEBRATING THE WEDDING OF THE DUKE OF JOYEUSE. Two of a series illustrating the ballet performed at the Louvre in 1581. Balthasar de Beaujoyeulx, *Ballet Comique de la Royne, fait aux nopces de M. le Duc de Joyeuse et Mademoiselle de Vaudemont, sa soeur* (Paris: A. Le Roy, R. Ballard, M. Patisson, 1582)*

HENRY, DUKE OF GUISE. Portrait engraving by Thomas de Leu (Museum of Fine Arts, Boston)

BARNABÉ BRISSON, Premier Président of the Parlement de Paris. Portrait engraving by Thomas de Leu (Museum of Fine Arts, Boston)

THE ASSASSINATION OF HENRY III. A cartoon of Jacques Clément, reproduced from François Courboin, *Histoire de la Gravure en France* (Paris, 1923)

Following page 156. PARIS: VUE DU LOUVRE by Jacques Callot, 1592–1635 (Museum of Fine Arts, Boston)

PARIS: LA TOUR DE NESLE by Jacques Callot (Museum of Fine Arts, Boston)

THE DUKE OF NEVERS RECEIVING A BOOK. Portrait engraving of Louis de Gonzague, Duke of Nevers, receiving a book. Christophe de Savigny, *Tableaux accomplis de tous les Arts Liberaux* (Paris: Jean et Francois de Gourmont, 1587)*

HENRY IV, King of France and Navarre. Portrait engraving by Thomas de Leu (Museum of Fine Arts, Boston)

* Reproduced from the collection of the Department of Printing and Graphic Arts, Harvard College Library, through the generosity of Mr. Philip Hofer.

INTRODUCTION:
THE BACKGROUND

INTRODUCTION:
THE BACKGROUND

THE DRAMA OF THE SIXTEENTH CENTURY

How many readers of John Keats have vicariously thrilled to his discovery of the "realms of gold" through Chapman's *Homer*? How many readers of history have wished that they might have seen some of the great moments of man's story, Socrates addressing the jury which condemned him, or Joan of Arc confounding the Inquisitors, or Washington rallying the ragged troops at Valley Forge? Letters, diaries, eyewitness accounts of such events are the priceless keys which open the doors of the historical imagination. With the aid of Pepys, for instance, the lover of history not only knows that Charles II was restored to the throne of England and Puritanism forced underground, he sees the wigs replace the shaved heads, the theatres flung open, the ravages of plague and fire; he hears the Puritans murmur that these scourges express God's wrath at the triumph of sin.

The *Mémoires-Journaux* * of Pierre de l'Estoile do for the Paris of Henry IV what Pepys does for the London of Charles II, and a great deal more, because L'Estoile was a serious student of politics and morals, and combined his acute observation with keen judgment of men and events. In his diary, which covers thirty-seven years, 1574–1611, the reader finds an eyewitness account of the wars of religion, the court of the Valois, and a full account of the reign of Henry IV, complete with an enormous cast of characters who take part in these events, their idosyncrasies, their clothes, their food, their jokes, diseases, and love affairs — so that the reader knows many of them more intimately than the family across the street. In effect, that family has ceased to be across the street, for the reader is living in the quarter of St. André-des-Arts on the left bank of the Seine opposite the Palais de Justice, and the Palais, seat of the Parlement de Paris, the highest court in France, has become the hub of the universe, as it was to the diarist, who earned his living as *audiencier*, or

---

* Based on the *Mémoires-Journaux de Pierre de L'Estoile, ed. Brunet, Champollion et al.* (Paris, 1875–1896). Translated and edited by the author.

3

clerk-in-chief of the Parlement. Seated with Pierre de l'Estoile in his *cabinet* the reader has a window on Paris; he sees too the events of the great world as they are seen at the Palais, where men are hotly disputing the merits of Mary Stuart's execution, or laughing at a sign which has been informally posted, "Lost! The Great Invincible Naval Army . . . [Armada] if anyone can give news of it . . . let him come to St. Peter's Palace where the Holy Father will give him wine."

The Reformation brought to every country where it reached major proportions a political and social upheaval marked by a series of crises so profound that the institutions of these countries were never the same again. During the first half of the sixteenth century many of the princes of north Germany, following the teachings of Martin Luther, established their states as virtually sovereign and independent of the Holy Roman Emperor, while Calvinism spread from Geneva — the Protestant Rome — to the Netherlands and France where it was embraced by important segments of the population ready to fight for it. In England, Henry VIII defied Rome and set up a national church under the crown, which was to become Protestant in doctrine under his son, Edward VI. Shortly after the middle of the century, Calvinism, under the leadership of John Knox, successfully challenged the crown and triumphed in Scotland, which, among other things, revolutionized the relationship of that country with England. Traditional enemies in the Middle Ages, the two British peoples became allies in the Protestant cause, though the alliance was fragile and often marked by friction.

The Roman church, belatedly awakened to the dimensions of the threat, launched a powerful counteroffensive about mid-century. The aim of this Catholic or Counter Reformation was to arrest the spread of heresy and reform the most flagrant abuses which had been the partial cause of the Protestant movement. Among the weapons in the Catholic arsenal were the newly formed Society of Jesus, a new spirit in the Papacy, and the military and financial power of Spain, then at its height under Philip II.

The events of the first half of the century made inevitable the life and death struggle of the second half, the so-called wars of religion, which were in reality civil wars in the full sense of the term, with political and dynastic issues as much at stake as those of theology and church organiza-

4

tion. The specific issues varied from country to country, as did the outcome. England avoided open civil war because of Queen Elizabeth's skill in satisfying desires in which most Englishmen were united, such as the desire for a national church, while compromising on issues on which they were seriously divided, such as the nature of that church. In the northern Netherlands, on the other hand, the issue of religion became entangled with the desire for national independence from Spain, a double cause which triumphed only after a generation of bitter fighting.

In no country were the religious wars more desperately fought than in France; in no country did they endure longer — nearly forty years — with more complicating factors involved; and in no country did they more clearly mark the end of one era and the beginning of another.

The religious issue in France was itself complicated by a situation unique in that country: the fact that, although France was a Catholic country, the church was a national institution which took very little leadership from Rome except in strictly doctrinal matters. The crown had long had a great measure of control over the clergy, and since the bargain between Francis I and Pope Leo X, known as the Concordat of Bologna (1516), the crown held the right of appointment to the key positions of the hierarchy and the great monastic establishments. This meant that the Counter Reformation, with its attempt to reassert papal power in general, and its relationship to Spain in particular, seemed to Frenchmen an ultramontane movement, that is foreign, beyond the Alps, which threatened the Gallican or national church. The result was that many Frenchmen, not in the least inclined to Protestant ideas, resisted the Counter Reformation while remaining loyal Catholics.

Calvinism at its height, about 1560, never constituted more than about one-fifth of the population among its adherents, but these included some of the great nobles, headed by the Bourbon branch of the royal family itself, and many of the newly prosperous middle class. Coincidentally, the dynastic situation was in a state of crisis: Henry II had died in 1559, leaving only very young children. His widow, Catherine de Medici, daughter of the great Florentine house, whose married life had been overshadowed by her husband's mistress Diane de Poitiers, suddenly found herself obliged to enlarge her role of *mère de famille* to include the government of a kingdom threatened from without and divided within. Her four sons, three of whom reigned in the next thirty years, were weak and un-

5

able to deal with this double challenge. During the very brief reign of the eldest, Francis II, 1559–1560, followed by the longer reigns of Charles IX, 1560–1574, and Henry III, 1574–1589, she was the real ruler of the kingdom most of the time, and was three times made Regent. The French crown was inevitably in a weakened position; an absolute monarchy cannot avoid challenge when the actual sovereign is unable to rule with a strong hand, for whatever reason. When we remember that France was surrounded by Hapsburg powers in Spain, Italy, the Germanies, and the Spanish Netherlands (Belgium) against which she had been fighting for over half a century, it becomes clear that she was faced with a considerable problem even before the outbreak of domestic troubles.

The civil wars began in 1562 as a result of the demands of the powerful Huguenot (Calvinist) party for concessions. Calvinists tended to be militant in demanding freedom of worship and the great nobles of the party had very effective military forces to back up their demands because of the large number of clients and feudal retainers who followed their lead. There were eight "wars," really one intermittent war punctuated by truces, between 1562 and 1585; in each of them the Huguenots won so many of the actual military encounters that the crown was forced to grant them increased concessions in each treaty. In the eyes of a Catholic people this did not strengthen the crown, nor satisfy their desire for heresy to be controlled if not exterminated.

It was this situation — the inability of the Valois to contain the Huguenots — which gave rise to an ultra-Catholic party under the leadership of the Guise-Lorraine family, whose alleged purpose was to rescue the country, and the crown, from heresy. Beyond that, the Guises hoped to take over the throne as "defenders of the faith" with the support of the majority of the people. Their reasons for thinking that they might succeed in this strategem were, first, there were at the moment no Valois heirs in the next generation — Henry III had no children and his younger brother, Francis, Duke d'Alençon, was unmarried and in frail health; and second, the next legitimate heir after the Valois was Henry of Navarre, chief of the Huguenot party.

The Lorrainers put out a number of pamphlets advancing their right to the throne on the grounds that they were descendants of Charlemagne (through his eldest grandson Lothair) while the Valois and the Bourbons were merely descendants of Hugh Capet who had usurped the throne from the Carolingians in 987!

The Guise party had begun to make plans in the late 1570's, after a treaty in which the Huguenots had gained the right to rule and fortify four key cities, but the movement did not assume definite form until after 1584, the year in which Francis Duke d'Alençon died, leaving Henry of Navarre heir apparent. They called their party the Holy League, *La Sainte Union*. It was the first rebellion to use methods we consider "modern" — an underground movement secretly organized by "cells" which accumulated arms and made preparation for "the day" when they would rise and take over the country by *coup d'état*. The leader of the League was Henry, Duke of Guise, son of the Duke who had figured so prominently in the earlier civil wars of the previous generation. Between 1585 and 1588 his agents and the fanatical Catholics were organizing their followers in all the cities of France, with Paris, naturally, their headquarters. During these years the weakness of Henry III, and particularly his misgovernment in financial matters, made the field fertile for recruitment to the League.

Faced by this challenge from the ultra-Catholics, now added to the Huguenot challenge, Catherine de Medici pursued the only possible course — that of playing them off against each other. She threw her weight to the weaker side when she dared to do so, or gave in to the dominant one when she did not. Catherine's preferred position, and that, events were to prove, of the majority of Frenchmen, would have been for France to remain Catholic in the traditional nationalist sense, a church virtually controlled by a strong crown. She was willing to pay the price for domestic peace and unity, namely to allow a certain degree of religious toleration to the Protestants. This position, known as *politique*, was eventually to triumph in the Edict of Nantes, 1598, but not until the nation had endured nearly forty years of civil war and seemed on the point of disintegration and domination by Spain.

SUMMARY OF THE LEAGUE REBELLION

The rebellion of the Holy League, led by Henry, Duke of Guise, his brothers, the Cardinal of Guise and the Duke of Mayenne, and his sister, the Duchess of Montpensier, lasted for almost six years, May 1588, to

March 1594, in Paris, the most fanatically Catholic of all French cities. Henry III, last of the Valois, was on the throne when it began. He was assassinated in its second year. Henry of Navarre of the House of Bourbon, a Huguenot, succeeded him as Henry IV, and it was he who finally brought the rebellion to an end. The peace of the kingdom was not finally restored and the Spaniards driven out until 1598, as it took four years to subdue the pockets of resistance remaining after the capitulation of Paris. The story is a real melodrama from the royalist point of view, with the "villains" having the upper hand up to the last minute, and it rises from lesser to greater climaxes before the denouement.

The first act consists of the spectacular uprising of the people of Paris on May 12, 1588, the Day of the Barricades, when the members of the League barricaded the streets of the sixteen quarters of the city with chains to prevent the movement of royal troops. The presence of these troops was indeed the immediate occasion for the long-desired movement to come into the open. The Parisian followers of the Duke of Guise had attempted several abortive uprisings in the past three years and were constantly importuning him to come to the capital and lead them. When it became known that Catherine de Medici had ordered several regiments, including Swiss mercenaries, into the city, everyone knew "the day" had come. So successful had been the preparations made, and so hesitant was the King to use the troops, that the League quickly got the upper hand. During the night of May 12 the King realized that he was faced with two unpleasant alternatives: to be taken prisoner in the Louvre, or to escape by the one gate still in royal hands. He chose the latter, and left with a handful of faithful followers in the early morning of Friday, May 13, cursing the city as he left, and vowing that he would re-enter it only by the breach. The victorious League took over the government of the city and reorganized the high court (Parlement) in the following weeks, and forced the King, who was at Chartres, to sign a humiliating treaty, the Edict of Union, July 1588, in which he signed away the substance of royal power to the Duke of Guise, although the latter's title was merely "Lieutenant-General of the Realm."

The choice of May 1588, as the occasion for the rebellion by the Duke of Guise — for he had planned it even before the royal movement of troops into the capital — was due to the fact that his chief supporter, Philip II, was about to send the Spanish Armada against England, thus cutting off Henry III from any possible assistance. Queen Elizabeth was the only source from which aid could come, as the Dutch were fighting for their own lives, Henry III lacked money to hire German mercenaries, and Philip controlled the rest of western Europe.

The second act curtain rises on a hopeful note for the King, virtually helpless in his own country, with the news that the Armada had been defeated (August 1588), and it was now Guise who was in an exposed position. Henry III, harboring a burning desire for revenge, but dissembling it, dismissed all his advisers and turned, for the first time in his life, away from his mother's tutelage. It was she who had chosen and trained the ministers and secretaries of state who were now discarded. He called the Estates-General, that old remedy of the French crown in time of trouble, into session at Blois in October, hoping to rally the nation's representatives to his banner and reverse the roles of the previous May. The delegates, however, especially those of the clergy and the third estate, were partisans of the Duke of Guise, and they showed themselves just as rebellious as the Parisians. The King then abandoned constitutional means and adopted a desperate course. On December 23 and 24 respectively, the Duke of Guise and his brother, the Cardinal, were assassinated in the royal chambers of the château at Blois at the King's orders. By this means Henry III hoped to confound their followers and become master in his own house.

But this act has a second scene. The Holy League was outraged and inflamed to a new pitch of enthusiasm by the murders, and instead of capitulating to the King the Parisians swore vengeance on the "tyrant." Under the leadership of the Duke of Mayenne they raised money and troops to fight the King, conducted a series of memorial services and religious processions in the Paris churches on a scale that had never been known, and launched a diplomatic offensive to enlist the aid of the cities and nobles of France, and also the support of the Papacy.

In a brief first scene of the third act, Henry III finally recognized Henry of Navarre as his true heir, and the two Henrys joined forces near Tours amid much rejoicing and emotion. Henry of Navarre's tears are described as "big as peas." Together they advanced to lay siege to Paris, heart and brain of the League.

In the chief scene of the third act, a Jacobin monk, Jacques Clément by name, one of the thousands of monks fanatically devoted to the League cause, procured admission to the royal camp at St. Cloud on the pretext of a message for Henry III from one of his partisans in the city, and took the opportunity to assassinate the King with a knife he had up his sleeve. The House of Valois had come to an end, and in the royal armies Henry of Bourbon was proclaimed Henry IV, King of France and Navarre.

The fourth act consists of a series of scenes which show that the extremists of the League, led by the Spanish agents, the clergy, and Madame de Montpensier, were more determined than ever to resist a heretic King. This faction is usually known as "the Sixteen," but actually consisted of a much larger, indeterminable number. Because they were in the pay of Philip II, the royalist writers also refer to these extremists as *éspagnolizés*, and sometimes as *zelés* because of their fanaticism. Owing to the continued dominance of this group in the capital, though many former *ligueurs* were cooling in their ardor, Paris withstood one of the worst sieges in history in the summer of 1590, with the *prédicteurs* (preachers of sermons) maintaining that it was better to kill and eat one's own children than to submit to a heretic king.

This same faction finally overreached itself in the autumn of 1591, when it attempted a purge of the more moderate elements by murdering three prominent citizens as *politiques*, royalists, including Barnabé Brisson, Premier President of the highest court in France. It was with some difficulty that the Duke of Mayenne restored order after this episode, and the extremists were never again willing to follow his lead, while his distrust of them was obvious. These divisions in the League between the more fanatical, Spanish wing and the Mayenniste, or French *ligueurs* had existed from the beginning, but as the years passed with no clear-cut Catholic candidate for the throne to substitute for Henry IV, and with the increasing economic hardship of Paris in striking contrast to the prosperity of the royalist suburbs, the friction came into the open, and the League was never able to heal its inner divisions and act as a unit again. The moderate or "French" League which followed the Duke melted away during 1592 and 1593, most of its adherents turning royalist. It was a situation where the middle course grew increasingly untenable, and the treasonable nature of the extreme wing made it repulsive to patriotic Frenchmen once it was seen in its true colors.

No one knew better how precarious was his leadership than the Duke of Mayenne himself. The final phase of the rebellion opens in January 1593 when he presided over a session of the Estates-General he had called to "elect" a Catholic King. It was obvious that as soon as Henry IV abjured Protestantism there would be no pretext left for the existence of the League. Every day delegations and letters from moderate *ligueurs* reached him begging for his conversion, and many prominent Catholic nobles and bourgeois and most of the bishops and archbishops had rallied to him in that expectation.

The Estates of Paris were, of course, illegal, since only a king had a right to convoke them, and they were a sorry and humiliating sight for Frenchmen. The nobility and higher clergy were conspicuous by their absence, and the scene was dominated by the Spanish envoys who tried to persuade the representatives to set aside the Salic Law and elect as sovereign the Infanta of Spain, daughter of Philip II and Elizabeth Valois, and therefore granddaughter of Henry II. This would have meant the total dismemberment of the kingdom, already so far on the way, and even the Estates of the League resisted it. They responded eagerly, on the other hand, to an invitation from the Catholic nobles associated with Henry IV, to attend a meeting to discuss the King's conversion. The Parlement de Paris, twice purged and supposedly *ligueur*, had the courage to denounce the Spanish proposals and declare that it was not in the power of the Estates — even had they been a legal assembly — to set aside the Salic Law, one of the "fundamental laws" of the realm. These fundamental laws, of which the Salic Law — preventing succession to the throne of a woman — is the best known, formed a sort of unwritten constitution for France under the *ancien régime*, and the Parlement was their guardian.

An important scene of the final act takes place in the cathedral of St. Denis, Sunday, July 25, 1593, when Henry IV, resplendent in a white satin costume and hat with his *panache blanc*, took what he himself described as *le saut perileux*, and attended Mass. The extraordinary vituperation with which the Paris preachers greeted the news merely showed that they knew the game was up and wished to prolong their rearguard action in order to damage the royal cause as much as possible.

In the final scene it is night in Paris in an unusually mild March, the streets are deceptively still. Men were not sleeping, however, they were waiting, some fearfully, knowing that the Duke of Mayenne had left the city some days before and that the royalists had been plotting to bring in the King, and wondering what their fate would be if this happened. Others were praying that Paris would "return to her obedience" quietly, that the long horror of civil war might end in reconciliation and unity. Just as the first light broke Henry IV entered the city by the very gate by which Henry III had fled. He was accompanied by his troops, which met only token resistance. Before the day was out the grateful city had thrown herself at his feet and he had issued a general amnesty, pardoning even those who had been most treasonable. He had sent the Spanish troops out of the city and allowed the most seditious Parisians to depart with them unmolested, so that they escaped the vengeance, not of the King, but of their fellow-Parisians who had waited six long years for a chance to strike back. The King himself sat in a window near the gate as the Spaniards left, and saluting their captains said, "Remember me to your master, but don't come back!"

So the curtain rings down on the traitors in flight, virtue triumphant, and a proud city reunited under a great king, about to begin a reign which set France on her future course as the leading nation of Europe culturally as well as in military and political power.

THE *MÉMOIRES-JOURNAUX*

From the point of view of political history the greatest value of Pierre de l'Estoile's diary lies in the first six volumes, covering the years 1574–1594. The *Journal de Henri III* is contained in the first three, 1574–1589. Volume IV contains L'Estoile's *recueils* or scrapbooks of brochures, proclamations, satirical verses, etc. for and against the League. This is a unique collection preserved by the diarist — many of the items with his comments in the margin — to point a moral to posterity: the horrors of rebellion. As these were all condemned to the flames when the monarchy was restored and there were severe penalties incurred if they were found in one's possession, their preservation was an act of considerable daring on L'Estoile's part.

The *Journal de Henri IV*, which begins with Volume V, takes up the story at the climactic point following the assassination of Henry III, when Henry IV became King but when he still had a long uphill fight to be recognized. Not until after his conversion in July 1593 did the League begin to crumble. The reduction of Paris, March 22, 1594, which begins

Volume VI, spelled the doom of the rebellion, although it was not until 1598 that the League finally collapsed and the Spaniards were driven out of France. Volumes VII through X contain much less about the League, however, as the movement was dead in Paris and L'Estoile is *témoin par excellence de Paris, ligueur, parlementaire et frondeur.** In these later volumes (VII–X) we find instead the concerns of the capital following the restoration of law and order, particularly the religious controversies over the Society of Jesus and the Huguenots, before and after the Edict of Nantes.

The final volume (XI) † relates the events following the assassination of Henry IV, and the reader is presented with a vivid picture of the regency of Marie de Medici and Concini, the personality of Louis XIII as a boy of eight, and the beginning of the new disintegration of the kingdom.

In addition to their political value, throughout the entire thirty-seven years the *Mémoires-Journaux* present a gold mine of social history — prices and crops, weather and natural phenomena, disease and the state of medicine, food, clothes, amusements, songs, jokes, personalities, and gossip — all the facets of Parisian life in the tumultuous century of the Renaissance, the Reformation, the Counter Reformation, and the Wars of Religion. With L'Estoile we live the life of the Paris bourgeois of the Parlement and through his eyes we see the greater actors and events of the times — William of Orange, Philip of Spain, Elizabeth, and Mary Stuart, the quarrels of the Popes with the Venetians, the fiasco of the Armada. The *Grand Guignol* of Paris always holds the center of the stage, but the greater drama of all Europe can be glimpsed beyond it.

This rich vein has long been drawn upon by students of sixteenth-century France, but two circumstances have kept it from being enjoyed by the public: the total lack of organization of the *Mémoires-Journaux*, with the most significant and the most trivial facts jumbled together throughout the eleven large volumes, and, for English-speaking readers,

---

* E. Lavisse (Ed.) *Histoire de France depuis les temps les plus récules* (Paris, 1900–1911) vol. VI, part 2, p. 453 (J. H. Mariéjol, the author of volume VI).

† Volume XII of the Brunet edition contains an alphabetical Index of proper names, a biographical and bibliographical commentary on L'Estoile, and Pierre's two short accounts of rebellions and events before 1574, which were not in diary form: *Mémoires de quelques princes et seigneurs hommageables à la couronne de France,* (619–1515) and *Mémoires pour servir à l'histoire de France depuis 1515 jusqu'en 1574.*

the lack of a translation. To fill this gap the present selection has been made, with the intention of bringing to the reader as directly as possible the Paris of Henry IV through the medium of an acute firsthand witness — Pierre de l'Estoile.

THE OBSERVER: PIERRE DE L'ESTOILE

Under the *ancien régime* in France the officers of the crown, especially those attached to the Parlements,* or high courts of each region, constituted a group which exerted great influence in every aspect of French life. Essentially successful *bourgeois*, they had been in a position to purchase their offices, thus relieving the perpetual financial necessity of the crown. Many had become ennobled by the same process, and were called the *noblesse de la robe*, or *de la robe longue*, to distinguish them from the feudal *noblesse de l'épée* or *de la robe courte*. In the late medieval and early modern period this class produced many individuals of ability who also served their king in divers other political capacities, such as Chancellor and Treasurer, and, with the notable exception of military affairs, gave more leadership to the country than the ancient nobility. In the cities they occupied the top of the social pyramid, although they ranked below the landed aristocracy of the region in which the city was located.

The L'Estoiles were well-known *gens de la robe* in Orléans throughout the fifteenth century, the most prominent being Regnault de l'Estoile, who became Lieutenant-Général du Gouvernement du Duché d'Orléans in 1460. Pierre's father, grandfather, and great-grandfather were all présidents in the Parlement de Paris. His grandfather, Pierre Tronson de l'Estoile, was a noted professor of law in his young manhood — later he joined the clergy — and included both John Calvin and Theodore Beza among his pupils. He was the author of several legal textbooks which continued in use in subsequent generations. His son Louis, father of the diarist, included among his titles Conseiller du Roi, Président au Cour des Aides, and Grand Rapporteur et Correcteur des Comptes de la Chancellerie de France.

Pierre's mother was Marguerite de Monthelon, daughter of François de Monthelon, Avocat au Parlement de Paris and Garde des Sceaux de

---

* If the reader is unfamiliar with the Parlements, he is advised to read the brief comment in attached glossary of terms, Appendix II.

la France. The Monthelons ranked high in the hierarchy, and a second François, Pierre de l'Estoile's uncle, was made Garde des Sceaux by Henry III in 1588 when he reorganized his council in the middle of the League rebellion. Through the Monthelons Pierre was connected with some of the leading Parlement families, the Chartiers, the Séguiers, and the de Thous. Marguerite's third husband was one of the Molés, the fourth one of the Cottons; with each new alliance she involved her eldest son more deeply with the most distinguished *gens du roi*. Pierre's four sisters who lived to maturity also married into the circle of the royal courts. The importance of this background cannot be over-emphasized if one wishes to understand the point of view of the diarist: throughout the *Mémoires-Journaux* it is the members of the parliamentary group who are described as *gens de bien*, Pierre's highest praise. Conversely his contempt is greatest for men of this group who betray that tradition by corruption, frivolity, and above all disloyalty.

Although the monarchy is sacred to L'Estoile, it is the crown with its appendages, the "fundamental laws" and especially the courts, and not the person of the king, which constitute its essence in his eyes. The defiance of Henry III by the Paris League is regrettable and unsuitable, but its attacks on the Parlement are outrageous and intolerable, in his opinion. Perhaps the greatest interest of the *Mémoires-Journaux* lies in the extent to which L'Estoile is the spokesman of the parliamentary bourgeoisie, a class which remained of prime importance in French history down to the revolution.

After Louis de l'Estoile, Pierre's father, had attained the pinnacle of success in the legal world and become Président in the Parlement de Paris, he moved to Paris, and there, probably in 1546, at what is now no. 10 rue de Tournon, Pierre was born. His early schooling to the age of twelve took place in Orléans with his cousins, under the tutelage of Matthieu Béroalde, a noted teacher of Hebrew, later a Protestant minister in Geneva. Agrippa d'Aubigné was one of his fellow-students and we learn from him that the connection of Béroalde with the L'Estoile family continued in later years, when they helped him to flee to Geneva from the persecutions of the League. Pierre pursued his studies further in Paris, and finished them with a year (1565) of special legal training in Bourges under the Scottish Alexander Arbuthnot. He returned to Paris the following year at the age of twenty, and as far as is known left the

15

city only once again — for a business trip to one of his country properties — before his death at the age of sixty-six.

Pierre de l'Estoile followed the established pattern on both sides of the family by entering the royal service. In 1569 he purchased the charge of Audiencier de la Chancellerie de Paris, a desk job of some importance in the record department of the royal courts, which brought with it the titles Conseiller du Roi, Notaire, and Secrétaire du Roi. He also carried on family tradition by marrying Anne de Baillon, the daughter of the Baron de Bruyères-le-Châtel, Trésorier de l'Épargne. She died in 1580, having borne him seven children, four of whom lived to maturity. In 1582 he married Colombe Marteau of the Gland family, members of the same judicial circle, who bore him ten more children and died giving birth to the tenth. Most of this set of offspring survived and as a result L'Estoile had the considerable burden of a large number of dependents down to his last years.

Six of his daughters lived to marry into the parliamentary circle. All their husbands were lawyers accredited to the Parlement de Paris, some became présidents. His daughter Anne married a Poussemothe, and their children took the name of L'Estoile at their grandfather's request, thus inheriting his library and the *Mémoires-Journaux*. Marie married into the Langlois family; one of her descendants was Maître d'Hôtel to Louis XIV. Françoise, who married into the La Motte family, had descendants who appear on the roster of the Parlement down to the revolution.

Four sons lived to manhood, but none really followed the family tradition. François became secretary to the Cardinal of Lyons, Alphonse du Plessis de Richelieu, brother of Louis XIII's minister; Pierre became a mediocre poet and client of the noble family of Montpensier; Matthieu became a monk; while little Claude, whose career as a page to the Duchess of Montpensier was terminated by his disfigurement in a fire, became one of the original members of the French Academy. As author of several plays, he was employed by Richelieu to make a critique of the *Cid*. In the later years of the *Mémoires-Journaux* there is considerable cynicism about offspring, and one feels that the failure of his sons to embrace a career in the royal courts may be its partial cause.

Most of these biographical details were obtained by the editors of the *Mémoires-Journaux* from public records. From Pierre de l'Estoile one would learn almost nothing of his family affairs until the final years of his life. Until then, as M. Brunet says, *il se met si peu en scène que l'on ignore presque totalement le rôle qu'il dût jouer*. The reason for this is that he did not think personal and family affairs important. What mattered was the rebellion of the Holy League against the French monarchy; no detail of that long and complex chain of events was too insignificant to be recorded, to point a moral to posterity. The sensational insurrections, murders, sieges, and other episodes of this drama L'Estoile regards as the main events in his life as they were of the capital. The majority of the parliamentary group remained royalist in spite of some adherents to the League who were resentful of the financial policies of Henry III and thus easy prey for the propaganda of the League. Pierre de l'Estoile's account is, in fact, the prime source of our knowledge of the grass-roots Parisian aspects of this story and the classic statement of the point of view known as *politique*. The essence of this position was that its adherents placed the unity of France and the power and independence of the crown above the Catholic cause, especially in the ultramontane form espoused by the Counter Reformation in general and the League in particular.

A very few entries in the *Journaux* reveal the impact in L'Estoile's personal life of the public affairs so thoroughly covered. In 1585 when Henry of Navarre and the Prince of Condé, Calvinist princes of the blood and next in line to the throne, were excommunicated by Pope Sixtus V and declared ineligible for the throne, a document in reply, bearing their signatures, circulated in Paris. This forceful statement repudiates the notion that the Papacy, or indeed any outside power whatever, has any right to interfere with the succession to the French crown. It is couched in strong nationalist, Gallican language. L'Estoile claims to be the author of this "reply" but gives no evidence of having been commissioned to write it. The internal evidence of the *Journal* would indicate that he did it on his own initiative as a spontaneous expression of his indignation.

In spite of his reluctance to play an open part in the controversy, or even to commit himself in the privacy of his diary, L'Estoile's royalist sentiments became known. He was one of the first to be taxed by the League in December 1588 when the Paris *politiques* were placed in jeopardy by the mutinous city seeking revenge for the murder of the Duke and Cardinal of Guise by Henry III.

In 1589 he incurred a considerable risk by copying and circulating royalist writings against the League, including satirical verses of Lieutenant-Civil Rapin — later co-author of the *Satyre Menipée* — who was a prisoner of the League. This must have increased the number of his enemies, for L'Estoile was one of three hundred *bourgeois* arrested on July 29, 1589, when the armies of Henry III and Henry of Navarre were at the gates and the League leaders — the Sixteen — feared treachery. He was held in the Conciergerie until August 7 and then released as the murder of the King "seemed to deprive the arrests of their alleged purpose."

From 1591 on Paris was dominated by the Sixteen under the general direction of the Spaniards and the clergy, and the *politiques* were in a position of acute danger. In November of that year L'Estoile was shown a list of known royalist sympathizers, each name marked with "p," "d," or "c," for *pendu, dagué, chassé*. L'Estoile's name appeared with a "d" on this *liste rouge*.

It must be remembered that while he was looked upon as an enemy by the League in Paris, in the camp of active royalists who were with the King, L'Estoile was suspected of being *ligueur* because of his continued residence in Paris when most royalists had fled, and even more because he continued to exercise his office under League domination although an alternate *chancellerie* with loyal personnel had been set up in Tours. Evidence of this embarrassing predicament is L'Estoile's necessity to do business in royalist St. Denis, in 1592, under an assumed name.

It is interesting to speculate on his submission to this situation, on the fact that he does not seem ever to have considered leaving Paris even under the worst excesses of the League. The scorn of fellow-royalists and the knowledge that they did not trust him must have been hard to bear. Perhaps he held the view later expressed by Henry IV: ". . . those of Tours looked after their own interests, those of Paris looked after mine." If L'Estoile thought this proposition through, however, no inkling of it occurs in his diary.

His continued residence in the capital is perhaps more simply explained by his opinion that to live was to live in Paris. To be exiled from the city was, to this wholehearted bourgeois, a fate worse than death. During the extreme hardship of the siege of 1590 he sent his mother, various children, and his pregnant wife (who was captured and held for ransom by the Spaniards) to the country, but managed to last out himself though he was at the end of his supply of food the day before the siege was lifted.

Most of his life L'Estoile lived in the quarter of St. André des Arts, at the corner of the rues Séguier and St. André, in the Hôtel de St. Clair, which had been the property of his father. In 1595 he bought a house on the rue de l'Hôtel de St. Denis, on a site now occupied by 25 rue des Grands Augustins. It was not for lack of other property that he stayed in Paris. He had inherited from his father two small holdings outside Orléans, the Seigneuries of Soullers and La Cour du Bois. By the death of his brother-in-law, who had no direct heirs, he acquired also the Seigneurie of Gland. It was to inspect the latter property that he made his single trip to the country in 1606.

The years after the end of the rebellion were increasingly hard for L'Estoile. He sold his office in 1601, intending to spend all his time on his library, collection of coins, and his diary, but the ten years remaining to him were full of painful illness, financial worry, irritating litigation, and disillusionment in family, friends, and even books.

Of the physical illness (probably cancer) the editors say merely that it was incurable, very painful, and that it manifested itself in occasional hemorrhages. From the *Journal de Henry IV* one learns further that it was an abdominal condition which went in cycles, so that at times he felt quite well and resumed his old habits of walking about the city, while at others he was confined to bed. We know also that he was completely cynical about the medical profession and never willingly consulted a physician. He found the mental depression which accompanied the disease the hardest thing to bear, and twice prepared for death, but recovered, regretfully.

His affairs were a source of great worry and irritation. Nicholas Martin, to whom he had sold his office, refused to pay what he had promised and L'Estoile sued him over a period of ten years. He felt himself cheated of revenues both in Orléans and at Gland; he was sued by five former associates and relatives; and the one man who owed him a substantial amount of money died while litigation was in process and the court favored his heirs. In the last two years of his life L'Estoile had to sell off parts of his precious collections to meet the burden of supporting his children in what he deemed an appropriate style. He wished to leave the children well established and was quick to resent indifference or lack of appreciation on their part. He ended by feeling that children are an affliction and a source of unhappiness.

His pleasure in his friends was affected by various unfortunate experiences, such as the "theft" of a valuable coin by a crony with whom he was accustomed to share his treasures. On this occasion he cries with Aristotle and Montaigne, "O my friends, there are no friends!"

Many accidents befell L'Estoile while he was struggling with these problems. Three times the ceiling of his study fell and he barely escaped injury; once was during a storm when the rain poured in and ruined some choice manuscripts. Twice there were serious fires in the house, and as a result of one little Claude, his "youngest and prettiest child," was disfigured for life. His eldest son died in battle, having almost broken his father's heart by joining the League, although he changed his allegiance just before his death.

Saddest of all to the sympathetic reader who has followed him every day for thirty-seven years is the disillusion with his books and hobbies. He came to regard them as "vanities," a waste of time, and resolved to read nothing but the Bible the rest of his life. It is this deeply religious cast of mind which enabled Pierre to bear his burdens and which turned near defeat into spiritual victory. His reiterated conviction that all things serve God's just purposes is the key to his life. He rounded out his days October 11, 1611, *craignant Dieu* like all those whom he most admired.

CHARACTER AND PHILOSOPHY OF LIFE

The chief impression of the personality of its author given by the *Journal de Henri III* (1574–1589) is of extreme prudence and caution. L'Estoile is slow to make up his mind and loath to commit himself. On most subjects he exhibits a great degree of objectivity and is shrewd at detecting ulterior motives and unmasking them.

In the quarrels of Henry III with the *bourgeoisie* of Paris L'Estoile shows sympathy for the King's predicament as well as disapproval of his tactics; he criticizes the attempts of subjects to defy their sovereign while respecting their desire to protect their rights. When he does make up his mind about the distribution of blame in the complex situation he defends his position carefully and intelligently. His unwillingness to blame the Huguenots for all the ills of France does not spare them his recognition that they are using the position of Henry of Navarre to advance their power, nor does his aversion to the ambition of the Guises prevent them from getting their due. When the Parisians gave all the credit for the victory of Auneau to the Duke of Guise, to the disparagement of the King, L'Estoile admits, "to tell the truth he deserved most of the glory." In spite of his deep attachment to Henry IV — the King's assassination caused him greater pain than all his personal ills — L'Estoile is aware of his defects, such as his extravagance, self-indulgence, and his tendency to lose in time of prosperity the stature gained in adversity.

In nothing is this objectivity more marked than in his religious views. His determination to remain Catholic never led him to condone the abuses of the church, and his Protestant leanings never took him to the point of considering the new church really reformed, witness his most cherished project, "to render the Catholic [Church] reformed, and the reformed [church] catholic." This fairness breaks down only as between the *larrons* [scoundrels] of the Paris League and the *gens de bien* of the Parlement.

A corollary trait is his respect for sound learning as opposed to superficial brilliance and for accurate information as opposed to hearsay, gossip, and popular misconceptions. He takes pains to check the sources of reports of matters at a distance which he cannot verify himself. In reporting an interview of Henry IV with Theodore Beza in Geneva he quotes from an eyewitness. His interpretation of Essex's trial is based on a letter from the Duke of Rohan in London to a friend who loaned it to L'Estoile so that he might copy it exactly.

He makes a point of ascertaining the facts for himself and scorns those who pretend to know what they cannot have witnessed. When it is not possible for him to be sure, his accounts are introduced by phrases like *suivant le bruit, on dit,* or *on croit que,* in the manner of Herodotus. It is because of this accuracy and objectivity that historians of the period have placed such reliance on the *Mémoires-Journaux*. The historian of Paris Paul Robiquet, in his *Paris et la Ligue sous Henri III*, says, "In comparing the Registers of the city with the *Mémoires-Journaux* it is impossible not to be struck by the perfect exactitude of the chronicler. Almost never is he found to differ with the original documents which constitute the true basis of our work." * The two multivolume collective histories of France in which each section is written by a specialist of the period, draw heavily on L'Estoile for the late sixteenth and early seventeenth centuries.

* Paul Robiquet, *Paris et la Ligue sous Henri III* (Paris, 1886), p. 300.

L'Estoile was humble about his own learning as compared to that of men like Cujas, Pithou, Scaliger, who knew Greek, although it is doubtful if many men of the age were better read than the diarist, especially on political and religious affairs. Much of the material of the *Journaux* is the result of what he himself calls his "curiosity." This must surely have seemed the dominant trait of his character to many who knew him. Not content with his collection of broadsides and other material concerning the League, he sold his office in 1601 for the express purpose of enlarging his collection of coins, pictures, and miscellaneous objects, and of entering into correspondence with men in England, Switzerland, Germany, and even the Ottoman Empire. His collections became a mild mania and he took delight in recording the price of each item as well as the details of its acquisition. In 1607 his *pacquets* (scrapbooks) numbered 1,200, his valuable coins over 200.

He shows the collector's pride in exhibiting his treasures and reports with pleasure when prominent visitors are brought to see him. In the first three months of 1607 he comments on the visits of four Germans, two fellow-collectors from Rouen, the British ambassador, and a Greek traveler with whom he had a most interesting discussion of the Greek Orthodox Church as compared to the western churches.

It is evident that in his last years L'Estoile had become a "curiosity" himself and men went out of their way to see him much as he went out of his way to see a child without arms or the site of an alleged miracle. In spite of illness and disillusion he crossed Paris a few months before his death to interview a man who had been attacked in the streets because there were rumors of a new St. Bartholomew.

In spite of his habit of talking to strangers and his interest in everyone's business, the *Mémoires-Journaux* give the impression that Pierre de l'Estoile had no intimates as a young man, and very few — those who share his religious interests — in his old age. He seemed quite solitary and detached from other people, including his family. In the early years the persons mentioned figure in public events almost exclusively. It is hard to document the impression that he was a man of brusque, rather ungracious manner, even truculent. One gets it from the sharp, caustic retorts he quotes himself as giving and in the type of humor with which he tells his story. Yet underneath he had a warm heart, which suffered keenly at injustice. He admitted that he was easily moved to tears. He gave to the poor even at considerable sacrifice, sharing his short supply of food with beggars at the door during the siege, and supporting a blind Huguenot whom he respected even when he was obliged to sell his prize books to pay his creditors. It seems probable that he was one of those persons whose virtues are less conspicuous than their faults, and that only in his diary can one see the more appealing side of his nature.

In spite of the bitterness and loneliness of his old age his perceptions remained clear and keen to the end. The account which he gives of the first months of Louis XIII's reign compares in shrewdness with that of the League thirty years earlier. He was able to write in his *Journal* up to a week before his death and the last pages show a vigorous critical mind. In general his judgment of important men and issues is that of posterity. Not only has his interpretation of the League rebellion been adopted by modern scholars, and his advocacy of religious toleration shared by most civilized peoples, but twentieth-century critics admire his heroes: the parliamentary *gens de bien* as typified by Achille de Harlay, Président of the Parlement de Paris, the political leaders like L'Hôpital and Henry IV, the philosopher Montaigne.

Throughout the *Mémoires-Journaux* one is very conscious that man is but a creature, although he is often deluded into thinking that he is the master of his own fate. Often L'Estoile pictures the Deity as deliberately allowing men to build up great schemes in order to show them how great is their sin and how complete their dependence on His will. This belief was a source of much satisfaction to L'Estoile and it grew with his advancing years. His curious, active mind required an explanation of life which would give it meaning when there appeared to be none, and especially one which would explain away the apparent triumph of evil. A skeptic about human goodness, his faith in God's perfection and justice made life intelligible and therefore endurable. The people of Paris were punished for the sin of disobedience to the king by the abuses of the League, Philip II's presumption was chastised by the defeat of the Armada. So great and unfitting a catastrophe as the assassination of a king of France by a "little monk, depraved" could only be explained by God's great and mysterious justice, taking a striking form so that the lesson could not be missed, even by those who did not wish to learn. There were some instances of God's hand in history which brought joy instead of sorrow, notably the role of Spain, the church, and the League in bringing

23

Henry IV to his rightful throne, though their intention was quite the contrary. The more wicked their actions the more certainly did they doom themselves. The end was the triumph of the Bourbon cause: Henry IV was "borne on their shoulders," "unsuspected of men."

The sudden fall of those who had been high and the ruin of ambitious schemes were evidence that "God disposes." The spectacle of the League princess Madame de Montpensier, jostled and ignored by the Paris crowds only a few months after she had been idolized, was a sight he stood long on a street corner to watch, "thus the vanity of this world, which God turns over and over as it pleases him."

It was not only the great events which showed God's concern with the world. Never was a man more prone to seeing "sermons in stones" than Pierre de l'Estoile; the falling of a bridge, crime, depravity, monstrous birth, even unseasonable weather were all seen as God's warnings to sinful men. Because they were ignored the greatest calamity of all fell upon France in the death of her good King (Henry IV), "the best in five hundred years." Without understanding this teleological and moralistic interpretation of life there would seem to be very little sense to the hodgepodge of the later volumes of the diary; the proportion of space given to lurid trials, the deathbed remarks of strangers, the sheaves of pamphlets on unrelated subjects — above all the hours spent going to see a house struck by lightning or a man accused of incest — these would seem ridiculous, the interests of a crank, if one overlooked the desperate search for meaning which impelled him to them.

The emphasis on death is an interesting feature of L'Estoile's mind. He was not a humanist. Man's task in this world was to prepare for the next. Although he never states in so many words that a man should not be judged until he has died, it is his practice to suspend judgment until he hears how that man has met death. When it is rumored that someone has met it badly he will take trouble to investigate, for if it is not true it would be wrong to register such a misfortune. If a man who had been vain and sinful died repenting, he rejoiced and made amends for any disparaging remarks he might previously have made. Gondi, worldly Bishop of Paris, Nemoux, one of the leaders of the Guise family, died nobly after evil lives, and a corrupt member of Parlement, for instance ". . . had vices, as we all have, which obscured his virtues, which God gave him grace to repent as he died . . . so he must be considered very happy, his sins being covered by the mercy of God."

If, on the other hand, a bad man met a bad end that clinched the matter; God had marked him as wicked by withholding the grace of repentance. Jodelle, "the vilest poet of our time . . . died as he lived, without God, thus proving the old proverb, *telle vie, telle fin.*" As an instance of God's favor, Henry IV, the night before his assassination,

. . . was seen on his knees praying to God all night, and when he got up withdrew again into his cabinet, and, staying much longer than usual, was interrupted, which annoyed him, and he said, "Will people still prevent my welfare?" A particular sign of the grace of God who seems to have warned him of his near end, a thing which comes only to those whom our Lord loves.

It was fitting and right that Henry IV should desert his jokes for prayer the day of his death, and that many of the St. Bartholomew murderers and League leaders should suffer hideous deaths. It bore out L'Estoile's conviction that there was a purpose in all things.

Like his King, the diarist knew his own end to be approaching in 1611, and having made the final preparations once in vain, spent the last six months of his life trying to maintain steadily the frame of mind which would assure him a place among the *gens de bien.*

Because the *Journaux* contain so much criticism of various religious orders and practices, and their author was so constantly concerned with theological controversy, the reader should not turn from Pierre de l'Estoile to his observations without some knowledge of the observer's personal religion. We know from discussions reported that his fairness to the Huguenots and his criticism of the "errors" of the Roman church caused him to be suspected of heresy on many occasions, and indeed he says in true Protestant style, "I confine myself simply to the words of Jesus Christ, which are of themselves so clear and intelligible, and admit no figure of speech. I reject all interpretations or glosses which spoil the text or are contrary, however subtle they may be."

About a year before his death, when he was very ill, he sent for a Jacobin whose funeral sermon for Henry IV he had admired, to hear his confession and administer the last rites. The priest comforted him, told him to confess his sins, ask God's pardon, and declare that he was dying in the Roman, Catholic, and Apostolic faith.*

On the first two points there was no difficulty, but as to the last on which he insisted and pressed me hard (saying that for salvation it was necessary to believe all that the church believed and that it could not err), I couldn't accord him such a statement, seeing that the contrary is true in many cases. But finally, beaten by feebleness of mind and body, which wouldn't let me argue further, I let it go on condition that he would prove to me that the doctrine and tradition of the Roman church of today conformed in every way to that of the primitive church . . . of St. Paul, who preached only Christ crucified, and saw no other foundation of salvation than that . . . in which faith I had always lived and wished to die, which he promised to do if God gave me a new lease on life but I doubt very much if he can do it, able man though he be.

In this same conversation, on what he believed to be his deathbed, L'Estoile set forth his rejection of what he considered the worst errors of the Catholic church: first, the reliance on saints as intermediaries for one's spiritual welfare.

I remember saying of the invocation of saints . . . that I recognized only one master and mediator, Jesus Christ, my Saviour . . . on which he didn't insist too much when I said that I realized the invocation of saints, and even of the dead, was a long established custom of the church, and that I would be glad to be enlightened by a learned man like him . . . not being able to make it agree with Holy Scripture where nothing is said of it, which made it difficult for me to believe.

The second serious error lay in the extravagant claims of the Papacy. According to Bellarmine, "it was to be seriously believed not only that the Pope could not err as Pope, but even that he could not err as an individual person . . . which . . . [I find] absurd as well as heretical."

Opposed to the saints, critical of the Papacy, convinced that the church can and does err, it is no wonder that L'Estoile was suspected of heresy and had to defend himself more than once. He resented very much that such subordinate issues should be taken for the substance of Christianity, and that a desire to reform abuses should be condemned instead of encouraged. Indeed he claims that the primitive church was the only true

* Pierre's account of his personal faith and the conversation with the Jacobin is to be found in *Mémoires-Journaux*, XI, 9-15.

church—the contention of all reformers. He was particularly annoyed that this good Jacobin should go around saying

. . . that I hold heretical opinions . . . which I never have, except on points where it differs from the word of God, which I will always prefer to all mandates and traditions of Popes or other men. . . . I hold it as indubitable truth that the church should never recognize anything contrary to Scripture, for if the same spirit presides over writings and tradition [the church] will not be contrary to itself. In conclusion, I am a child of the Roman church . . . but I do not ignore how much it has degenerated from the primitive . . . I cannot advocate error, as God forbids it. I will always embrace reform with a glad heart but will never consent to her dissipation (even if she be a harlot as the Huguenots say), she is my Mother. . . . Meanwhile I pray God for her improvement but will not leave or go out to join the other, in which I see as many faults . . . as in this one, and think that if it had lasted only half as long it would better be called Deformed than Reformed. . . . Three things prevent the union [of the two], lack of charity, too little zeal for the glory of God, and stubbornness, last stronghold of the ignorant. I will hold to this old trunk of the Papacy therefore, even though mutilated. . . . One may find salvation in the Roman church corrupt as she is . . . here I stop . . . for if I had thought otherwise I would have left . . . for nothing would have made me leave . . . if not the superstitious and idolatrous ceremonies of the League. Now . . . I am resolved to live and die in it, following the teaching of my late father (*homme de bien* and *craignant Dieu*) who, knowing the abuses, supported reform and didn't find it necessary to go out of the church.

His father's last words to Pierre had been to stay in the church while resisting its abuses and superstitions. "This last will of so good a father has always been engrained on my heart and soul . . . praying to God to give me grace to live and die as well as he, in the faith of Christ crucified, his only hope, and mine too, which I desire to pass on to my children."

In the last analysis L'Estoile's religion is faith in God, belief in Christ's message, and fear, meaning respect and abstinence from presumption. All man's science is ignorance, the love of God is his all. To a man who was a skeptic in worldly matters, this conclusion was the ultimate result of all speculation, political, philosophical, or religious.

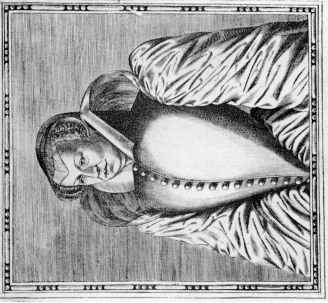

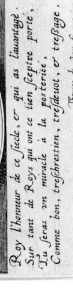

HENRY III

CATHERINE DE MEDICI

BALLET CELEBRATING THE WEDDING OF THE DUKE OF JOYEUSE

Barnabæ Briſſonii
in ſenatu Pariſienſi præſidis
Icon

Quid mirum, ſi cælex Briſſonem turba trucidat?
Non potuit iuris gloria, iure mori.

N. Rabel. in c. p.

Thomas de leu fecit.

BARNABÉ BRISSON, PREMIER PRÉSIDENT

HENRY · DVC · DE · GVISE

Engeance de l'Hercule, et des Horreurs Nataux,
Mort qui te fais pleurer d'un Infiny d'humains:
Que riront fer ce Prince; Helas ſes beaux deſſeins,
Ne pouuoient fleſchir tes violentez Fatales.

Thomas de leu. Fe. et excu.

HENRY, DUKE OF GUISE

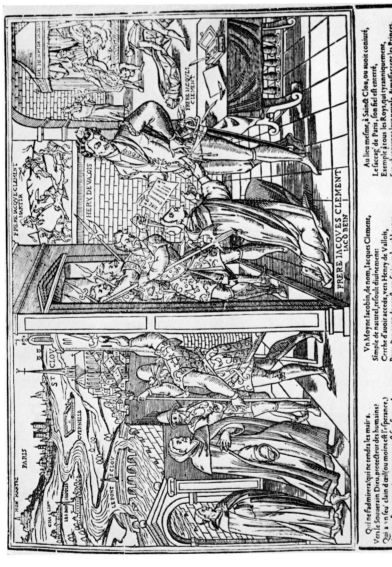

THE ASSASSINATION OF HENRY III

The *Mémoires - Journaux*

THE YEARS LEADING
TO THE LEAGUE REBELLION
MAY 1574 – MAY 1588

1574

THE LAST VALOIS KING

MAY

DEATH OF KING CHARLES IX.

Sunday, May 30, 1574, the day of Pentecost, at three o'clock in the afternoon, Charles IX, King of France, worn out by a long and violent illness and loss of blood, which had caused his death to be predicted for more than three months, died in the Château of Vincennes near Paris, at the age of twenty-three years, eleven months and four or five days, after reigning about thirteen and a half years full of continual war and strife. He left one daughter, about nineteen months old, named Isabella of France, by his wife Madame Isabella of Austria,* and the kingdom of France troubled by civil wars (on the pretext of religion and the public welfare) in most of its provinces, especially Languedoc, Provence, Dauphiné, Poitou, Saintonge, Angoumois, and Normandy, where discontented Huguenots and the Catholics associated with them have seized various towns and strongholds which they hold with great force.

MEETING OF PARLEMENT AT THE PALAIS THE DAY AFTER PENTECOST.

Monday, the last day of May, the Court of Parlement assembled in the morning, in spite of the holiday, and deputed certain présidents and conseillers to go to the Château of Vincennes to request Madame Catherine de Medici, mother of the late King, to accept the regency and undertake the government of the kingdom until the arrival of her son King Henry, who was in Poland. To this effect, the same afternoon . . . [she] willingly accepted the task, according to the intention of the late King, her son, who had decreed it a few hours before his death.

That same afternoon the body of the late King, who had lain in his bed . . . with his face uncovered for everyone to see . . . was opened and embalmed by the physicians and surgeons and placed in a metal casket.

* Elizabeth of Austria.

31

JUNE

GATES OF THE LOUVRE LOCKED AND WHY.

Wednesday, [June] 2nd, the Queen Regent had all the entrances to the Château of the Louvre locked, except the main gate . . . which had a large troop of archers stationed inside and one of Swiss outside. . . . Rumor has it that she did this in fear of enterprises and secret conspiracies discovered at Easter, which had already resulted in the execution of Tourtet . . . La Mole . . . and Coconas . . . in the Place de Grève in late April, and in the imprisonment of the Marshals Montmorency and Cossé.*

REGENCY OF THE QUEEN MOTHER.

Thursday, June 3, letters establishing the regency of the Queen were announced in a full session of Parlement and later printed.

Friday, June 4, three well-known gentlemen were sent by the Queen, in her own name and that of M. le Duc d'Alençon and the King of Navarre . . . to Poland to announce to the King the death of his late brother, congratulate him on his accession to the crown of France, and to urge him to hasten his return to his kingdom, to establish himself and to obviate the great evils and inconveniences which might be brought about by any further delay. . . .

At this time there circulated secretly in Paris a satirical epitaph of the late King, Charles IX, allegedly from the hand of a Huguenot who could not forget St. Bartholomew, although many attributed it to a very Catholic lawyer in the Parlement de Paris. This fell into my hand this Saturday, June 12:

> More cruel than Nero, than Tiberius more scheming,
> Hated by his subjects, mocked abroad,
> Brave when his chamber could shelter afford.
> Malicious to his sister, defiant to his mother,
> Envious of the exploits of King Henry, his brother,
> Foe of the youngest.† Prompt to avenge,

---

* This was one of the conspiracies of the youngest Valois brother, "Monsieur," Francis, Duke d'Alençon, against his brothers. Coconas was notorious for his cruelty during the massacre of St. Bartholomew.

† Alençon.

Without honor and faith, inconstant save in revenge.
Abominable blasphemer, adulterer bold,
The wealth of the churches, stolen, he sold.
Wild waster of his own wealth and others' millions,
He filled the Order * with the lowest of villains,
And France with ignorant prelates and minions.
His entire reign was a horrible carnage
And he died like a mad dog locked in a cage.

JULY

Thursday, July 8, the heart of the late King Charles was carried to the Célestins in Paris by M. le Duc, his brother, and there interred with all the solemnities and ceremonies usual in such cases. On the Sunday following, his body was brought to Notre Dame de Paris, and the next day to Notre Dame in St. Denis, where it was buried with the magnificent obsequies observed at the funerals of kings of France.

DISPUTES OF THOSE OF PARLEMENT WITH CERTAIN LORDS FOR RANK AT THE KING'S FUNERAL.

During these ceremonies, and in the procession, certain altercations broke out between Messieurs of the Court of Parlement and M. Jacques Amyot, Bishop of Auxerre, M. Pierre de Gondi, Bishop of Paris, M. Albert de Gondi, Count of Retz, Marshal of France, and other seigneurs of the late King's bedchamber. . . . Finally the Parlement won out and held, as usual, the nearest places to the effigy of the late King. . . .

GEOFFREY VALLÉE AND HIS FINE BOOK.

In this month of July, a miserable atheist and crazy man (one never finds the one without the other), named Geoffrey Vallée, was hanged and strangled in Paris, and his body reduced to ashes, for having printed and circulated a little book of his own writing entitled *The Happiness of Christians, or the Flail of the Faith.* . . .

By order of the Court, the copies of this splendid book of one leaf — of which the title alone shows the wisdom of its author — were burned

---

* Order of St. Michael, a special chivalric order established by Louis XI in 1469. The Valois used it to honor their favorites.

33

at the foot of the scaffold, and the author put to death, contrary to the opinion of many in the Court, who thought he ought instead to be shut up in a monastery like the idiot he was and proved himself at the execution by crying aloud that the people of Paris put to death their God on earth, but that they would regret it, and warning them to guard well their vineyards this year.

AUGUST

THE KING OF NAVARRE AND M. LE DUC RELEASED BY THE QUEEN MOTHER AND TAKEN BY HER TO GREET THE KING.*

Sunday, August 8, the Queen Mother left Paris to go to meet the King at Lyons, and took with her Monsieur, brother of the King, and the King of Navarre, her son-in-law. Following certain instructions from the King, she partially released them, and let them travel as if free, after extracting a promise that they would attempt nothing against the King and the state. . . .

DEPARTURE OF THE KING FROM POLAND, AND HIS ROUTE HOME.

Meanwhile the King had secretly fled the kingdom of Poland about the middle of June with eight or nine companions, to the great annoyance of the Senate and lords of that country. . . . He arrived at the Austrian border about the 25th of June. He was magnificently received by the Emperor in Vienna, and was accompanied through all the imperial lands by the Emperor's two sons. . . . When he arrived in Venetian territory he was greeted by ambassadors from the Signory, which assumed all his expenses during his visit. . . . On the 18th of July he arrived in the city itself, and was given the richest apparel and most elaborate welcome that even that city had ever seen. . . . [He took the route] of the princes, and, on August 11, arrived at Turin where he was greeted in great joy and high style by his aunt, the Duchess of Savoy.

SEPTEMBER

THE KING IN LYONS.

Monday, the 6th of September, the King, having come by the pass of

* Alençon and Navarre had been forcibly detained by Catherine since St. Bartholomew. Later both were able to escape and rejoin their followers, which led to the resumption of the civil wars.

Mont Cenis, arrived in his city of Lyons, where he was seen and received with great joy by the inhabitants and various seigneurs, all rejoicing at his return safe and sound from Poland. . . .

Friday, September 10, the King gave audience to the ambassadors of the Count Palatine and other German princes, who had come on behalf of the Prince of Condé . . . to request His Majesty to permit the exercise of the religion they call Reformed, and to remit their goods and titles. The King replied that all his predecessors, the kings of France, had always maintained the title and actions of Most Christian, and that following their example he wished to live and die in the Roman, Catholic and Apostolic Church, which he also understood to be received of all his subjects. As for the Huguenots, he would pardon them their past offenses on condition that they would lay down their arms and surrender to him all places seized by force . . . contrary to the duty of good subjects, and would live as obedient Catholics in the future. Otherwise he commanded them to leave the country, and he would allow them to take their goods with them and provide them with letters patent to assure their safety.

SEVERITY OF THE KING, NOT WELCOMED BY THE NOBILITY.

Thus the King, seeking all means to pacify the kingdom, behaved more severely and made himself more inaccessible than his predecessors, which the nobility found unusual and unwelcome. (These measures came from a council unsympathetic to the native nobility.) For instance, he would not permit them to talk while eating, nor to approach him . . . without prearrangement and formality. . . .

PARIS CELEBRATES THE KING'S RETURN.

Tuesday, September 14, the Court of the Parlement de Paris, the Chambre des Comptes . . . the Corporation of the city, and all the other companies, went to Notre Dame for a Solemn High Mass and *Te Deum* as a sign of rejoicing to celebrate the King's return to his kingdom. After dinner there were fireworks set off in front of the Hôtel de Ville, cannonades, trumpets, drums, magnificent inscriptions, and other signs of celebration. The bell of the clock in the Palais pealed all day, and the night was turned to day by the fireworks.

DEATH OF THE DUCHESS OF SAVOY.

Saturday, September 18, Madame Marguerite de France, Duchess of

Savoy, died in Turin, to the great regret of the Duke her husband, and of all good men, because of the great graces and rare virtues with which this lady was endowed. Among her other perfections she was very devout, and possessed of such a marvelous charity that when on occasion certain French gentlemen traveling through her domains found themselves short of funds, and asked her to lend them money, not only did she give them freely more than they asked and comforted them, and took care of all their needs, but said, "My friends, trust always to the good Lord, keep His holy name before your eyes, He will deliver you from all adversity, if you will keep faith in Him. It is not I whom you should thank, it is He who uses me to serve Himself. I give you gladly what you ask because I am the daughter of great and generous kings who taught me not to lend but to give freely to whoever implores my aid." In short, she was a true Christian. . . .*

CAPTURE OF FONTENAY IN POITOU BY THE CATHOLICS.

Monday, September 20, the town of Fontenay in Poitou, held by the Huguenots, was taken by surprise and [thereafter] murder, sack, and violation of women made this poor town miserable and desolate. Du Moulin, a minister of the town, a learned man who knew Latin, Greek, and Hebrew, was hanged and strangled.

THE LIFE OF SAINT CATHERINE.

At this time the *Life of the Queen Mother*, which has been renamed by the people the Life of Saint Catherine, was printed and circulated. Lyons is full of copies. The Queen Mother has read it laughing with rage, and saying that if they had consulted her she would have given them lots more material . . . and they could have had a bigger book. She disguises in this Florentine manner her annoyance at the Huguenots who show their feelings in this way, since no other is open to them. The truth is that this book was received as well by Catholics as by Protestants, so hated is the name of this woman by all the people. They even say that not only is everything in it true, but that it contains only half of what she has done. . . .

* Daughter of Francis I; sister of Henry II.

OCTOBER

THE MÉMOIRES DE FRANCE UNDER CHARLES IX.

In this time there appeared the *Mémoires of State and Religion under Charles IX*, in three volumes, which is a confused jumble, too precipitately published to contain the truth, of opinions, discourses, letters, negotiations, and *mémoires* against the honor of the late King and his council (on account of St. Bartholomew) and against the present King and his mother. There are, nevertheless, many things worth knowing about in these volumes and some singular treatises which will be useful in writing the history of our times. . . . But there are also a good many infected with the disease of the century, which is passion and partisanship, especially in the accounts of the massacres of those of the religion, which seem to be based on the rumors of the Palais which often have dead those who are alive and kicking, or on the *Réveille-Matin* of the Huguenots which is worthless.*

NOVEMBER

PROTESTATIONS OF MONSIEUR AND OF THE KING OF NAVARRE AT MASS.

Monday, November 1, day of All Saints, the King, the King of Navarre and the Duke d'Alençon received together their Lord's Body. The two latter princes, kneeling before the King, protested their loyalty, begged him to forget the past, and swore . . . to be faithful to the last drop of their blood. . . .

RUMORS OF PARIS.

There was a fear in Paris about this time of a plot to take by surprise certain suburbs of the city, such as Pontoise, Beaumont, Meulan, Poissy, and other ports and crossings of the Seine, Marne, Oise, and Yonne rivers so as to facilitate the advance of the German mercenaries which are said to be brought into France by the Prince of Condé and other seigneurs who have been refugees in Germany since the day of St. Bartholomew,

---

* Modern scholars concur in L'Estoile's opinion of this collection. It reveals attitudes and opinions necessary to the understanding of the period but cannot be taken as an objective history.

1572. . . . On this account certain measures were taken . . . but it was discovered that these were just rumors of Paris, that is, lies, and that the Prince and all his followers haven't the means to put even one well-armed company into the field.

TRIP OF THE KING TO AVIGNON.

Tuesday, November 16, the King left Lyons to go to Avignon . . . on the way the retinue of the King and Queen of Navarre, going down the Rhone by boat, was wrecked at the bridge of the Holy Spirit. Many fine things were lost and thirty or forty persons fell into the water. Twenty to twenty-five were drowned, including M. Alphonse de Gondi, steward of the said Queen.

LACK OF MONEY.

On the trip money was in such short supply that most of the King's pages were without cloaks, having been forced to leave them in pawn to get the necessities. If it hadn't been for a treasurer named Le Comte, who loaned the Queen Mother five thousand francs, she wouldn't have had a single lady to wait on her . . . one speaks of nothing else at court these days except this devil, money. . . .

DECEMBER

METAMORPHOSIS OF MARSHAL DAMVILLE * AND THE DUKE D'UZÈS.

Marshal Damville . . . took the town of St. Gilles and marched to the gates of Avignon, which threatened the court . . . D'Uzès was sent by the King to oppose him. In this we see a strange metamorphosis: the said Damville in the late troubles was formerly Catholic and led the royal troops against the Huguenots, but he is now one of their chiefs, while the other, formerly Huguenot, now professes to be Catholic, and bears arms for the King against his former associates. . . .

MONEY DEMANDED OF THE CITY OF PARIS.

Sunday the 19th of November, Pinard, secretary of state, arrived in

* Son of Anne de Montmorency, Damville was a prominent Catholic associated with the Huguenots in the civil wars. The Montmorencys were the leading non-royal noble family of France.

Paris, where it was rumored he was sounding out the Prévost des Marchands and the Echevins about the possibility of raising 600,000 francs from the inhabitants of the city . . . he got a cold response. . . . In fact the King, with the Pope's permission, had raised a million pounds from the churches of France and another was about to be raised in 1575. . . .

DEATH OF THE CARDINAL OF LORRAINE IN AVIGNON.*

Sunday, the 26th of December, at five o'clock in the morning, Charles Cardinal of Lorraine, aged 50, died of a fever and headache which he contracted by marching in the procession with bare head and feet . . . [this is] the poison that is now being mentioned.

The day of his death and in the night following there was a great and terrible wind . . . in most of France, whose like had never been seen. The Catholic Lorrainers said that it was a sign of God's wrath, and that He had removed such a great and wise prelate. The Huguenots, on the contrary, said that it was the devil's sabbath, the demons being assembled to receive him. . . .

To speak without partiality, the Cardinal of Lorraine was a prelate of parts, with as many graces and abilities as France has ever seen. As to whether he used them well or abused them, the judgment is up to Him before whose throne we must all appear. . . .

REMARKS AND VISIONS OF THE QUEEN MOTHER AFTER THE CARDINAL'S DEATH.

That day the Queen Mother said, as she sat down to dinner, "We will have peace from this hour, now that the Cardinal is dead. He was the obstacle, many said, though I could never believe it, as he was a great and good prelate, in whom we and all France suffer loss." But privately she said, "Today died the worst of all bad men". . . . As she was raising her glass she began to tremble violently and cried, "Jesus! I see the Cardinal of Lorraine! . . . In the night also she had apparitions . . . so that now there is so little talk of him at the court that he might never have existed . . . which is worthy of notice. Only certain Huguenots remember him, for the evils that he had brought on them in his lifetime. . . .

* Charles de Guise, Cardinal of Lorraine, was the second son of Claude de Lorraine, first Duke of Guise, and brother of Francis, Duke of Guise, with whom he dominated France during the reign of Francis II. Mary Stuart, Queen of Scots, wife of Francis II, was their niece. The Cardinal was the brains of the ardently Catholic faction while he lived. He was also a great patron of letters, and the sponsor of such men as Michel de L'Hôpital.

1575

UNPOPULARITY OF ITALIANS

JANUARY

On the 10th day of January, the King left Avignon . . . to assault Liveron, where he saw the stubborn resolution of the Huguenots to defend themselves, even to the women, who fought in the breaches no less courageously and valiantly than the men . . . which made him raise the siege. This was also influenced by the knowledge that Marshal Damville had retaken the town and fortress of Aigues-Mortes.

At this time certain companies of [German] mercenaries, in Champagne and Picardy, were ravaging the country, and protested that they were unwilling to fight against the Huguenots, who were of their own religion. . . .

FEBRUARY

CORONATION OF THE KING.

Friday, February 11, the King arrived at Rheims, where he was crowned on Sunday, the 13th of the month, just a year after his coronation in Poland, to the day and hour. When the crown was placed on his head he said aloud that it hurt him, and it started to fall off twice, which was remarked as a bad omen.

MARRIAGE OF THE KING.

Monday, the 14th of this month, the King married Mademoiselle Louise de Lorraine, formerly called Mademoiselle de Vaudemont. . . .*

Many seigneurs, including some of the greatest in the land, found this marriage an unworthy one, and too hastily entered into. . . . But it was said that the year before, passing through Lorraine on the way to Poland, [he] had seen her and found her so beautiful and full of grace that he had continued in his [desire to marry her]. . . . The Queen Mother

* Niece of the Duke of Lorraine.

40

found this marriage good, hoping from it abundant posterity, which is the thing the said Queen desires most (according to some) or least (according to others) in the world. . . .

MARCH

DEATH OF SELIM, EMPEROR OF THE TURKS.

Thursday, March 3, came the news of the death of Selim, Emperor of the Turks, who was succeeded by his son Amurath. The latter, suspicious of his two younger brothers, had them strangled.

RUMORS OF PARIS.

Other news the same day was of a great army of Protestant mercenaries . . . a false rumor, circulated expressly to raise money. . . .

APRIL

VINES FROZEN.

Tuesday, April 19, the vines were frozen in the suburbs of Paris, which raised the price of wine to three or four sous a pint. There is also an influx of beetles which have ravaged the vineyards and all sorts of fruit trees. . . .

MAY

THE TRUE CROSS STOLEN.

Tuesday, the 10th day of May, the True Cross was stolen from the Sainte Chapelle in the Palais, which astonished and troubled the people of the city. Right away it began to be said that it had been taken by no less a person than . . . the Queen Mother (of whom the people have such a horror that there is no terrible thing they will not impute to her). . . . The common opinion is that it has been sent to Italy as collateral for a large loan of money, with the approval of the King and his mother.

AMUSING INCIDENT ABOUT THE KING OF NAVARRE.

Thursday, May 26, M. Henri de Bourbon, King of Navarre, was enjoying himself in the chamber of his aunt the Princess of Condé, and listening to a gentleman named de Noailles playing the lute. This man was supposed to be in love with the Princess and she with him. He sang a song with this line in it, "I see nothing that pleases me apart from your divinity," and repeated long and soulfully the word "divinity," with eyes fixed on the Princess. At this the King began to laugh, and said, "Don't apply that line to my aunt, she's too fond of humanity," with a meaning look at Noailles.

When the King heard this story he took pleasure in it, saying, "There is a fine occupation for my good brother. If he had no others we would have peace!". . .

JUNE

THE QUEEN MOTHER'S ILLNESS AND THE CAUSE OF IT.

Sunday, the 19th of June, there arrived in Paris the Duke of Lorraine and M. de Vaudemont, father of the Queen, to celebrate the marriage of the Marquis of Nomenie . . . with Mademoiselle de Martigues. . . . On this occasion there were many festivities at the court. At one of these the Queen Mother ate so much that she feared she would burst. They say it was too many hearts of artichoke and cock's kidneys, of which she is inordinately fond.

HUGUENOT ENTERPRISES.

At the end of this month the Baron of Langoirant, Huguenot, surprised the town of Périgeux . . . they pillaged and looted and held men for ransom, in their usual manner, and took great booty from the churches.

The King hears news every day of such surprises and attacks in some parts of the country . . . which were regarded very sourly indeed by those around him, and in spite of his dissimulation he couldn't help letting his brother and the King of Navarre know that he held them responsible. . . . They on their side couldn't disguise how much they desired their liberty. The Huguenots were so bold and proud that instead of seeking for peace, as was their duty, they trumpeted war, nothing but war, justifying themselves by the evil and deceptive treatment they'd had in the past, and especially by the St. Bartholomew, which they couldn't forget. . . .

JULY

EXECUTION OF CAPTAIN LA VERGERIE. NOT APPROVED BY THE KING.

Tuesday, the 6th of the month, a captain named La Vergerie was hanged and drawn in four quarters. He was condemned to death by Chancellor Biragues * after a very short trial. . . . The gist of it was that, finding himself in a group which was discussing the quarrels of the students and the Italians, he said that one must side with the students and that the Italians should be chased out or have their throats cut, and also those that supported them, because they were the ruin of France. . . . The King saw him executed, although it is said that he didn't approve this iniquitous judgment, which scandalized the people, as if one wanted to establish a foreign domination in France, to subject and tyrannize over the country against the laws. . . .

Verses attacking the Italians.

When these cowardly rascals came to France
They were thin as sardines, and empty, save of evils,
But by their fat pickings, and not by chance,
They've become as rich and fat as boll weevils.

Those Gallic fathers, formerly unconquered,
Would blush with shame, even if conquered
By a brave, honored warrior who ruled in Rome.
But we without shame submit supinely
While a woman masters us entirely.
When a woman rules, it is a coward's home.

When these gentlemen first did come
We could easily have put them on the run,
But good courage was lacking for that fate.
Now that each one of us would do it,
I fear there's none has force to do it.
Always France becomes wise too late!

The wars and the taxes, the business of France
By Peroni, Gondi, and Biragues are run,
Right before our eyes, without just balance,
Without valor or pity, they rob us for fun.
Today Italy tyrannizes over France
Who bears the yoke too easily.
The one piles up treasure, the other eagerly,
Famished, sucks out its blood and substance.

* René de Biragues, Italian favorite of Catherine and Chancellor of France. He is often attacked along with the Gondis in the popular press.

Miserable Frenchman who cannot expel
From his own house the exacting stranger
And learns to bear demanding Italy well.
We who are free [Franc] become enslaved,
Bossed by a woman, whose vicious control
Reduces our France to a desert, depraved.

Some of these *pasquils* were addressed directly to Catherine:

Catherine whose odor
Makes rancid all France,
Either make our state better
Or return to your Florence!

SEPTEMBER

ESCAPE OF MONSIEUR, THE KING'S BROTHER.

Thursday, the 15th of September, François de France, Duke d'Alençon, sole brother of the King, who had been held virtually a prisoner . . . left Paris in a coach, at six in the evening . . . and went to Dreux in his *appanage* after being joined by forty or fifty of his followers, armed and mounted. . . . The King, all his court, and the people of Paris were much disturbed by this escape.

Saturday, September 17, Monsieur issued a Declaration, founded (as they all pretend to be) on the preservation of the laws of the kingdom, but in reality it is a revival of the quarrel of the "Public Good," which can only be appeased by a larger and richer *appanage*.*

The King said [of this declaration] to his mother and the King of Navarre, "I know what these things are worth. Plenty of them involved me when I was with the late Admiral and the Huguenots. . . . He will start out by thinking he's in command but bit by bit they will make him their servant. . . ."

LIGHTS IN THE SKY OVER PARIS.

Wednesday, the 28th of September, strange lights and fires were seen in the skies around Paris between nine and ten in the evening, they seemed to produce clouds of smoke and to represent armed men and horses. The

* League of the Public Good was an uprising of the great nobles against the Crown in the fifteenth century.

court and the city were astonished, and many people thought they augured a sinister future for the city.

This day the Queen held a conference with M. le Duc, her son, at Chambourg. He said that he would not negotiate further until the Marshals Montmorency and Cossé were released [from the Bastille]. She sent a message about this to the King in Paris, asking him to set them free. This was done Sunday, October 2.

DEFEAT OF THE MERCENARIES BY THE DUKE OF GUISE, AND HIS WOUND.

Tuesday, October 11, came news to the King of the defeat of two thousand men, some mercenaries, some Frenchmen, by the Duke of Guise . . . at the crossing of the Marne near Dormans. The King had a solemn *Te Deum* sung. . . . This battle's reputation was greater than the reality, only fifty men fell, counting both sides. . . .

The Duke of Guise received a wound during the battle, from a simple foot soldier, from his left ear across his cheek. It is said in Paris that the King and the country received more harm from this wound * than benefit from the supposed victory in the battle. . . .

NOVEMBER

HABITUAL DEVOTIONS AND CONDUCT OF THE KING.

At the beginning of November, the King visited all the churches of Paris to pray and give alms with great piety. He abandoned at this time his embroidered shirts, of which he had made such a point, and wore his collar reversed, in the Italian style. He went in a coach, with his wife the Queen, to the convents in the vicinity to add to his collection of little lap dogs . . . which gave him and the Queen great pleasure, and equal displeasure to the ladies to whom these dogs belonged. He also took up the study of grammar, [he said] "to learn to decline." This word seemed to presage the decline of his power. . . .

NOTABLE SAYING OF THE KING.

. . . At this time the companies of soldiers raised by the King's command wandered around the country looting, stealing, and sacking the

* It was this wound which became the distinguishing feature of Henri de Guise and gave him his nickname, *Le Balafré*.

45

poor people, without any discipline whatever, and His Majesty received many complaints about them. He even was told of a captain of Provence who had set himself up as an independent leader, and commented, "See what happens in civil wars, formerly even a Constable or a Prince of the Blood could not have formed an independent party, now mere valets can get away with it."

DECEMBER

MEETING AT THE HÔTEL DE VILLE ON THE SUBJECT OF LOANS TO THE KING.

Monday, December 12, a meeting was held at the Hôtel de Ville . . . about the demand of the King for the city to aid him by the imposition of a tax on the bourgeois of the city, to pay for the upkeep of three thousand Swiss which he had hired . . . especially for the defense of Paris against the rebels. . . . It was decided to point out to the King the poverty of the people and the necessity of internal peace.

When this word was taken to the King by the Prévost des Marchands, accompanied by a number of prominent citizens . . . he protested, on his part, of the pains he took every day to pacify the troubles, complained of the exorbitant demands of his enemies, and of the need to meet them by force which would only be possible through the aid of his good and loyal subjects. . . .

When this was reported back to another meeting of the city Corporation, the 23rd of the month, it was resolved . . . to oblige the King with two-thirds of what he had asked. . . .

ORIGIN OF THE LEAGUE

JANUARY

HOW THE KING PASSES HIS TIME.

At this time, in spite of the affairs of war and rebellion that he has on his hands, the King doesn't fail to make many excursions in the vicinity of Paris with the Queen his wife, to visit the convents and other houses of pleasure, and comes home very late in the night, through mud and bad weather. On Saturday, the 7th of January, his coach broke down, and he traveled more than a league on foot in the vile storm of that night, arriving at the Louvre after midnight. . . .

DELUGE IN MAINE AND ANJOU.

Monday, the 30th, news came to Paris of a small deluge in Maine and Anjou, which frightened people and did a lot of damage, as well as of an earthquake in Boulogne-sur-Mer in the night of Friday the 27th, which terrorized the countryside with lightning and thunder.

Among other incidents, they tell of a certain man who clung to the mast of his ship during the storm, who was struck by a thunderbolt and thrown into the sea with such force that he was burned and drowned.

FEBRUARY

Friday, February 3, M. Henri de Bourbon, King of Navarre, who has been pretending since Monsieur's escape to be on the outs with him, and to have nothing to do with the Huguenots, and who had gotten away with it by his skill and pleasant manner — even to the point where the most ardent Catholics . . . even the killers of St. Bartholomew . . . were taken in . . . left Paris on the pretext of going to hunt in the forest of Senlis. . . . That night he took the route via Vendôme to Alençon, where he abjured the Catholic religion . . . and withdrew to Maine and Anjou to join Monsieur and his cousin, the Prince of Condé. He resumed the open practice of the religion that he had been forced to give up by holding an infant at a solemn service of baptism.

The rumor is in Paris (which has since been confirmed to me by one of his own followers, an upright man) that the said King said not a word from the time he left Senlis until he had crossed the Loire, but the minute he crossed it he uttered a great sigh and, lifting his eyes to Heaven, said, "God be praised, He has delivered me! In Paris they caused my mother's death, they murdered M. l'Admiral and all my followers. They would have done the same to me if God hadn't protected me. I'll never return unless I am dragged." Then, joking in his usual manner he said that he regretted only two things he had had to leave behind in Paris, the Mass and his wife: he could manage without the first, but not without the second, and he wished her in his arms.

The day he left Paris, he went to the St. Germain fair fully booted and spurred, in the company of the Duke of Guise, with whom he was most affectionate . . . standing a full quarter of an hour with his arm around him for all the people to see. They, seeing only as far as the end of their noses, thought it a good sign to see this reconciliation. He urged the Duke to go hunting with him, but the Duke, who has nothing of the small-town Parisian in his make-up, absolutely refused. . . .

Two days before his departure there was a rumor that he had already fled; even the King and his mother were of this opinion . . . but the next day, when they were resigned to it, he showed up at the Sainte Chapelle, and said in his usual way that he had brought back the man they were seeking . . . who could easily escape if he wanted to, but that such a thought had never crossed his mind. He wanted to reassure them, so they would be spared anxious moments in the future, that he would never leave their Majesties except at their express command, but would live and die at their feet and in their service. This is the real characteristic of the Béarnais. . . .

MARCH

Tuesday, March 13, Beauvais la Nocle, chief of the representatives of the Huguenots and associated Catholics, arrived in Paris, and the next day negotiations began between him and the King's council. . . . These continued until the 20th of the month, when the said council was so enraged at the exorbitant demands [of the Huguenots] that they got up and left, and it looked as though all conciliation were impossible. But M. de Montpensier, arriving the 22nd from a conference with Monsieur, appeased this great wrath, so that the 24th [deputies of the King] went to the Duke [Alençon] at Moulins to tell him what the King was willing to concede, and the terms of the pacification. . . .

At this time notes were sent to the bourgeois of Paris informing them of their share of the 200,000 pounds granted to the King to pay the Swiss . . . at which there was a great protest . . . because many persons were listed at an assessment away beyond their means and unreasonable. . . .

APRIL

At the beginning of April the Huguenots began to lay siege to the town of Nevers, and succeeded in extracting 30,000 francs. . . . On the other side, the partisans of the King in various parts of the country, behaving without any military discipline, using the fact that they were not paid as an excuse, pillaged, ravaged, sacked, killed, burned, violated, and held for ransom at their will many towns and villages. Thus is the poor people buffeted and ruined by both parties, for if there are villains in the one, there are plenty of brigands in the other.

The 15th of April, Palm Sunday, the King had announced in all the parishes of Paris that he had had a new cross made, similar to the one which was stolen from the Sainte Chapelle last year, and that embedded in it there was a piece of the True Cross of Our Saviour . . . and that everyone should go to kiss and adore it during Holy Week as usual. The people of the city were very joyful at this, being devout and credulous in such matters. . . .

Wednesday, April 25, the Queen Mother left Paris and went to meet Monsieur, her son, and the lords of his party . . . and brought them the Edict of Pacification to sign, which had already been signed by the said Queen and the King.

Monday, April 30, the King went to the Parlement and requested that each of the présidents and conseillers, according to his means, should promptly lend him money to expedite the payment of the foreign troops, so that they would leave the country. . . . At this they said that they would help as much as possible. . . . The King was angry at those who tried to offer less than he thought they should, and commissioned MMs. de Thou and Séguier, First and Third Présidents, Nicolay and Bailly, First and Third Présidents of the Chambre des Comptes, Neuilly and de Thou, First Lawyer of the King, to collect more. These men gained the favor of the King and the hatred of the people, who posted defamatory placards about them in all parts of the city, threatening even to massacre them. . . .

Among others was the following, posted . . . on the house of Président Séguier:

Can't you be satisfied, Présidents de Thou and Séguier, with approving the pact made with the enemies of God and the people, and having introduced the pretended reformed religion into the kingdom? Stop short before you ruin the poor people with your so-called loans and evil counsel to the city to raid the incomes of widows and orphans. . . . Change your tune or die, for it is not right that you should live at your ease on the ruin of others.

MAY

PUBLICATION OF THE PEACE. *

Tuesday, May 8, the terms of the peace were published . . . the King wished to go to Notre Dame and have a *Te Deum* sung . . . but the clergy and the people would have none of it, out of annoyance at the concessions made to the Huguenots by this Edict.

Nevertheless the next day a solemn *Te Deum* was sung by the royal choir, in the absence of the canons and choir of the city, who refused even to attend. . . . The King attended . . . with the Parlement, and had fireworks set off in celebration in front of the Hôtel de Ville, but with a notable lack of attendance by the people, who were very angry at this so-called peace. . . .

THE BONDS OF THE CITY SEIZED.

Toward the end of the present month of May it was discovered that the

* The terms of this Edict of Pacification, signed at Beaulieu, and usually called the Peace of Monsieur, were as follows: 1) Henry III expressed regret about the massacre of St. Bartholomew and promised to rehabilitate the victims, so far as possible; 2) the reformed religion could be practiced anywhere in France except in Paris and wherever the court might be, while it was there; 3) eight fortified towns were conceded to the Huguenots and their allies; 4) all the Parlements in France would have a new chamber added for religious cases, to consist of half Protestant members and half Catholics; 5) Alençon received Anjou, Touraine, and Berry, and Damville was restored to power in Languedoc.
This Edict was the model for the Edict of Nantes twenty-two years later.

King had seized money supposed to be paid out from the municipal bonds . . . at which the people murmered loudly, all the more because the King was asking loans on loans, taxes on taxes, and on top of it all helped himself to the income from these bonds which was the sole means of support of many.

To meet this situation meetings were held at the Hôtel de Ville on the 26th, 27th, and 28th of May . . . among others . . . the Conseiller Abot freely and frankly condemned the King's evil policies, and urged that protests be made. . . . These were duly presented to His Majesty by Charron, Prévost des Marchands, on the first day of June . . . and he replied that he would pass the remonstrances along to the princes of the blood and members of his council, and would see that they all were satisfied, that is to say, "Hang them all and shut up about it."

JUNE

Thursday, the 7th of June, the King, accompanied by the princes, seigneurs, and men of his council, went to the Palais to have published in his presence the Edíct setting up a new chamber [in the Parlement] to be called Bipartisan [mi-partie], in accord with the Edict of Pacification. This was so odious to the court that if the King had not been present they would have flatly refused to do it.

At this time various gentlemen met at Péronne . . . and it became known that there was some league and agreement between the Pope and the King of Spain, and certain French nobles, united against the Huguenots and the Catholics associated with them.

In the meanwhile those of the Religion,* seeing that many towns would not permit the exercise of their faith, contrary to the Edict, and refused them entrance entirely, and knowing that those of Péronne were in league with Amiens, Abbéville, St. Quentin, and other cities to prevent the Edict from being carried out . . . seized the town of La Charité. . . .

Friday, June 22 . . . Maurevert, that well-known assassin . . . who fired the shot that killed the Admiral † . . . demanded money from the Queen Mother to make him leave the country. She, knowing his desperate

* French royalist Catholic writers of the period always mean Calvinism when they speak of "the Religion."

† Coligny, August 1572. His murder by the Guises was the occasion of the massacre of St. Bartholomew.

nature and fearing a betrayal (and she had good reason to know him) promptly gave him a thousand pounds. . . . When he laid hands on the money he holed up in his house and would not leave, daring to defy the crown because of the assurances of the Duke of Guise to defend him against his enemies. . . .

JULY

HUGUENOTS OF ROUEN FLEE BEFORE THE CROSS OF THE CARDINAL OF BOURBON.

Monday, July 23, the Cardinal of Bourbon, who was Archbishop of Rouen . . . went to the place where the Huguenots were holding their service, following the Edict of the King which gave them permission, but the minister and the congregation, fearing something worse, ran out pell mell as his cross approached. . . .

At this time the King bought the estate of Olinville . . . for 60,000 francs, from Benedict Milon, treasurer and intendant of finances, and gave it to the Queen his wife, and furnished it with 100,000 francs' worth of new furniture. It used to belong to the late Jean de Baillon, treasurer, the most capable man of finance France has ever had. . . . Milon had bought it for 30,000 and sold it to his master for sixty.

Because the said Milon had grown in a night, like a mushroom, from a poor boy, son of a metalworker of Blois, to such luxury that instead of soldering locks as his father did, he was soldering the King's money, various satirical verses were written about him. . . .

There is beginning to be a lot of conversation about the *mignons*, who are much hated and scorned by the people, as much for their haughty manners as for their effeminate and immodest appearance, but most of all for the excessive liberalities of the King toward them. Popular opinion holds that this is the cause of [the people's] ruin. . . .

These fine *mignons* wear their hair long, curled and recurled artificially, on top of [which they wear] little velvet bonnets like those of the girls in the brothels; their shirts are long and loose, so that their heads look like St. John's on the platter. . . . Their occupations are gambling, blaspheming, jumping, dancing, quarreling, fornicating, and following the King around. They do everything to please him, giving no thought to honor or to God, contenting themselves with the grace of their master. . . .

AUGUST

Thursday, August 2, Their Majesties, notified of a secret League and conspiracy among various towns and seigneurs of the realm to prevent the execution of the Edict, even by force of arms, made the Duke of Guise, the Duke of Mayenne his brother, and the Duke of Nemours their father-in-law, sign and swear to support and carry out the said Edict. The King did this because he had reason to believe that these three seigneurs were the chiefs of the League, which was nothing other than the beginning of a rebellion against the state. . . .

THE BISHOP OF PARIS IN WRONG WITH THE CLERGY.

Monday, the 13th of this month, the Bishop of Paris [Gondi] arrived back from Rome, bringing with him a bull from the Pope, giving permission to take from the ecclesiastical revenues of France 50,000 pounds of income. All the clergy were up in arms about this and the preachers denounced it in their sermons. . . .*

At this time the King went on foot to all the churches of the city . . . accompanied by only two or three persons, holding in his hand his great prayerbook, murmuring prayers to himself as he walked. They say this was done on the advice of his mother, to make the people see how devout he was, so that they would be more willing to give him money. But the people of Paris, although they are easily imposed on in matters of religion, were not taken in, and composed the following *pasquil* which was posted on the street corners. . . .

SEPTEMBER

THE PARLEMENT ATTACKED.

[The first six days] of September, placards appeared all over Paris attacking the men of Justice for conniving in opening the door to . . . Huguenots . . . but the truth is that these people would be willing for the whole world to be Huguenot provided that they could rule, and make their League and conspiracy against the state successful.

* It was notable that the higher clergy, who owed their positions to the Crown, were not drawn into the League, while the lower clergy, and especially the monastic orders, formed its hard core.

THE PEOPLE IS A STUPID BEAST.

At this same time there circulated in Paris under the name of the People (which is a stupid animal, stubborn and ungrateful, more inconstant than the weathervanes) the following titles given by them to their King. . . .

Henry, by the grace of his mother, imaginary King of France and Poland, Concierge of the Louvre, despoiler of the churches of Paris, son-in-law of Colas, master of the wardrobe and hairdresser, merchant of justice, habitué of the sewers, and protector of thugs. . . .

OCTOBER

MEMORIAL OF DAVID, PURPOSE OF THE HOUSE OF LORRAINE AND REAL BASIS OF THE LEAGUE.

At the end of the month there began to circulate the Memorial of the late M. Jean David, lawyer, found among his papers after his death in Rome. He had gone there as an agent of the Holy League, founded on the pretext of religion, but in fact on the pretensions of the House of Lorraine who claimed descent from Charlemagne, and that the House of Capet were usurpers. . . .

NOVEMBER

Monday, November 5, the King and his wife the Queen went from Paris to Olinville, where two days later Monsieur his brother arrived, with a very small retinue. They greeted each other with affectionate caresses. . . .

This sudden and unexpected reconciliation of the King and his brother caused great alarm, especially among the Huguenots . . . (since St. Bartholomew it takes little to alarm them). . . . It didn't diminish their suspicions to learn that Don Juan of Austria had been in Paris, disguised under a Portuguese passport, staying with the Spanish ambassador . . . on his way to see the Duke of Guise. . . .

PARIS RECEIVES NEWS OF THE SACK OF ANTWERP.

Saturday, November 10, there arrived in Paris the piteous news of the sack of the city of Antwerp by the Spaniards on the 4th of this month.

At noon the Spaniards left their fortress in fury and charged the poor inhabitants . . . when they had made themselves masters they burned the Hôtel de Ville and eight hundred houses, killing, massacring, sacking, and burning three or four million pounds of merchandise that they couldn't carry away with them.

This went on for about two weeks and left seven or eight thousand dead of all sexes, ages, and qualities, for the Spaniard victorious is usually so insolent and cruel that he will spare nothing to get revenge. Great and pitiful was the desolation of this poor city, one of the most beautiful, rich, and magnificent cities of the world, as everyone knows.

SCANDAL OF THE ITALIAN PLAYERS

JANUARY

THE KING'S DECLARATION TO THE ESTATES ON THE FIRST DAY OF THE YEAR 1577.

Tuesday, the first day of the year, the King declared to the deputies of the Estates gathered at Blois that, following their advice and request, he wanted in his kingdom only the exercise of the Roman, Catholic and Apostolic religion, that he would revoke everything which was contrary to this in the latest Edict of Pacification. . . .

The King of Navarre, the Prince of Condé, and Marshal Damville, when they learned this, and in addition that he had sworn to and signed the Holy League on last December 12, made preparations for war . . . fortified La Charité, and began taking towns and châteaux in the vicinity . . . which astonished the King and the Estates.

Thereupon the nobility, as usual, stood firm for their king, having nothing in mind but the maintenance of the state and the crown; the clergy favored this policy because they were partisans of the House of Lorraine, which is the heart of the League, even against the King himself. . . . The people, who have of themselves no motion except as the great give it to them, followed, as they always do, the first breath of wind, usually against their manifest welfare.

FUNERAL OF THE EMPEROR MAXIMILIAN.

Wednesday, January 9, a memorial service was held in Notre Dame for the late Maximilian of Austria, Emperor, father-in-law of the late King Charles IX, with the great and magnificent ritual customary in such cases. . . .

MURDER COMMITTED WITH IMPUNITY PUBLICLY IN THE PRESENCE OF THE KING.

Sunday, January 13, the rumors of war and the unbridled license of the armies and the lack of discipline and order that prevails in France gave a soldier the boldness to kill a brave Gascon captain, right in the Château of Blois, almost under the King's own eyes. . . .

SECOND SESSION OF THE ESTATES.

Thursday, the 17th of January, the second session of the Estates was held at Blois, and the King heard the propositions and speeches of M. Louis d'Espinac, Archbishop of Lyons, for the clergy, the Baron of Seneçay for the nobility, and M. Pierre Versoris for the Third Estate. The first two spoke well, to the satisfaction of all. Versoris was long and boring, and to put it in a word, said nothing and annoyed everybody. . . . All agreed in asking the King to permit no other religion in his kingdom but the Roman, Catholic, and Apostolic.

The clergy and nobility, with moderation, begged His Majesty to manage so that there would be no renewal of war . . . the clergy offered to support five thousand foot-soldiers and twelve hundred cavalry. The nobility offered their services and their arms. Versoris [and others] . . . for the Third offered their bodies and goods, to the last drop of blood . . . especially Versoris, who as a dependent of the House of Guise trumpeted war against the Huguenots more openly and scandalously than anyone else. . . .

At the same time Aimar, Président of Bordeaux, and Bodin, lawyer of Laon, deputies of the Third Estate for their towns and provinces, spoke very well and pertinently for the maintenance of peace, against Versoris and his faction.*

FEBRUARY

THE LEAGUE.

Friday, February 1, the *quarteniers* of the city of Paris went from house to house carrying the text of the articles of the League and asking the householders to sign up in its favor. M. de Thou, Premier Président,

* Jean Bodin, French political philosopher, author of *The Republic*.

signed with considerable qualifications, as did other [members of Parlement]. Others rejected it and refused flatly. . . .

THE GELOSI.

In this month the troupe of Italian comedians called *I Gelosi*, which the King had imported from Venice for his amusement, whom he was subsidizing . . . began to perform their shows at the Château of Blois. . . .

Sunday, February 24, the King received word that the Huguenots had formed a counter-League with the Kings of Sweden and Denmark, the Swiss and German Protestants, and the Queen of England . . . but he entered more violently than ever into jousts, tourneys, ballets, and masquerades, where he was usually dressed as a woman, with a low-cut collar which showed his throat, hung with pearls . . . it is said that if his father-in-law hadn't just died he would have spent 200,000 francs on these activities, so are luxury and waste enthroned in the heart of this prince! . . .

MARCH

By the beginning of this month there is almost no more talk of the League in Paris, everyone being thoroughly disgusted . . . seeing that the King and the Queen were using it in a fantastic way to pull money out of the people which they couldn't do in any other way.*

There appeared also at this time a delightful discourse entitled "Revision of Opinion and Abjuration of a Gentleman Who Had Signed the League" . . . which exposed plainly the artifice, imposture and vanity of the said League. . . .

MAY

THE LOOTING OF BUSSY D'AMBOISE: A PREMIUM ON VICE.

At the beginning of the month of May, Bussy d'Amboise, to whom Monsieur had given the town of Angers, began to loot and pillage the provinces of Anjou and Maine with four thousand armed men who got very rich on their booty. . . . Later he presented himself to His Majesty

---

* It was the irony of Henry III's situation that the League, which was greeted enthusiastically at first, lost favor as soon as the King appeased the Guises by joining it. He tried to use it for his own purposes, without success.

at Tours, and so plausibly excused himself for this public tyranny . . . that His Majesty said that he held him to be one of his best and most faithful servants and that he would be maintained in all his offices and pensions, which caused great complaint among the people.

FESTIVAL OF THE QUEEN MOTHER. THE MODESTY OF THE COURT.

Wednesday, May 15, at Plessis-les-Tours, the King gave a festive party in honor of M. le Duc, his brother . . . at which the ladies of the court waited on table dressed as men in green silk suits which cost 60,000 francs. . . .

Then the Queen gave a great banquet at Chenonceaux which cost her — so they say — 100,000 pounds which she borrowed from the Italians . . . at this splendid affair the ladies of the court appeared half naked. . . .

BUFFOONS BETTER RECEIVED BY THE PEOPLE THAN PREACHERS.

Sunday, May 19, the Italian comedians, *I Gelosi*, began to perform in the Hôtel de Bourbon in Paris . . . where there was such a jam of people that the four best preachers in Paris put together haven't so many at their sermons.

Tuesday, May 28, Monsieur began the furious assault of the town of Issoire, which he took on June 12.

His soldiers, remembering the many gentlemen killed at La Charité, avenged themselves by pillaging and burning this town. The King, at Chenonceaux, heard about this, and the gaining of Marshal Damville to his party, rechristened the estate the Château of Good News. The King of Navarre, the Prince of Condé and their partisans, on the other hand, finding it hard to bear the ill-treatment and lack of faith toward them and their religion . . . called this the Year of Bad News. . . .

JUNE

PARLEMENT FORBIDS I GELOSI TO PERFORM. COMPARISON OF THE LADIES OF THE COURT TO SOLDIERS.

Wednesday, June 26, the Court assembled and issued an order forbidding the Italian comedians, *I Gelosi*, to perform any more in Paris. Some said (even some of the younger ones . . .) that their comedies taught nothing but fornication and adultery, and served as a school of debauchery for the youth of Paris, of both sexes. And in truth their influence was so great, principally among the young ladies, that they took to showing their breasts — like soldiers — which shook with perpetual motion and served as a bellows to their forge.

JULY

Saturday, July 27, *I Gelosi*, comedians from Italy, having presented to the court letters patent from the King authorizing them to perform despite the court's decision, were refused appeal and charged not to bring the question up again on pain of a fine of 10,000 pounds . . . but at the beginning of September following they opened again at the Hôtel de Bourbon in defiance of the court, with the express permission of the King, the corruption of the times being such that clowns, buffoons, prostitutes, and *mignons* have all the credit and influence.

Toward the end of this month of July the fortress of Mont-Saint-Michel was surprised by the Huguenots, with the connivance of three monks at the abbey, and twenty-four hours later it was retaken by the dexterity of the Catholics, who threw the three traitors into the sea.

OCTOBER

THE INNKEEPERS AND THE ITALIANS.

At the beginning of the month of October, the tavern- and innkeepers of Paris and its suburbs were summoned to the Palais to learn their quotas [of a new tax just announced by the King and approved by the court]. They murmured loudly in protest, some refusing flatly to pay, at first, but under threat of imprisonment and fines they finally gave way, one by one. . . . This new impost adds up to 100,000 pounds for the city of Paris, and more than 500,000 for all of France. It is one of the new devices of the Italians to raise money, which is dissipated as soon as it is raised.

THE QUEEN ILL OF ANNOYANCE, A FALSE REPORT.

Monday, the 7th of October, the King left Poitiers and went to Amboise, where his wife the Queen lay sick, it was said, of annoyance because she could not have children, and had heard that the King would repudiate her on this account. This was entirely false.

On Thursday, the last day of October . . . the King received the deputies of the Estates-General of Flanders, who came to beg Monsieur to take them under his protection, a duty from which the said gentleman excused himself.*

NOVEMBER

Thursday, November 7, a comet began to appear about noon, with a long tail trailing to the east. It rose higher and higher after sunset and set about ten in the evening. This went on for forty days. The crazy astrologers said that it presaged the death of a queen or great lady in some terrible manner. The Queen Mother was in a state of terror that she would be the victim. . . .

DECEMBER

WEDDING AT THE HOUSE OF MARCEL.

Tuesday, December 10, Claude Marcel, formerly a metalworker of the *Pont-au-Change*, and now counsellor to the King and one of his superintendents of finances, married one of his daughters to the Seigneur de Vicourt. The reception was held at the Hôtel de Guise, and was attended by the King, the three Queens,† M. le Duc, and the leading members of the Guise family. After supper the King made the thirtieth in a masquerade of thirty gentlemen and thirty ladies of the court, all dressed in cloth of silver and white silk embroidered with pearls of great number and price. These masquerades created such confusion that the majority of the wedding-guests were forced to leave, and the more modest ladies withdrew . . . which was wise, for there occurred such violence and villainy . . . that if the walls and tapestries could talk they'd have quite a tale to tell. . . .

At the end of the year a beautiful young girl was discovered in the monastery of the Cordeliers in Paris, disguised as a man . . . they had all thought she was a man . . . she was beaten in the courtyard of the Conciergerie, which I witnessed myself. . . .

* This is the first mention of the connection between Alençon and the Flemish Estates. In the following years he led troops against Spain in the Low Countries, with the reluctant cooperation of his brother and Queen Elizabeth.

† The three queens at the Valois court in this period were the Queen Mother, Catherine de Medici, Queen Louise, wife of Henry III, and Marguerite, Queen of Navarre, sister of Henry III and wife of Henry of Navarre, later Henry IV.

1578

FEUDS OF THE VALOIS

JANUARY

BOLDNESS OF BUSSY D'AMBOISE.

Monday, January 6, 1578 . . . a Mademoiselle of Pons, in Brittany, was conducted from the Louvre by the King, his hair elaborately curled, to hear Mass in the Bourbon chapel. He was followed by all his *mignons* all dressed as extravagantly as he was. When they arrived they found Bussy d'Amboise, *Mignon* of Monsieur, dressed simply and modestly himself but with six pages in cloth of gold and hair curled just like the King's men, and he said aloud that this was the season when the more showy the costume the braver one was supposed to be. This was the origin of the hatreds and quarrels that broke out soon afterwards. . . .

Friday, January 10, Bussy, who had picked a fight the night before with the Seigneur de Grammont . . . sent three hundred mounted followers to the St. Antoine gate, and Grammont as many of the King's followers, to fight it out to the death . . . this was prevented at the King's command. But in spite of this Grammont went, after dinner the same day, to seek out Bussy in his lodging . . . and there ensued a brawl between those within and those without, a capital example of insolence. . . . When this was learned by the King, he sent the Marshal de Cossé and Captain Strozzi . . . to bring Bussy to the Louvre . . . as well as Grammont. Each was locked in a separate room till the next morning when they were forced to become reconciled . . . at the King's express order. He did this instead of bringing them to trial and punishment as he should have, if there were any true justice in France and at the court.

This same day . . . the King made a fine declaration and remonstrance in the presence of a large number of lords and gentlemen on the subject of these quarrels which break out every day, even in his presence (this is supposed to be a capital offense according to the laws). He said that he was much displeased . . . and to prevent them in future he was announcing certain regulations . . . which he intended to enforce. They were in fact printed and circulated a few days later, but badly carried out, as is customary with all good measures of reform in France.

FEBRUARY

Saturday, February 1, the young Seigneur Quélus, accompanied by other beloved *mignons* of the King, drew his sword and charged Bussy d'Amboise, chief *mignon* of Monsieur, near the gate of St. Honoré. . . .

Monsieur was much offended by this action [and because Bussy was forced to withdraw from Paris] threatened to leave the court of the King. It was with great difficulty that his mother changed his mind, temporarily. . . .

Monsieur was determined to depart, and commanded his men to have his carriage ready to leave for Angers. His mother and the King, fearful of what might follow, assured themselves that he was in his room . . . and seized La Chastre, Rochepôt, and Cimier, followers of the Duke. They were locked up in the Bastille. Things looked very bad until Monsieur de Lorraine reconciled the King and his brother the next day. They swore to be friends and brothers. Bussy and the other favorites of the Duke swore likewise to Quélus, Saint-Luc, and other *mignons* of the King . . . dissimulating their feelings and putting on a good show. . . .

Monsieur, for his part, pretended to go along with them, but on Friday the 14th, at seven in the evening . . . he left the Abbey of Ste. Geneviève, where he had gone to dine with the abbot, by descending the walls of the city on a rope, joined some of his favorites, and galloped off to Angers.

This ignominious departure astonished the people as well as the court . . . and the next day the Queen set off to try to find him and bring about a further reconciliation. . . .

MARCH

THREE FRENCH CARDINALS CREATED IN ROME.

Saturday, the first day of March, the Papal Nuncio visited the King and informed him that the Pope, his master, had created three new French cardinals, M. Charles, son of the Duke of Lorraine, to be called the Cardinal of Lorraine, M. Louis, Archbishop of Rheims, brother of the Duke of Guise, to be called the Cardinal of Guise, and M. René de Biragues, Chancellor of France, to be called the Cardinal of Biragues.

Saturday, March 29, the [old] Cardinal of Guise died, last of the six original brothers in his generation . . . this good prelate was called the Cardinal of Bottles, because he loved them well, and concerned himself exclusively with affairs of the kitchen, which he understood very well, much better than those of state and religion. . . .

APRIL

SALES OF OFFICES OF JUSTICE.

All the offices in France are being sold to the highest bidder, but most of all those in the courts, against all law and reason. It is the habit to sell at retail what one has bought wholesale. . . . The most abominable is the traffic in benefices, the great majority being held by women or married men . . . even to infants still at the breast, so that it would seem that they come into the world bearing a cross and mitre. . . . In short, it is not possible to imagine a crab more twisted and contradictory than the government of France. . . .

FIGHTS OF THE MIGNONS. DEATH OF QUÉLUS AND HIS LAST HOURS.

Sunday, April 27, to finish off a quarrel begun the day before, Quélus, one of the great favorites of the King, and young Entragues, favorite of the Guises . . . met at five in the morning . . . near the Bastille [with their friends] . . . and there fought so furiously that young Maugiron and Chomberg were left for dead. Riberac died the next day from his wounds. . . . Quélus, who received nineteen blows, lingered thirty-three days and finally died on May 29. . . . The great favor of the King did him little good, though His Majesty sat all day by his bed, and promised 100,000 francs to the surgeons if they could pull him through, not to mention another 100,000 to the fine favorite to give him the will to live. In spite of all this he passed from this world, saying with his last breath . . . "Oh, my King, my King," with no word for God or His Mother. . . . The King held his head in his arms, after he was dead, and removed the earrings he had given him with his own hand, as he had formerly put them on.

These and similar ways of behaving (unworthy of a great and magnanimous king) were the cause of the gradual growth of contempt for this prince, and the increased hatred of his favorites, which gave a great advantage to the House of Lorraine . . . and built up their party, that is, the League. . . .

MAY

Toward the end of April Monsieur called into service companies of infantry and cavalry from all parts of his *appanages,* to go to Flanders and fight in the service of the Estates . . . which the King pretended to be against, because the Spanish ambassador was threatening him with war. . . . He announced that none of his subjects could leave the country without express permission, under pain of imprisonment and seizure of all their goods . . . but with the other hand he lent Monsieur some money to help him. . . .

Saturday, the 3rd of May, the King sent the Seigneur Beauvais-Nangis with four companies of foot-soldiers to St. Denis, to reassure [the people], because they had been so harassed by armed men of Monsieur, supposedly on the way to Flanders, that the monks of the Abbey had sent all their treasure to Paris for safekeeping.

This was a sorry commencement for the enterprise, which began with brigandage, and ended by the hand of God falling on these thieves and villains.

THE GUISES LEAVE COURT, AND WHY.

Saturday, May 10, the Dukes of Lorraine, Guise, Mayenne, and Aumâle, with the Marquis d'Elboeuf and the new Cardinal of Guise, left Paris and withdrew to their own estates, discontented and indignant at the King's *mignons.* . . .

BEGINNING OF THE PONT NEUF.

In this same month of May . . . while the river was low . . . the Pont Neuf was begun. [It goes] from the Nesle [tower] to St. Germain. It was under the direction of young Du Cerceau, royal architect, and M. Christophe de Thou, Premier Président. . . . It was made of blocks of granite.*

* Baptiste Androuet Du Cerceau, member of a prominent family of architects in the service of the French crown. They were Huguenots, and distinguished by their loyalty to the

JUNE

THE KING BATHES IN THE SEA.

Tuesday, June 3, the King and the Queens went . . . to Chantilly, where they were entertained for three days magnificently by Marshal Montmorency . . . then they went via Rouen . . . to Dieppe, where the King bathed in the sea, on the advice of his doctors, to cure his gall bladder, which had troubled him.

BIRAGUES RECEIVES HIS RED HAT.

Tuesday, June 24, Feast of St. John, the Chancellor Biragues, accompanied by more than two hundred cavalrymen, some Italian, some French, came to the great church of Paris to receive from the hand of the Papal Nuncio the red hat sent by His Holiness . . . the elaborate ceremonies . . . were attended by many members of Parlement and officers of the crown, all very richly dressed, with much circumstance, without which these cardinalates wouldn't amount to much.

JULY

FIRST VOYAGE OF MONSIEUR TO FLANDERS.

Monday, July 7, M. le Duc left the town of Verneuil at midnight, accompanied by Bussy, Cimier . . . and other gentlemen of his suite, totaling ten mounted men . . . and in two days arrived in Arras. From there he went to Mons where he was welcome and very well received. . . .

MURDER OF THE MIGNON ST. MÉSGRIN.

Monday, July 21, young St. Mésgrin, rich, handsome, one of the frizzed *mignons* of the King, was attacked by thirty unknown men as he was leaving the Louvre about eleven at night. They left him on the street for dead, but miraculously he lived till the next day, suffering from thirty-four or thirty-five wounds, each one bad enough to be fatal. The King had him buried in the same place . . . and with the same pomp as the late Quélus, his former companion in favoritism.

---

faith as well as to the King. The De Thous were one of the ranking families of the hierarchy of the Parlement. The Pont Neuf was completed under Henry IV.

CAUSE OF THIS MURDER.

His Majesty was informed that the Duke of Guise was responsible for this murder . . . because of the rumor that this *mignon* had been carrying on with his wife . . . and that the man who had struck the final blow bore the face and the beard of his brother the Duke of Mayenne.

OPINION OF THE KING OF NAVARRE.

It was said that the King of Navarre remarked, when this event was reported to him in Gascony, "I understand the action of my cousin Guise, in being unwilling to be cuckolded by a *mignon* like St. Mésgrin. This is how all these little gallants of the court should be treated, who dare to make love to princesses."

DEMANDS OF THE KING ON THE CLERGY.

At the end of this month the King demanded of the clergy of France an extra amount of money . . . on pretext of the expenses incumbent on him in conducting the Queen of Navarre, his sister, to the King of Navarre, her husband — at which the clergy protested strongly. They made a number of remonstrances both by word of mouth and in writing. . . .

Meanwhile the King went to hear Mass in all the parishes of Paris, to show the priests and theologians, who accused him of not caring for the Church, that he was a very devout Catholic, and that the clergy neither could nor should refuse him.

AUGUST

DEPARTURE OF THE QUEEN OF NAVARRE.

Saturday, August 2, the Queen of Navarre took the road to Gascony to rejoin the King her husband (with great regret according to rumor). She was accompanied by the Queen, her mother, the Cardinal of Bourbon, M. le Duc de Montpensier, and Guy du Four, Sieur de Pybrac, Président in Parlement.

In this month of August, the armed companies of Monsieur, allegedly en route to Flanders, romped through Picardy and Champagne, pillaging, sacking, stealing, violating women, killing, and burning. . . .

OCTOBER

DEATH OF DON JUAN OF AUSTRIA.

At this time news came to Paris of the death of Don Juan of Austria, who died in Naumur of a severe dysentery, agreeable news to the Estates of the Low Countries, and equally annoying and disagreeable to the Spaniards and their allies.

Thursday, October 16, when the King was at Olinville for hunting, he received word from the Queen his mother of the good and gracious welcome she had been given by the King of Navarre at Nérac. . . .

In this interview between the King of Navarre and the Queen, M. le Cardinal de Bourbon said a few words to his nephew [Henry of Navarre] intended to make him change his religion. The King replied in his joking manner (recognizing the language of the League) . . . "My uncle, they say around here that there are people who want to make you King — tell them to make you Pope! It would suit you better and then you'd be greater than they are, and [than] all the kings there are." * When this story was told to the King [Henry III] he laughed loud and long. . . .

NOVEMBER

At the beginning of the month of November . . . the nobles and people of Brittany, Normandy, Burgundy, and Auvergne joined together and resolved never to pay any more imposts, aids, subsidies, loans, taxes, or any other charges which had not been in force at the time of King Louis XII. They cried out loudly against the King for his daily exactions. . . .

THE KING RECOGNIZES THE LEAGUE BENEATH ITS MASK; HIS STRATAGEM.

When His Majesty learned of these things [the provinces' resolutions] he said, "These are the fruits of the League . . . but I will check its operation, if I can. These men are great at managing people, but I'll show them I'm a greater master still." And indeed he began at this time to deal with Monsieur and the King of Navarre, *sub rosa* . . . giving the latter a yearly subsidy of 100,000 francs. . . .

* Charles de Bourbon, younger brother of Antoine de Bourbon, and uncle of Henry of Navarre, declared "King" by the League in 1589 after the death of Henry III. The uncle was preferred to the nephew, partly on the grounds of religion, and partly on those of age — the Cardinal was sixty-six, and the future Henry IV was thirty-six. The Cardinal was used as a foil by Henry of Guise, and died the following year.

DEATH OF BUSSY D'AMBOISE

JANUARY

CREATION OF THE ORDER OF THE HOLY SPIRIT.

Thursday, the first day of January 1579, the King established his new Order of the Knights of the Holy Spirit in the Church of the Augustinians in Paris, with great pomp and magnificence. In the next two days he entertained and held council with the new knights. They wore black velvet doublets, ornamented and slashed with cloth of silver, their shoes and belts of white velvet, the whole covered by a black velvet mantle bordered with gold fleurs-de-lis, lined with scarlet satin, and a smaller cape of cloth of gold . . . a large necklace . . . from which hung a gold cross elaborately worked and enameled, in the middle of which was a white dove, symbolizing the Holy Spirit. . . .

It is said that the King instituted this order to tie those whom he needed to him with a new and even stronger tie . . . because so many of his subjects, agitated by the winds of the League . . . tended to rebellion. . . . He thought to fortify himself with these new knights and the *mignons*, who would be sworn directly to his obedience and would accompany him constantly, in case of trouble. . . .

The Huguenots, always suspicious, feared that this covered a new stratagem to trap them. Others, more malicious, blamed it on decadence and voluptuousness, said that it was a cover for the love affairs and debauchery of the King and his *mignons*. This was the language of the League. . . .

FEBRUARY

STUDENTS MOCK THE KING AND HIS MIGNONS.

Wednesday, February 4, the King . . . attended the fair at St. Germain . . . and had various students arrested for parading at the fair wearing long shirts and big collars made of white paper in mocking imitation of the King and his *mignons,* and shouting insolently, "By their costumes one recognizes the beasts." *. . .

MARCH

At Easter time of this year, 1579, the King had made and installed the marble and bronze screen around the principal altar of the Sainte Chapelle. At the same time the organ was done over, and is now the most beautiful and excellent in the world. . . .

APRIL

FLOOD OF THE RIVER ST. MARCEAU IN PARIS.

In the night of Wednesday, April 1, the St. Marceau River, as a result of the recent heavy rains, crested at a height of fifteen feet, tearing down many walls, mills, and houses, and drowning various persons, as well as many animals. The people of Paris rushed out by the thousands in the following days, to see this disaster, with combined fright and curiosity. The water rose to the top of the high altar in the church of the Cordeliers. . . .

The following Saturday, the court of Parlement went in procession to Notre Dame and held a solemn Mass with prayers to God that it might please him to end this scourge. . . .

SICKNESS AND DEATH OF MARSHAL MONTMORENCY.

Friday, April 10, Marshal Montmorency came back from Rouen and went to stay at the Louvre; the next day he was suddenly taken with an attack of apoplexy . . . and [later] died, to the great regret of all good men and the saner part of the nobility of France.

MONSIEUR IN PARIS.

Sunday, April 26, M. le Duc arrived in Paris, with a large and elaborately dressed company. The King met him outside the walls of the city, and conducted him to the Louvre, where they spent much time together in great harmony and brotherly affection. . . .

* It was the style at the court of Henry III to wear a large, elaborate white collar called "fraise," which resembled the intestines of a cow in shape. There is a pun involved, "fraise" being the membrane which encloses the intestines.

MAY

MAUREVERT, ASSASSIN, WOUNDED.

Friday, May 1, Maurevert, meeting a cousin of his with whom he had been having a quarrel, was attacked, and a bullet ripped his left arm, breaking all the bones, so that it had to be amputated a few days later. The amazing thing is . . . that he was not killed, so that it looks as if God were preserving him for some special punishment, to make an example of him. . . .

JULY

FIRST VOYAGE OF MONSIEUR TO ENGLAND.

Monday, July 3, M. le Duc left Paris, with a very small retinue, to go to Boulogne-sur-Mer, where he spent three weeks. From there he went to England, with the safe-conduct of the Queen, by whom he was joyously and magnificently received in her palace, where they spent eight days together making plans for their marriage.

The poor state of the Duke's equipment gave rise to various amusing verses, which were circulated in Paris. . . .

AUGUST

DEATH OF BUSSY D'AMBOISE.

Wednesday, August 19, Bussy d'Amboise, prime favorite of M. le Duc . . . who behaved so arrogantly because of the favor of his master . . . was killed by the Seigneur de Montsoreau and the Lieutenant-Criminel de Saumur, in a house belonging to the said Montsoreau, to which Bussy had been conducted by the said Lieutenant in order to carry on his affair with Montsoreau's wife. Bussy had been making love to her for a long time, but she had conspired to have him taken . . . by her husband.

[Montsoreau] was accompanied by ten or twelve armed friends, all of whom threw themselves at Bussy. The latter, seeing himself betrayed, and being all alone . . . nevertheless defended himself to the last moment, proving what he had often said, that fear had no place in his heart. As long as a piece of his sword remained in his hand he fought with it, and then with the handle, and then with tables, chairs and benches, with which he dispatched three or four of his enemies. When he had no weapons left, and was overcome by sheer force of numbers, he ran to a window to throw himself out, but was killed before he could do it.

This was the end of Captain Bussy, highhanded, of invincible courage, proud and bold, as brave as any captain in France of his age (which was thirty years), but vicious and scornful of God, which was his undoing . . . as usually happens to men of blood. . . .

He so dominated his master, the Duke, that he boasted that he could make him do anything he wanted, even to keeping the keys to his treasury and helping himself to it. . . . He was a lover of letters — though he was rather unskilled in them — and enjoyed especially Plutarch's *Lives*. Whenever he would read of a noble or brave exploit of a Roman captain he would say, "There is nothing here that I couldn't do just as well in the same circumstances." He also used to say that though he was only a simple gentleman, he had the heart of an emperor. Indeed this was the reason that Monsieur finally turned against him, hating him as much as he used to love him, and even giving his consent (according to the rumors) to his undoing. In which we see the illustration of an ancient proverb about princes, "Most happy those who do not know them, unhappy those who serve them, and unhappiest those who offend them."

Saturday, August 22, the houses of various Protestants in Paris were marked with a cross, which made them fearful, especially because of the anniversary. When the news of Bussy's death came, it began to be said that the Huguenots were afraid of Bussy's ghost, who had done them much harm the day of St. Bartholomew . . . even killing his own cousin St. Georges, who had loaned him a large sum of money.

SEPTEMBER

THE KING CRITICALLY ILL WITH AN EARACHE.

Thursday, September 10, the King . . . was extremely troubled by a severe earache, so that all the monasteries in Paris were praying for his recovery. A courier was sent to the Queen Mother to notify her, because for twenty-four hours all the doctors despaired of his life, all but the Great Physician. His condition was blamed on his excesses, because he spent his nights carousing and indulging in all sorts of activities injurious to his health. . . .*

* L'Estoile at times revels in the details of what he considers the court's debauchery; at others, his puritanism triumphs and he contents himself with a veiled reference.

1580

CIVIL WAR AND PLAGUE

JANUARY

EDICT OF THE ESTATES OF BLOIS.

Monday, January 26,* the Parlement published, after long deliberation, the Edict which resulted from the Estates held at Blois in the year 1577. This contained many fine and noble ordinances which, if it had pleased God and the King to enforce them, would have brought great relief and satisfaction to the Estates and people of France. But it is to be feared that it will be said of them as of the Ordinances of Orléans and others, "not valid after three days." . . .

FEBRUARY

Wednesday, February 3, the King dined with the Cardinal of Bourbon in the Abbey of St. Germain-des-Près, the next day with the Cardinal of Guise, in the Hôtel St. Denis . . . and so on each day, as long as the fair lasted.

THE PEOPLE PILLAGED FROM BOTH SIDES.

At this same time, in revenge for the cruelties [of the Huguenots] in Mandes, the Catholics of Toulouse rose in arms and attacked the Protestants. The Bipartisan chamber . . . had to flee in the night, and the Huguenots, on their side, began to sack the houses of the Catholics. . . .

REFORM OF THE CUSTOMARY LAW OF PARIS.

Tuesday, February 22, M. Christophe de Thou, Premier Président . . . in company with [various other members of Parlement] began the reform and classification of the customary law of Paris in the great hall of the Bishopric of Paris, which was hung with splendid tapestries for the occasion.

* There is a gap between the foregoing entry of September 1579 and this of January 1580.

MARCH

BEGINNING OF THE PLAGUE.

At this time the plague appeared in Paris. It was forbidden, by order of the Parlement, to sell any household goods, either in public places or privately. Many fevers are prevalent, and even the very old are attacked. Many sudden deaths are reported also.

Tuesday, March 29, a funeral service was held for Sebastian, former King of Portugal, and his uncle Henry, Cardinal of Rome, with all the usual solemnities, in the great church of Paris.

APRIL

Wednesday, April 6, a man of Toulouse named La Valette was hanged and strangled in front of the Hôtel de Bourbon . . . in his long robe, for having pretended that he was a doctor of law. He was also guilty of a number of poisonings, and indeed a number of bottles of different kinds of poison were found in his possession. . . .

JUNE

CONFISCATION OF HUGUENOTS' GOODS.

Monday, June 6, the King, hearing that [the Huguenots] were trying to raise new mercenary troops in Germany, published letters seizing the goods of all Huguenots who bore arms against the Crown, or who left the country without permission.

THE PARIS GRIPPE OF THE YEAR 1580.

From the second day of this month of June through the 8th, ten thousand people in Paris have come down with a form of grippe and catarrh called the *coqueluche* . . . including the King. This malady is characterized by headache, stomachache, intestinal trouble, and much pain in all parts of the body. It raged through the country all during the year; hardly a house or village escaped. It was a forerunner of the plague. The best that the doctors could figure out was to tell the afflicted to abstain from wine . . . but finally they found the best thing was to stay in bed and to eat and drink very lightly and take no medicine at all. They say more than ten thousand have died in the last three months of this same disease in Rome.

LA NOUE FAVORED BY TWO KINGS.

At this time the Seigneur de la Noue [who had been captured by the Spaniards, while fighting in the Low Countries] obtained a safe-conduct for his wife to join him, from King Philip, and a declaration from King Henry, exempting him from the Edict confiscating the goods of Huguenots. The Seigneur Strozzi said to the Spanish ambassador that if the King of Spain or any of his subjects were to maltreat M. de la Noue or deal with him in any way not becoming to a noble prisoner of war, he, Strozzi, would destroy every Spaniard that fell into his hands.*

JULY

The plague, this summer, is worse in Paris, and the Prévost de Paris and Prévost des Marchands are taking steps to do something about it. . . . They created a new officer called Prévost of Health, who is to go about finding those who are afflicted and have them taken to the Hôtel-Dieu. . . . Malmédy, the King's mathematician, philosopher and learned physician, undertook the general question of what treatment should be given. Tents and temporary lodgings for the patients began to be constructed in Montmartre, Saint-Marcel, and other suburbs. . . . To meet the expenses of these buildings, a tax was laid on all the inhabitants of the city; some contributed extra funds out of generosity, as a form of charity.

The disease was more frightening than dangerous, for there were not more than thirty thousand deaths in Paris and the faubourgs in the entire year 1580. But the fear was so great that the majority of the people of Paris who had the means to do so left the city . . . to the point where there was great complaint from the streetcriers and merchants, who were hard up for cash and spent their time throwing dice on the street corners, and even in the great hall of the Palais. . . .

* François de la Noue, known as *Bras-de-fer*, one of the most respected of the Huguenot nobles and a famous warrior.

AUGUST

OFFICES FOR SALE.

In this month M. Barnabé Brisson became Président in the Parlement, succeeding M. Pomponne de Bellièvre, M. Jacques Faye became Lawyer of the King, replacing the said Brisson, and M. Pierre du Rancher became Master of Requests, succeeding the said Faye. They say that Brisson paid to Bellièvre 60,000 pounds, Faye to Brisson 40,000, and Du Rancher to Faye 25,000. I leave it to be imagined what the people of France can expect in the way of justice from these officers. . . .

SEPTEMBER

RECIPES FOR CHILDREN, RENDERED USELESS BY GOD'S JUDGMENT.

In this month of September the Queen, by the advice of the royal physicians, went to Boulogne to take the baths . . . with the assurance that it would enable her to have children. She also observed faithfully a regime prescribed by them for the same reasons. But none of this availed, nor the pilgrimages either — in which they put so much stock. . . .

OCTOBER

DEATH OF PRÉSIDENT SÉGUIER.

Monday, October 24, M. Pierre Séguier, Second Président in the Parlement de Paris, died in his house in Paris at the age of 76. He left five sons, M. Louis Séguier, Dean of the Church of Paris [Notre Dame] and Conseiller in the court; M. Antoine Séguier, Lieutenant-Civil; M.——Séguier,* Master of Requests, and M. Hieronymous Séguier, *audiencier* in the *chancellerie*, which office he created for this son although it was notoriously not in the public interest. He excused himself on the grounds of the great affection he had for his children and the need to establish them well. . . .

He was a lawyer in the Palais for twenty-five or thirty years, with the reputation of being one of the ablest and best-spoken; then he held the office of Royal Advocate and finally Président. He had four daughters

* L'Estoile omits the first name of this member of the family.

whom he married off very advantageously, having nothing else in mind.

Aside from what he left his children he died worth 200,000 pounds . . . a remarkable feat for a man who knew nothing but the *tric trac* of the Palais. . . . He was remarkably gifted, a good judge, merciful . . . but worldly and a courtier if ever there was one, serving the great and his own opportunity. . . .

NOVEMBER

FIRE AT THE CORDELIERS'.

Saturday, November 19, at nine in the evening, a terrible fire started in the altar screen of the church of the Cordeliers, and the whole church, which was made of wood, was consumed in three hours . . . even the marble sepulchers around the outside were reduced to powder, and those in bronze melted. The Cordeliers started a rumor that it had been set by the Huguenots, but it was later discovered that it was due to the negligence of a novice, who had left a lighted candle too near the screen. . . .

DECEMBER

In this year 1580, in spite of plague and the wars which assailed his people from all sides, the King never stopped visiting all the convents of Paris in the evenings, making love to the nuns . . . the people attributed all the ills of the kingdom to his wicked life. . . .

Meanwhile those of the House of Lorraine solicited some of the leading Huguenots, and tried to persuade them to join the League. The Duke of Mayenne approached the Baron of Salignac, among others . . . promising the free exercise of their religion even in the armies . . . to which the Baron replied that he neither could nor would be of any other party than that of the King. . . . When this was reported to the Queen Mother she thanked him, and assured him that all things would be put in order (whether she was sincere or not, God knows), but no one can see any sign of it.

Thus the zeal of the Guises for the preservation of the Catholic, Apostolic and Roman faith, and the projects of the League to exterminate heresy in France!

1581

WEDDING POMP
INCREASES DISCORD

MARCH

MASQUERADES OF THE KING, SUNDAY IN MID-LENT.

Sunday, March 5, the King, after a long fast at St. Germain-en-Laye ... returned to Paris ... went with his *mignons* D'Arques and La Valette * and various young ladies of his private acquaintance, all masked, and rioted through the city to all the houses where he would find good company. . . .

EMBASSY TO ENGLAND.

Wednesday, the 8th of this month, Prince Dophin and the lords Marshal de Cossé, de Carrouges, La Motte-Fénelon, de Lanssac, Pinart, Secretary of State, Président Brisson, with various other gentlemen in their retinue, went to England to see the Queen and to discuss with her and her Council the articles of the proposed marriage between Her Majesty and Monsieur, the King's brother. They were very well received and grandly treated by Her Highness. . . .

STORM AND TEMPEST IN PARIS ON EASTER DAY.

March 26, Easter Day, a great storm and violent wind arose over Paris, beginning at seven in the morning and lasting until noon. It was accompanied by thunder, lightning, hail, rain, and snow in rapid succession, and astounded the people, being this special day, and because it did much damage, as much in the city as in the villages. . . . It felled chimneys, broke windows in the churches, uprooted great trees, and toppled steeples . . . many thought that it was a flail of divine punishment over the heads of Frenchmen, abandoned as they are to all sorts of luxury, waste, and vices which rouse the ire of God. . . .

* D'Arques was later made Duke (Joyeuse) and Peer, and married to the King's sister-in-law. La Valette became Duke d'Épernon, the most important of the King's favorites. (See below, *passim*, 1587.)

MAY

BRIGANDAGE AUTHORIZED AS A DEVICE TO RAISE MONEY.

Wednesday, May 17, the Queen Mother returned from a fruitless visit to her son, M. le Duc. (He had been spending six or seven months in Gascony with the King of Navarre and was determined to lead his expedition to Flanders. She tried to stop it in every way possible but could do nothing with him.) When she arrived in Paris she procured 70,000 crowns from the Prévosts des Maréchaux of the kingdom. This was the result of a bargain she had made with them to maintain them in their offices and privileges to rob the people in return for a certain consideration.

On this same May 17, the King had published and announced by public crier letters patent commanding governors of cities and provinces to seize all military men who were leading or recruiting men of war . . . unless they had his Majesty's express permission, signed by his own hand and sealed with the great seal. . . . He did this because he had been warned by the King of Spain that if his brother went to Flanders to aid the rebels, he [Philip II] had the means at hand and the intention to . . . take vengeance on France. But of all these orders were was not a single execution, the King contenting himself with having them published, as is usual with princes in such matters. . . .

JUNE

Monday, June 29, the King, in St. Maur, where he had retired due to the continuation of the plague in Paris, gave audience to the ambassadors newly returned from England where they had been arranging for the marriage of M. le Duc his brother. It is all decided upon and definite, according to the rumors which Their Majesties spread about, which were believed at the court and in the city.

JULY

THE KING AT THE PALAIS, ON ACCOUNT OF THE EDICTS.

Tuesday, July 4, the King went to the Palais to hold his *lit de justice*, and have registered in his presence the nine new Edicts creating new offices and new imposts on the people. . . . the Premier Président said aloud that, according to the King's law which assumed absolute power they could pass, but, according to the laws of the kingdom which were governed by reason and equity they neither could nor should be published. In spite of these remonstrances the Chancellor Biragues, who was not Chancellor of France but Chancellor of the King of France, published them at once, at the King's command.

A GREAT PRINCE THRUST ASIDE FOR A MIGNON.

At this time the ambassador of Ferrara, in the name of M. Alphonse d'Este, heir apparent of the Duke of Ferrara, came to the court to ask the hand of Marguerite de Lorraine, the Queen's sister, in marriage, but he was sent home without satisfaction. The said lady was promised instead to D'Arques, most cherished of the King's *mignons*, with a dowry of 400,000 crowns. . . .

SEPTEMBER

OF THE NEW DUKE OF JOYEUSE, THE GREAT PRIVILEGES AND HONORS GIVEN HIM BY THE KING; OF HIS WEDDING AND THE EXCESSIVE LUXURIES AND EXPENSES THEREOF, BY THE WILL OF THE KING.

Thursday, September 7, the day of decisions in red robes, Seigneur D'Arques, first *mignon* of the King, came to the Parlement . . . where the letters were published which raised his *vicomté* of Joyeuse to the rank of a duchy and peerage . . . with the provision that he would take precedence over all other peers except the princes of the blood or sovereign houses, such as Savoy, Lorraine, Cleves. All this was because of his approaching marriage to Mademoiselle Marguerite de Lorraine, daughter of Vaudemont, sister of the Queen. They were betrothed at the Louvre, Monday, September 18, in the Queen's apartments, and married the following Sunday at St. Germain l'Auxerrois, at three in the afternoon. The King escorted the bride, followed by the Queen, princesses, and ladies of the court, so richly dressed that nothing so sumptuous has ever been seen in France.

The costumes of the King and the bride were so covered with pearls and precious stones that it was impossible to count them; they cost about 10,000 crowns. There were seventeen different parties and festivities held day after day following the wedding, given by the various princes and seigneurs at the King's command . . . and at each one the lords and ladies appeared in a different costume, most of them of gold and silver cloth enriched with embroidery and precious stones of infinite number and great price. The expense was so great, with the masquerades, jousts on foot and on horseback, music, dancing, entertainment, and presents, that the rumor is that the King won't get out of it for less than 12,000 crowns. In fact, the cloth of gold and chariots, and luxury even in the livery of the servants, was no more spared than if they had been in God's honor. Everyone was aghast at such luxury and needless expense in a time which was not the best in the world, but very hard for the people, eaten and worn to the bones by the ravages of soldiers in the countryside and by the new taxes and subsidies in the towns.

For the librettos and music which they provided for the masquerades, combats, and other entertainments of the wedding the King gave the poets Ronsard and Baïf 2,000 crowns apiece, as well as silk suits for the occasion. He also provided a dowry of 400,000 crowns for the bride. . . .

Toward the end of this month of September, the King and his mother sent M. de Bellièvre * to Monsieur, brother of the King, to attempt to appease his annoyance at the great expense of the King for the wedding of his *mignon* D'Arques. The Duke was complaining that his brother had not been willing to help him with men or money for his enterprise in Flanders, and said that it would have been a much better use for such an amount of money than the gratification of a favorite.

OCTOBER

ENTERTAINMENT OF THE CARDINAL OF BOURBON.

Tuesday, October 10, the Cardinal of Bourbon gave his party for the Duke of Joyeuse in the Abbey of St Germain-des-Près, including a great and sumptuous barge on the river Seine, in the form of a triumphal chariot, in which the King, the bride and bridegroom, and the princesses were to go from the Louvre to the Pré-aux-Clercs. It was an affair of great pomp and expense. The triumphal barge was escorted by other boats disguised as sea horses, tritons, salmon, tortoises, and other marine creatures, numbering twenty-four in all. In some of them, concealed in the bellies of the monsters, were trumpets, clarions, hautboys, and violins,

* Pomponne de Bellièvre was charged with many delicate missions by Henry III and later by Henry IV, especially in dealings with the League.

played by excellent musicians, and operators of fireworks, who during the crossing were supposed to set them off to the great pleasure of the King and his company, as well as of the fifty thousand Parisians of all ages and sexes lined up on the banks in great anticipation of a beautiful and rare sight. But something went wrong and they were not able to perform as expected. The King waited from four to seven at the Tuileries without being able to see any action at all, though he said he could clearly see that there were beasts commanded by other beasts. . . . This feast was judged the most pompous and magnificent of all, and the said Cardinal had had an artificial garden created near the Abbey, full of flowers and fruits as if it had been the month of May or July.

FEAST OF THE QUEEN.

Sunday, October 15, the Queen gave her party at the Louvre, which ended with a ballet of Circe and her nymphs, the best planned and executed of all those which had been given.

ROYAL COMBATS OF ALL SORTS. MUSIC, BALLET, AND CAROUSELS.

Monday, October 16, in the great and beautiful walks of the Louvre gardens, the King held a tourney of fourteen Whites against fourteen Yellows, at eight in the evening, by torchlight, with great magnificence and at great expense; Tuesday, the 17th, another with lances and [other weapons] on foot and on horseback; and Thursday, the 19th, to end all the festivities, a ballet in which Spanish horses advanced, retreated, and turned to the sound of trumpets and clarions, for which they had been trained for five or six months beforehand.

All this was beautiful and agreeable, but the best of all that was done was the music, both vocal and instrumental, the most harmonious and beautiful that anyone present had ever heard. The fireworks were also spectacular, shining with incredible brilliance and delighting the audience. It is true that one of the buildings where the harnesses and other equipment of the performing animals was kept caught fire, but there was no other damage.

With this finally ended the bombast and extraordinary and mad expense which it pleased the King to make for the marriage of his *mignon* and brother-in-law. He has since said that he regretted it (with good reason), and that if he had to do it over, he would spend much less, which would spare his poor people and his reputation, both at home and abroad. But it is usual for princes to recognize their mistakes too late. . . .

NOVEMBER

EMBASSY OF THE GRAND TURK IN PARIS.

Wednesday, November 9, two ambassadors of the Grand Turk arrived in Paris, where they were magnificently received. One had a special commission to invite the King to attend the circumcision of the eldest son of the Sultan, which will be solemnly celebrated next May in the city of Constantinople; the other came to reconfirm the ancient alliance between the Ottoman Emperors and the Kings of France. They were lodged in the rue de Seine in the Faubourg St. Germain, and left Paris on December 10, laden with rich presents.

CHASTELLENIE OF ÉPERNON RAISED TO A DUCHY.

Monday, November 27, the *mignon* La Valette . . . came to the court of the Parlement . . . for the erection of his Chastellenie (which the King had purchased from his brother-in-law the King of Navarre especially for him) into a duchy and peerage. The letters patent declared that as the said La Valette would marry the other sister of the Queen, he would precede all other dukes and peers after the princes and Joyeuse.

DECEMBER

MARRIAGE OF THE PRINCE OF CONTI.

Sunday, December 17, the Marquis of Conti, younger brother of the Prince of Condé, was married to the Countess of Montafier at the Louvre. No luxury or extraordinary pomp accompanied this wedding, as if the excessive show of the wedding of Joyeuse had exhausted everything that could be done in this line, and there was no further point to it. . . .

FUNERAL OF AN
HOMME DE BIEN

JANUARY

SWISS EMBASSY IN PARIS.

Monday, January 15, the thirteen ambassadors of the thirteen Swiss Cantons came to beg the King to pay them the five or six hundred thousand crowns due them in back pay. Among their supplications they mingled certain veiled threats to quit the French alliance and join the Spaniards, who were making them great offers. They were appeased with fine promises, including that of a fair proportion of the money by next Easter. To soften them further each one was given a gold chain worth 200 crowns and 300 to cover the expenses of the trip.

FEBRUARY

VOYAGE OF MONSIEUR AND HIS ENTOURAGE FROM ENGLAND TO ANTWERP.

Thursday, February 8, Monsieur, the King's brother, having spent three months in London with the Queen of England, from whom he had received all the honors and courtesies that a prince of his quality can expect from a great queen, embarked for Antwerp where the Prince of Orange and the Deputies of the Estates of Flanders awaited him. To continue her favor to him during the trip, the Queen loaned him three well-equipped warships and had him escorted by Milords the Counts of Leicester, Howard, and Hunsdon, and various other English gentlemen.

He arrived at Antwerp Saturday the 17th of February, and the following Monday was given a reception and formal procession as lavish and magnificent as those for the Emperor Charles V, and his son Philip, King of Spain, at their welcomes. . . . Feasting and fireworks were held for four days, money was coined with his name and arms and distributed to the people, and he was given the title of Duke of Brabant and Marquis of the Holy Roman Empire.

MARRIAGE OF LA VALETTE, WITHOUT EXPENSE, AND WHY.

Tuesday, February 15, the elder La Valette, brother of the Duke d'Épernon, was married at the Louvre very simply and with no publicity . . . at the express command of the King. It had been reported to him that when the Swiss ambassadors came to ask for the money owed them, and they had been told that they must be patient because the King had no money, they had replied that they could not believe that his coffers were not overflowing, because only a few months before he had spent . . . more than 1,200,000 crowns for the marriage of a simple gentleman, the Duke of Joyeuse. Surely if he could spend such a sum for triviality there must be plenty for the important affairs of the kingdom. . . .

MARCH

THE PEOPLE OF PARIS TAXED AND MOCKED.

At the beginning of the month of March the King asked for private loans from the *bourgeois* of Paris, to pay for his pleasures and those of the *mignons* . . . in this way he exploited the people, who are not so stupid that they are not well aware of it. They complain, but can do nothing else, having to give way to a force greater than theirs.

FIRE IN THE SKY.

Monday, March 8, about nine in the evening, a great and splendid light shone in the sky over Paris. It was greeted with astonishment and fear that it presaged some great evil.

MARQUISATE D'ELBOEUF RAISED TO A DUCHY.

Thursday, March 29, the Marquisate D'Elboeuf was raised to a duchy and peerage by letters patent of the King, verified in the Parlement. This was at the insistence of the members of the House of Guise, who were much displeased to see the Dukes of Retz, Joyeuse, and Épernon, mere favorites of the King, precede the Marquis d'Elboeuf, prince of the House of Lorraine and their cousin, in rank and honor. . . .

JUNE

THE DUKE OF JOYEUSE, ADMIRAL.

Tuesday, June 19, the Duke of Joyeuse was received at the Parlement to take the oath as Admiral of France, which office was sold by the Duke of Mayenne [brother of Guise] at the King's request, for 120,000 crowns, which the King paid for his *mignon* and brother-in-law.

VOYAGE OF THE KING AND QUEEN TO CHARTRES; THE COUNCIL OF TRENT.

Monday, June 26, the King and Queen made another trip to Chartres. After making prayers and oblations to have a child, they gave a silver lamp . . . and 500 pounds of income to keep it burning day and night. . . . They hardly stopped in Paris after this because they were on their way to Fontainebleau to meet with the Council of State and prepare the response to the Pope and the King of Spain, whose ambassadors were pressing the King to accept the articles of the Council of Trent in France and to establish the Inquisition.

JULY

HOLY DECLARATION OF THE KING, IF HE HAD CARRIED IT OUT.

Monday, July 18, the King, from Fontainebleau, declared that from now on he would sell no more offices of justice, but would give them free to learned men, capable and of good life. He did this, it is presumed, on the advice of M. de St. Germain, theologian of the Sorbonne, whom he keeps near him to advise him in matters of conscience. Indeed, he had the Parlement publish this declaration of his holy will on the 23rd of the month. But shortly afterward, with the appetite of his *mignons* and other harpies, he forgot himself and sent to the Court an Edict establishing two new conseillers in each prévostal district of France. . . .

THE DEFEAT OF STROZZI BY THE SPANIARDS, AT SEA.

At this time there came to Paris the first news of the defeat of Signor Philippe Strozzi, who since May had been making war on the King of Spain on behalf of Don Antonio, in the Azores, with many well-stocked warships and a company of fine gentlemen, all volunteers. The said Don Antonio was the last member of the ancient royal family of Portugal, and was claiming the throne of that country against King Philip, as was also the Queen Mother [Catherine de Medici], who had sent the said Strozzi to his aid. For a long time the rumors of this engagement went up and down, as it is hard to get news from so far . . . but finally certain word came that Strozzi, having courageously attacked with only three or four vessels, was met by a great number of Spanish ships . . . and was finally killed, and his ship sunk by the Spaniards, while all the rest of the French forces retired without fighting, through cowardice or through treason. For if he had been as bravely followed as he had led the Spaniard would have been put to flight. Great was the mourning at court for the loss of so brave a captain and close relative of the Queen Mother. He was regretted by all except the bastard Spanish-dominated members of the League, who were beginning to build on the ruins of France their future grandeur, based on their imaginary pretensions to the throne. . . .

SEPTEMBER

THE PEOPLE OPPRESSED, DESPITE FINE WORDS.

At this time the King sent members of his *Conseil d'État* and [of the Parlement] traveling through all the provinces to hear the complaints of the people, which were great, for the purpose, he said, of relieving their sufferings. But the upshot was that an additional 1,500,000 crowns was raised from the walled towns, and the *taille* increased by half for the next six years. (Whether the King decided this on his own or because of bad advice is not known, probably the latter.) There was such an outcry at this time that some even went so far as to wish the army of Monsieur in France, turned against his brother, the King, and to revive the war of the Public Good.

DEATH OF M. DE MONTPENSIER.

In this month of September M. Louis de Bourbon, Duke of Montpensier, died in his estate at Champigny, to the great regret of the nobility and all good men in France. He was a good prince, very generous, lover of public peace, and a very faithful servant of his King.

87

NOVEMBER

DEATH OF PREMIER PRÉSIDENT DE THOU.

Tuesday, November 1, M. Christophe de Thou, Premier Président of the Parlement de Paris, died in his house in Paris. . . . His death is blamed on his anger against the King who had made him do many things he did not believe in . . . unhappiness and anger combined with his years to send him to the tomb. He died in his seventy-fifth year (having been married to the lady Isabeau de Tuleu his wife forty-nine years and seven or eight months), full of years, full of goods, full of honors, with as much reason for satisfaction as any man of the times. He was buried on Monday, the 14th day of the present month of November, in splendid pomp in the chapel which his late father had built and furnished in the church of St. André-des-Arts, his parish. The Bishop of Meaux . . . read the service, and the whole body of ecclesiastics attached to the Sainte Chapelle marched in the long procession, which passed by the Cordeliers' and St. Cosme, the length of the rue de la Harpe, where the King and the Queen watched it from the house of the Prévost de Paris, then it turned into the Quai des Augustins and finally into the rue St. André-des-Arts. The University marched in a body. . . . All the présidents and conseillers who were then in Paris marched in black robes, preceded by a dozen or so Masters of Requests. Présidents Prévost and Brisson, and Messieurs Anjorrant and Chartier, the senior conseillers of the Grande Chambre, held the four corners of the canopy, which was of black velvet and white satin with his arms in gold. The princes of Nevers, Guise, Mayenne, D'Aumale, Nemours, the Dukes of Joyeuse and D'Épernon, and various other distinguished gentlemen, marched behind the Parlement, immediately in front of the casket. . . . The city fathers sent two dozen torches decorated with the arms of the city. The Prévost de Paris was escorted by a dozen sergeants. There were five bishops in the procession. . . .

The nave and choir of the church of St. André-des-Arts were draped in black, with his arms in gold on black velvet hanging in the middle and on the pulpit. Our master Prévost, theologian, gave the funeral sermon, which has been printed.

[The Premier Président] leaves two sons and two sons-in-law, M. Philippe Hurault, Seigneur de Cheverny, Garde des Sceaux of France, and M. Achille de Harlay, Seigneur de Beaumont, Third Président in the

Grande Chambre, to whom the King gave the office of Premier Président. . . . He leaves also two brothers, Nicholas de Thou, Bishop of Chartres, and Augustin de Thou, Lawyer of the King in Parlement. . . .

The said Premier Président died regretted by all as a good judge and very worthy of his high rank in the commonwealth. He was very diligent and accessible to all who had business with him, and prompt in expediting justice, which pleases the *procureurs* who regard him as the first and last of his kind at the Palais. But it is hard to please all the world and there are some who hold against him ambition (which is natural) and avarice and misuse of his office (which is pure calumny). . . .

THE SWISS RENEW THEIR ANCIENT ALLIANCE.

Monday, November 28, the ambassadors of the Swiss Cantons arrived in Paris to renew the alliance with the King, in spite of the machinations of the King of Spain, who has been trying for four or five years to gain them to his side by every means possible, even saying that he would pay them the arrears owed by the King [Henry III] and pay them twice as much in the future. . . .

The King sent the Prévost des Marchands and the Échevins of his city of Paris, in their red and tan robes, to escort them from the Porte St. Antoine to the Hôtel de Ville. And every day they were there the said Prévost and Échevins provided them with thirteen pasties of Mayence ham, thirty quarts of white Hippocras and claret, and forty wax candles. This was done at the King's order, and he gave the city 4,000 crowns to defray the expense of it.

Sunday, December 4, they all heard Mass in the great church of Paris, the King being present also, after which the articles of the League and Confederation were read, word for word, and solemnly sworn on the Holy Gospel by both sides. The King gave them a magnificent banquet in the Bishop's lodging, and had many shots fired in celebration. The princes and great seigneurs who were in Paris at the time also gave them splendid entertainments . . . and they finally departed for home very content with their fine reception and generous presents. . . .

In this month of November the river Seine overflowed its banks violently, because of the continuous rain. There was so much water everywhere that there was talk that it was the second Deluge.

DEATH OF THE OLDEST MAN IN PARIS.

Sunday, November 13, a good old man named Jacquet Mereau, who made his living in real estate, died at the age of one hundred and eight years. He was held to be the oldest man in Paris.

DECEMBER

GENERAL PROCESSION.

Thursday, the first of December, the King had a general procession held in Paris, in which the chariot of Ste. Geneviève and the relics of the Ste. Chapelle were displayed. The King and the three Queens watched as the fathers of the city and the members of Parlement marched in their red robes. It is said that this is the climax of his year-long prayers . . . that it would please God to give him children to succeed to the crown of France, for which he has an intense desire.

At this time the King, starved for money, laid a new exaction on all the wholesale wine merchants of Paris . . . on one a thousand crowns, on another 800, and so on . . . according to the rumors of their means. Each received a command to pay his quota within twenty-four hours on pain of prison, with no remonstrances. A little while before similar taxes had been laid on the men involved in the salt trade. . . .

REFORM OF THE CALENDAR.

In this month of December 1582 the reformation of the calendar made by the Pope was confirmed by royal command and Edict. It removed ten days, so that what had been the 10th of December became the 20th, with provision that creditors could not take advantage of the ten days to constrain their debtors, nor any contract be shortened, but must run its course. . . .

1583

RELIGIOUS EXCESSES
IN PARIS

JANUARY

RENEWAL OF THE PARLEMENT DE PARIS.

On the 7th day of January, M. Achille de Harlay entered into the exercise of his new estate of Premier Président, and M. Jean de la Guesle into that of Président of the Grand' Chambre, formerly held by the said de Harlay. The eldest son of de Guesle, Charles, took over the office of Procureur-Général of the King, formerly held by his father. . . .

FLOOD WATERS CAUSE THE COST OF LIVING TO RISE.

In this month of January the Seine river overflowed, due to the great and continuous rains. It rose almost as high as last November, and as a result wheat rose to 11 francs, feed grain to 8, and hay to 15.*

KINGS IN THE MATTER OF MONEY ARE INEXORABLE. A BLOW TO THE BONDS OF THE CITY.

At this time the King levied a tax of 1,5000,000 crowns on the cities of the kingdom . . . of which the quota of Paris is 200,000, which the King, without any consultation or deliberation, commanded the Prévost and Échevins to collect from the bourgeois of the city. . . . An assembly was held at the Hôtel de Ville . . . where it was resolved . . . that his town of Paris could not furnish such a sum. The King was much irritated at this response and forthwith commanded de Vigny, treasurer of the city, to take it out of the income of the municipal bonds, which was about to be paid out.

* Although L'Estoile does not say so here, it seems probable from other entries that he means the price per bushel.

THE KING'S DREAM, REMARKABLE FOR WHAT HAS HAPPENED SINCE.

January 21 . . . the King returned to the Louvre, and had the lions, bears, bulls, and other animals he has kept for purposes of amusement killed. This was due to a dream he had had in which these animals were eating him up. This dream seemed to presage what we have seen since, when the furious beasts of the League threw themselves on this poor prince, tore, and ate him, with his people.

THE UPRISING IN ANTWERP.

January 28 there came to Paris news of the terrible rioting and fighting in Antwerp between the French and the inhabitants, on the 17th of this month. This was on the occasion of the French, under M. le Duc d'Alençon, trying to make themselves masters of the city and loot it, as the Spaniards did six or seven years ago. . . . Fifteen or sixteeen hundred were killed, including three or four hundred French gentlemen, all of the flower of the nobility, a terrible loss. Other Frenchmen, found unarmed, were arrested and put out of the town. . . . The Duke . . . retired to his camp . . . where he was without provisions. . . . He was much criticized for such a rash and ill-advised enterprise which really cannot be called by any other name than treason, although if it had been successful it would be called something else! Indeed, by this day the name of Frenchman lost greatly in the eyes of foreigners, and Monsieur, the King's brother, much of his reputation. . . .

FEBRUARY

OF THE KING FREQUENTING THE STREETS, AND OF THE REPROACHES OF ROSE.

On the day of Mardi gras the King and his *mignons* went about the streets masked, going from house to house and committing a thousand insolences, up to six in the morning of Ash Wednesday. On that day most of the preachers of Paris openly blamed him for this in their sermons. This annoyed the King very much, especially the reproaches of Rose, doctor of theology, whom he sent for.* Rose tried to avoid going, saying that he feared maltreatment . . . but he finally appeared and received a light reprimand from the King . . . with the order not to do it again. . . . The King not only pardoned him but, several days later, sent him 400

* William Rose, Bishop of Senlis, one of the founders of the Paris League. He was among the most violent of the League preachers during the rebellion.

crowns "to buy sugar and honey, to help pass Lent, and to sweeten your bitter words."

MARCH

THE KING AT THE PALAIS FOR HIS EDICTS. THE LEAGUE.

Monday, March 1, the King, accompanied by his two *mignons* and a few other gentlemen, went to the Palais to have published in his presence a number of financial edicts which the Court had refused to register, on the grounds that they tended to the manifest oppression of the people. . . . [They were registered] although the money is used only for the profit of the Italians and the *mignons,* and even more does it give advantage to those of Guise, who stir the people up more against the King on this account. The League is beginning now to develop their *mystique* of [Henry III's] iniquity.

THE CONFRAIRIE DES PÉNITENTS, THEIR PROCESSIONS AND CEREMONIES.

In the present year 1583 the King instituted a new brotherhood which is called the Penitents, of which he and his two *mignons* are members. . . . The first ceremonies were held on the 25th of March, Feast of the Annunciation, with a solemn procession at four in the afternoon from the monastery of the Augustinians to the great church of Notre Dame. They marched two by two . . . dressed in white cloth from Holland . . . the King among them, without any guard, indistinguishable from the others. The Cardinal of Guise carried the cross, the Duke of Mayenne, his brother, was Master of Ceremonies . . . the King's singers marched in the procession, dressed like the others, singing the litany melodiously.

When they arrived at Notre Dame they all sang the *Salve Regina* accompanied by beautiful music. The hard and continuous rain which fell all day long did not in the least hinder these ceremonies. This occasioned a gentleman of quality to write the following quatrain about the King's wet robe, which, being found very timely and apropos, is being repeated everywhere:

> After having pillaged France
> And put the people to sack,
> Isn't it a fine penitence
> To wear a dripping wet sack?

93

THE BOLDNESS OF PONCET'S PREACHING, FOR WHICH HE WAS IMPRISONED.

Sunday, the 27th of the said month of March, the King had the monk Poncet arrested. He had preached a Lenten sermon at Notre Dame the day before, in which he attacked this new brotherhood, calling it a brotherhood of hypocrites and atheists.

On the same day the King had over a hundred pages and lackeys at the Louvre beaten because they had mocked the procession of the Penitents by putting white handkerchiefs over their heads, with holes cut for their eyes, and had imitated the ceremonies in an obscene and disrespectful manner. . . .

APRIL

AUTHOR OF THE BOOK: STEMMATA LOTHARINGIAE.

At this time M. François de Rosières, Archdeacon of Toul, subject of the Duke of Lorraine, was imprisoned in the Bastille at the King's command for having said many things against the truth of history and against the honor of the King and his predecessors in his book entitled *Stemmatum Lotharingiae ac Barri Ducum, Tomi Septem.*

. . . Arrived at the Bastille, he threw himself on both knees and begged for mercy. . . . And although such a crime can really only be wiped out by loss of his life (as M. de Cheverny, Garde des Sceaux, told him in no uncertain terms), His Majesty, at the request of his mother . . . pardoned him. . . .

It is the most inept and impertinent book possible, and the worst advocate of the House of Lorraine and the League that has appeared. It would have been worth their money to have it repressed rather than published. . . .

THE MARSHAL OF MONTMORENCY DEFIES THE KING.

In this month the King grew angry at the Marshal of Montmorency, Governor, or to speak plainly King, of Languedoc, because he wouldn't give up his office to the Marshal of Joyeuse, father of his *mignon* and brother-in-law . . . but Montmorency defied the King, and made himself so strong, with the support of the local nobility, that he could not be dislodged even by force without provoking civil war. . . .

JULY

DUNKIRK BESIEGED AND TAKEN BY THE SPANIARDS.

In the month of July, Dunkirk, which had been held by Monsieur, was besieged by the Duke of Parma and taken. The opinion is that this was done by secret agreement between Monsieur and the King of Spain, who paid him well for it.

AUGUST

AFFRONT TO THE QUEEN OF NAVARRE WHICH HAS COST FRANCE DEAR. JOKING REMARK OF THE KING OF NAVARRE.

Monday, the 8th day of the present month of August, the Queen of Navarre left Paris after having spent eighteen months — with great pleasure — at her brother's court, to rejoin the King of Navarre, her husband, in Gascony. This was at her brother's command. In fact the King had said that it would be better for her to be with her husband than at the court, where she served no useful purpose. . . . The King sent a company of sixty archers after her . . . and arrested two of her ladies, whom he accused of moral misdemeanors, as well as her secretary, her doctors, and others of her suite, ten in all. They were taken to Montargis, where the King himself interrogated them on the behavior of the said Queen, including a child she was supposed to have had while at the court. . . . He didn't learn anything of consequence and finally sent them back to the Queen with permission for her to continue on her way.

[Henry III] wrote to the King of Navarre about these matters . . . but when the latter resolved not to take her back . . . he wrote again and urged him to reconsider because he had discovered that the charges were all false and greatly damaging to the honor of the Queen. But the King of Navarre said he would follow the information of the first letters . . . and would not take her back. The King was much irritated by this time and sent M. de Bellièvre with letters signed by his own hand to command the King of Navarre . . . to obey him. In one of these letters the King said, "That he knew that kings were liable to be deceived by false reports, and that even the most virtuous princesses were not always exempt from calumny, and he would remind him that false accusations had even been made against the late Queen, his [Navarre's] mother."

95

When he saw this letter the King of Navarre took to laughing, and said to Bellièvre, "The King does me too much honor in these letters. In the first he called me a cuckold, and by this one, son of a prostitute."

HIÈRONIMITES.

In this month the King . . . had built in the Bois de Boulogne a chapel for a new religious group which he calls Hièronimites . . . he loses himself each day in new devotions with them, living the life of a monk more than that of a king.

SEPTEMBER

PROCESSIONS IN PARIS ON ALL SIDES.

September 10, eight or nine hundred people came in a procession to Paris, dressed in white with veils over their heads, bare feet, and carrying in their hands either a large burning candle or a wooden cross. They marched two by two, as pilgrims do. They were inhabitants of the villages of St. Jean des Deux Gemeaux and D'Ussy, in Brie. They were escorted by two gentlemen of the village, on horseback, with their ladies following in a coach. The people of Paris gathered in great crowds to see them offering their prayers and gifts in Notre Dame, and were moved by pity and admiration for their long and devout voyage in bare feet. . . .

[Later in the autumn there came five other such companies] in supplication that it would please God and Our Saviour . . . to soften His wrath and turn away the plague, which is severe and widespread in the whole kingdom.

NOVEMBER

LADIES OF PARIS IMPRISONED FOR THEIR LUXURIOUS CLOTHES AND BAUBLES.

Sunday, November 13, fifty or sixty bourgeois ladies were taken prisoner for having broken the edict about the reform of dress by their lavish attire and jewels . . . this was excessive as the edict really only required a fine to be paid . . . in the following days the *commissaires* of Paris collected quite a lot of money from other offenders, depending on the degree of the offense and the financial standing of the victim.

DEATH OF CARDINAL BIRAGUES.

Thursday, November 23, M. René de Biragues, Cardinal and Chancellor, died at the age of seventy-six . . . in Paris. He was laid out dressed as a bishop, with his red hat at his feet, and his Penitent's costume beside him. He remained thus for eight days, and great crowds of Parisians went to see him.

This Cardinal was Italian in nationality and in religion [*sic*], well versed in affairs of state but very little in those of justice . . . for the rest he was liberal, voluptuous, a man of the times, absolute slave of the King's whims, having often said that he was not Chancellor of France but Chancellor of the King of France. . . . He died poor for a man who had always served kings . . . and did better for his friends and servants than for himself. He said, a little before he died, that he would die Cardinal without title, priest without benefice, and Chancellor without seal.

THE KING, OFFENDED BY AN AFFRONT TO THE HONOR OF GOD (A RARE THING IN PRINCES), DISMISSES DU PERRON, AND IN THIS ACTS AS A VERY CHRISTIAN KING.

Friday, the 25th of this month, M. du Perron,* great talker and philosopher, made a fine discourse on the proof of the existence of God . . . with clear and cogent reasons . . . which the King enjoyed and praised. . . . But Du Perron . . . carried away by conceit . . . said to the King, "Sire, I proved today by good and sufficient reasons that there is a God. Tomorrow, if it please your Majesty to hear me again, I'll prove by equally good reasons there is no God." The King flew into a rage at this, dismissed Du Perron and forbade him his presence. This just anger was very cheering to all good men, and it was regarded as the best and most Christian thing he had ever done in his whole life. . . .

DECEMBER

BURIAL OF BIRAGUES.

Tuesday, December 6, M. René de Biragues, Cardinal and Chancellor of France, was magnificently buried. . . . The princes of the houses of

---

* Jacques Davy, Cardinal du Perron, 1556–1618, convert from Calvinism, made Bishop of Evreux by Henry IV in 1591. He was influential in obtaining papal absolution and recognition for the King in 1595. The most prolific of Catholic apologists, Du Perron opposed Du Plessis-Mornay in the famous debates at Fontainebleau in 1600.

Bourbon and Guise wore mourning, followed by all the chambers of the Parlement, the officials of the city, and the body of the University of Paris. . . .

December 13 a great and impetuous windstorm blew up over Paris, which lasted about two hours. About three days later the following "prediction" appeared and was circulated in the city. It is attributed to the Huguenots. Whether it is put into their mouths to make them more and more odious to the King, or whether they are really responsible . . . is not certain. But from whatever quarter it comes, it is just as stupid and ridiculous as malicious and seditious.*

* This "prediction" illustrates a device used by all factions in the propaganda of the wars of religion, that is, to fabricate documents containing the arguments and vocabulary which one's own interests require of the group or person to whom they are attributed. In this case the Huguenots are predicting that the churches of France will be dissipated, all Catholics persecuted and robbed of their property, and German Protestant mercenaries brought in to establish the Huguenot control of the country. The purpose of it was to justify the widespread fears of Huguenot intentions, and rouse further opposition to them and to those — *politiques* — who were willing to make concessions to them in the interests of peace and national unity.

1584

DEATH OF ALENÇON

JANUARY

REFORM OF OFFICES; TRIALS OF TREASURERS.

January 12, the King with his Conseil d'État . . . returned to St. Germain-en-Laye to continue the reformation that he says he wishes to make of all offices, as many of the long robe as of the short. He has withdrawn and abolished many offices, to the great discontent of those who had purchased them and are not reimbursed when dismissed. He had it in for the treasurers and tax collectors especially, holding them to be notorious crooks (and he is not mistaken). He has had many of them tried in a special court created for the purpose. . . .

FEBRUARY

M. LE DUC IN PARIS.

February 11, M. le Duc arrived from Château-Thierry . . . and celebrated three days of carnival with his brother, the King. The Queen Mother had him staying with her . . . and supervised their reconciliation, which was very demonstrative and gracious on both sides. They wept, embraced each other and their mother, three times, at her request.

MARDI GRAS CELEBRATED.

On the day before Lent they [the King and the Duke] went together through the streets of Paris, followed by all their favorites and *mignons*, mounted and masked, disguised as merchants, priests, lawyers, etc., tearing about with loose rein, knocking down people, or beating them with sticks, especially others who were masked. This was because on this day the King wished it to be a royal privilege to go about masked. They went to the fair in St. Germain and committed infinite insolences, rioting and disturbing the good people who were there until six o'clock in the morning.

MARCH

PILGRIMAGE OF THE KING ON FOOT.

Friday, March 9, the King left Paris to go on a pilgrimage to Notre Dame de Cléry. He went on foot, accompanied by forty-seven Brothers Penitent — the youngest and most capable of walking — all dressed in their habit of Penitent.

GONDI'S HOUSE BOUGHT BY THE QUEEN FOR HER SON.

About this time the Queen Mother did business with Hièrome de Gondi. [She planned] to purchase his newly built house in the faubourg St. Germain-des-Près . . . for M. le Duc her son . . . which came to nothing because of the Duke's death soon afterward. In fact, she left Paris, March 14, in a great hurry to go to the Duke in Château-Thierry where he lay very ill and bleeding violently from the nose and the mouth.

PENITENTS OF ALL SORTS AND COLORS.

Holy Thursday, March 29, in the evening, the King held his usual procession of Penitents, visiting the churches of Paris all during the night. Another band of about eighty Penitents, dressed in blue, also held a procession, but separately, that night. These latter were also barefoot and were accompanied by fine, harmonious music.

HUGUENOTS TAKEN BY SURPRISE AND PUNISHED.

The next day, Good Friday . . . a minister named Du Moulin, his students, and certain other Huguenots were arrested and taken to the Conciergerie. They had been assembled . . . about twenty-five strong, to celebrate communion in their manner. . . . The 14th of April following, at their trial, the Court banished [Du Moulin] and another teacher from Paris forever, and from the kingdom of France for nine years. . . .

APRIL

DEATH OF THE PHYSICIAN MALMÈDY, UNWORTHY OF A CHRISTIAN.

On the same day [April 18] the physician Malmèdy, being at Roussey, near Étampes, committed suicide by cutting his throat in despair over the crushing debts he had . . . a type of death unworthy of a Christian man, who was very learned, a great doctor and philosopher.

MAY

VOYAGE OF THE DUKE D'ÉPERNON TO THE KING OF NAVARRE, AND THE REASON.

The 16th day of May the Duke d'Épernon left Paris with a commission from the King to go to Gascony to take letters from His Majesty to the King of Navarre begging and urging him to come to the [King's] court and attend Mass. This was because the King's brother the Duke of Alençon was desperately ill and the news of his death awaited from hour to hour, and he [Henry III] wished to recognize [Navarre] as his true successor to the throne . . . and to give him all the honors, privileges, and fine treatment that his position required. The rumor is that [D'Épernon] left with 200,000 crowns given him by the King. . . .

MONSIEUR'S POSSESSIONS BROUGHT TO PARIS BY THE QUEEN MOTHER.

Toward the end of the month the Queen Mother went to Monsceaux and from there to Château-Thierry to be with M. le Duc, her son, who was gravely ill. She returned on June 1, and had sent down by water all the valuable possessions of her son, now abandoned by the doctors as being beyond human help.

JUNE

DEATH OF MONSIEUR, THE KING'S BROTHER. CEREMONIES AND OTHER DETAILS.

Sunday, June 19, about noon, Monsieur, brother of the King, died in Château-Thierry of a great hemorrhage. . . . June 21 his body was brought to Paris to St. Magloire, in the faubourg St. Jacques.

June 24, Feast of St. John, the King left the Louvre after dinner, wearing a great cape of violet Florentine serge, with a train wider than it was long, borne by eight gentlemen, to go to the said church and sprinkle holy water on the body of his late brother. He was preceded by a great number of gentlemen and princes, all in mourning. The princes rode white horses caparisoned in black . . . the bishops in scapularies of black Florentine serge, and the Cardinals in violet. Before the King marched the Swiss guards, beating their drums, which were muffled in black, and the Scottish archers . . . in their usual livery except for black hats and capes and their halberds draped in black. He was followed by the Queen, his wife, in a closed coach . . . and eight more coaches with the ladies of the court.

Monday, June 25, the body was brought to Notre Dame in Paris. The service was held on the 26th, and the next day [Alençon] was buried with great pomp and royal magnificence. . . . The white pall bore the arms of Alençon. . . .

THE KING, THE DUKE OF GUISE.

On the Monday, when the body was being taken to the church, the King, dressed in violet, sat in a window on the corner of the Parvis, near the Hôtel-Dieu, for four or five hours while the procession went by, showing himself to all the world, his face uncovered. With him was the Duke of Guise, who seemed very sad and melancholy on the surface and in what he said, though his thoughts were probably quite otherwise. . . .

M. Renault de Beaune, Archbishop of Bourges, gave the funeral sermon, and said nothing worth listening to, he never did so badly in his life. . . .

THE LEAGUE.

This prince, who was only thirty-one years old when he died, was generous and warlike, French in name and character, bitter enemy of foreigners, especially the Spaniard, who feared him. He was not fond of the House of Lorraine, to whom this death was a great source of encouragement. It came at a very opportune time for them, facilitating and advancing the designs of their League, which from then on began to grow stronger and France to grow weaker. . . .

OFFICERS OF THE LATE MONSIEUR ILL-RECEIVED BY THE KING, COMFORTED BY THE WORDS OF THE QUEEN MOTHER.

On Wednesday, June 27, the King dined at the Château of Madrid and spent the night at St. Germain-en-Laye, where the officers and servants of his late brother presented themselves to His Majesty. He sent them to the Queen Mother saying "that it was not possible for him to look upon them favorably." The Queen Mother wept when she saw them, and promised them her favor — in words.*

COUNTIES AND DUCHIES REUNITED TO THE CROWN BY THE DEATH OF MONSIEUR.

By the death of Monsieur, the King's brother, all the duchies, counties, and other estates which had been given to him as *appanages* in great numbers were reunited to the crown. The annual revenue will add up to 400,000 crowns.

JULY

DEATH OF THE PRINCE OF ORANGE.

July 21 news arrived in Paris that on the 11th of the month the Prince of Orange had been killed by a pistol shot in Delft, Holland. [It was fired] by a Burgundian of Dôle, named Balthasar Gérard . . . man known to the Prince. . . .

INTRIGUE OF THE JESUITS. AMBASSADOR OF SPAIN. THE DUKE OF PARMA.

At his trial he [Gérard] confessed that a Jesuit in Rome had urged him to the act, also to the assassination of the late Duke of Alençon, brother of the King, on the grounds that these two were the chief enemies of the Roman, Catholic and Apostolic religion, and that if God extended him the opportunity to remove [them] he would commit an act so generous it would provide him with immortality. In fact . . . that he would be lifted by waiting angels straight to Paradise. [He further said] that he had returned from Rome resolved to execute the enterprise, and had gone to Château-Thierry . . . but being unable to carry it out, he had gone to Paris and discussed the matter with the Spanish ambassador. The latter had given him much encouragement, promising him great compensation on the part of his master if he were successful. Returning to Flanders . . . he had discussed it with the Duke of Parma, who had promised him equally great rewards in this world as the rewards in Paradise promised by the Jesuit. Thereupon he had gone to Delft. . . .

* It was characteristic of the Valois family that their personal relations were full of hatred and bitterness. This was especially true of the relationship between Margot, Alençon, and Henry III. Many contemporaries account for these hatreds by the partiality of Catherine de Medici for Henry III.

After his trial was over, his right arm, which had fired the shot, was burned to the shoulder, and his body torn apart very cruelly (as he deserved) . . . without any angels appearing for his escort. . . .

THE RELIGION OF ALL THOSE WHO REBEL AGAINST THEIR PRINCE, ON WHATEVER PRETEXT.

This was the end of this Prince, not less feared than hated by the Spaniard and the House of Lorraine, who, to fool the people, covered their designs with the cloak of religion, though the truth is that their religion and his [Orange's] was nothing but ambition . . . the one, under the beautiful but specious name of liberty, and the others, under the title of the Holy League . . . this was the true foundation of both leagues.

WILLIAM PARRY.

At the same time one William Parry, gentleman and doctor of laws in London, was put to death in the said city for having made an attempt on the life of the Queen, and for attempting to start an uprising against the state and religion of England. This was at the instigation of the Pope and the Jesuits. And although he suffered the fate he deserved — that all assassins of princes deserve — Messieurs the Jesuits persuade the people as much as they can that these men are martyrs. They claimed that [Parry] had suffered for his religion, and that his bones, to be seen at the gates of London . . . were holy relics. Actually they were symbols of rebellion, assassination, and treason, crimes detested even by barbarians, condemned by nature even where there is no written law. . . .

AUGUST

HIGH PRICES OF OFFICES.

In this month of August, offices of conseiller in the Parlement de Paris are selling for 7,000 crowns; those of the Chastelet for 4,000; Maistre des Requestes for 9,000 and 10,000. . . .

SEPTEMBER

SYNODS OF MONTAUBAN AND LORRAINE. AMBITION RULES.

In this month of September, the Huguenots assembled in Montauban, the *Ligueurs* in Lorraine . . . both hoping to advance their cause by capitalizing on the death of Monsieur. The Huguenots, having as their chief the first prince of France, aim by that fact to increase their number and establish their religion in the kingdom. The *Ligueurs*, on the other hand, [hope] by the extermination of the said religion and the ruin of its chief, to facilitate the usurpation of the crown. The ecclesiastics of the one religion and the ministers of the other are very active; divided in religion but united in ambition. . . .

OCTOBER

PLAGUE AT THE COURT.

October 19, the King left in great haste from Blois and the Queens from Chenonceaux, because two or three of the Queen's ladies had caught the plague. . . . While dining with the King at Fontainebleau, Rucellai, commenting on the fear of the King and the Queens . . . dared to say, "Your Majesty ought not to fear this disease, because the court is a worse disease and will never give way to another." The King was very angry at this, and Rucellai retired immediately, fearing what would happen, and annoyed that the words had escaped him.

[October 30] the Count La Val and M. du Plessis-Mornay arrived in Paris to inform the King of the resolutions taken at Montauban, and to bring the declaration of the King of Navarre, to wit, "that he wouldn't consider changing his religion for all the monarchies in the world." This did not please the King, who said that he would have done better not to say it, that such a declaration was against his own [Navarre's] interests, but that he wouldn't listen. He [Henry III] was afraid that when he wanted to listen it might be too late.

NOVEMBER

RETORT OF THE KING TO A REMARK OF THE DUKE OF GUISE.

On the last day of this month, when the King was enjoying himself making the beautiful horse he was riding jump and perform, he turned to a gentleman of Champagne, a client of the Duke of Guise, and said, "Has my cousin Guise seen in Champagne monks who can make their horses jump like this?" He said this because it had been reported to him that the Duke, speaking of the devotions of the King, had said that he lived like a monk and not like a King. And it is true that this good prince would have done better to ride horses more often and say his beads less.

DECEMBER

VIOLENT WINDS, THE BREEZES OF THE LEAGUE.

December 5, throughout most of the kingdom, but especially in the region of the Loire, there arose winds so great, violent, and overwhelming that steeples were knocked down, chimneys broken, houses ruined, and oaks a hundred years old torn up by the roots and carried away. These have been called the breezes of the League.

ANJORRANT.

Anjorrant, dean of the Court, more than eighty years old . . . died very suddenly. He had been at the Palais both morning and afternoon of that very day. It is said that he, his valet, and his mule (whose knowledge was roughly equal) had about two hundred years between them.

LE SUEUR, DU PUIS, VIGNOLLES.

. . . all three conseillers in the Court, died. . . . Opinion at the Palais considered Le Sueur a beast, Du Puis an atheist, and Vignolles a drunkard.

PYBRAC.

May 27 of this year 1584 died the Seigneur de Pybrac, one of the rarest spirits of the century, and among the most learned. But ambition cut his throat, as is usual with clever, easy talkers. . . .

M. D'AIGREMONT, CONSEILLER IN THE GRANDE-CHAMBRE.

Monday, July 30, between five and six o'clock in the evening, M. Jacques Violle . . . was seized with apoplexy as he was dismounting from his mule to enter his house after returning from the Palais. He died almost at once, and was regretted sorely, as *homme de bien*, a good judge, and very worthy of his office. . . .

1585

HENRY OF NAVARRE
DEFIES THE POPE

JANUARY

NEW REGULATIONS.

At the beginning of this year, 1585, the King made new regulations for his household. Those who were in daily attendance . . . he dressed in black velvet, and replaced their former hats with black velvet bonnets. They were to wear a gold chain around their necks while on duty. The members of the Conseil d'État were to put on great robes of purple velvet which he had had especially made when they sat in the said Conseil. Because he was alarmed by the enterprise of those of the Houses of Guise and Lorraine against his person and his crown, he reinforced the guards . . . and kept a certain number of armed men near him day and night. . . .

FEBRUARY

AMBASSADORS OF FLANDERS WELL RECEIVED BUT REFUSED.

At the beginning of the month of February, deputies of the Estates of Flanders came to put the Low Countries under the protection and safeguard of the King, and to ask his aid against the oppression and tyranny of the King of Spain and the Duke of Parma. . . . The King received them honorably, lodged them well and treated them splendidly . . . but he sent them home without satisfaction in their demands, saying that he had enough on his hands already. . . .

MAGNIFICENT EMBASSY FROM ENGLAND.

February 23, the ambassadors from England, of whom the Earl of Warwick is the chief, arrived in Paris followed by two hundred cavalry, splendidly attired. The King received them well and paid all their expenses — it is said to the tune of 500 crowns a day. The leading men were lodged in the Hôtel d'Anjou, near the Louvre. . . . They brought the King the necklace of the Order of the Garter, covered with pearls and precious stones, worth more than 100,000 crowns, which the Queen of England had sent to her good brother. What they were really charged with was to get His Majesty to take Flanders under his protection, and offered, in the name of the Queen, to contribute a third of the expense involved.

THE KING MADE KNIGHT OF THE GARTER, FEASTS.

On Thursday, the last day of February, the King, dressed in the habit of the Knights of the English order, received the necklace from the hand of the Earl of Warwick in the church of the Augustinians in Paris, and took the oath of the Order. That evening he gave a magnificent and royal feast to the said Earl and his suite. . . .

MARCH

The first Sunday in Lent, which was March 10, 1585, the King gave another magnificent ballet. Twenty-four persons, sumptuously dressed and masked, performed, including the most beautiful (and least honest) ladies of Paris. This was chiefly to give pleasure to the English lords (which was the point of all these festivities). The ladies did this by their beauty and their subtle wiles. This party lasted from ten in the evening to three in the morning. . . .

THE LEAGUE ON HORSEBACK, WHICH IS ANOTHER FORM OF MASQUERADE, BUT UNPLEASANT.

At this time the enterprise of the Holy League began to be known. This was headed by those of the Houses of Guise and Lorraine, supported by the Pope, the King of Spain, and the Duke of Savoy, his son-in-law. It was rumored throughout the kingdom that the Duke of Guise and his brother, the Duke of Mayenne . . . were raising men of war and armaments. At first there was considerable doubt about the true nature of this enterprise, some thinking that it was an underhanded way of the King to send aid to Flanders, others that it was to join the forces of the Spaniard, the Savoyard, and the Pope . . . who were besieging Geneva and had sworn to ruin it. Still others said that the Guises . . . wished to back up their claims to the Duchy of Brittany, the Duchy of Anjou, and the counties of Maine, Touraine, and Provence, as well as other estates of the crown of France. But it soon became apparent . . . that this army was to provide teeth for their Holy League . . . under pretext of which they declared themselves protectors of the Roman, Catholic, and Apostolic Religion against those of the new opinion, or Pretended Reformed Religion, introduced in this realm by those who are called Huguenots and practiced with the King's permission. Holy League, I say, invented by the late Charles, Cardinal of Lorraine, who, seeing the line of Valois about to expire . . . hoping to exterminate the House of Bourbon . . . because of their profession of the [Protestant] religion, thought by this means to take over the crown of France. He claimed that it had been usurped . . . by Hugh Capet . . . from Lothair, last of the House of Charlemagne . . . and that [Capet] had no right except that of violence and usurpation.

THE KING TEMPORIZES, UNWILLING TO BELIEVE WHAT HE CANNOT SEE.

The King was warned of all these preparations throughout the kingdom . . . even by the Duke of Bouillon . . . while he amused himself with balls and masquerades . . . but he replied that he neither believed nor feared it. Nevertheless, after thinking about it, he began to be on his guard, but so casually . . . that the suspicion grew that there must be a secret understanding between him and those of Guise.

CHÂLONS TAKEN OVER BY THE DUKE OF GUISE.

March 21, the Duke of Guise . . . took over the town of Châlons-sur-Marne and placed a garrison there which was devoted to him. . . .

THE KING CHANGES THE CAPTAINS IN PARIS, AND WHY.

March 30, the King, having found out the intentions of the Guisards, and wishing above all to assure the safety and conservation of his good city of Paris, aware that the majority of the merchants and the little people of the city held to the League . . . had the Prévost and Échevins assemble the *dixaines* * . . . and announce the appointment . . . of new captains

---

* *Dixaine* is a subdivision of a Parisian quarter, originally a group of ten households. Orders of the Bureau de la Ville or of the Crown concerning police measures were issued to *quarteniers* and *dixainiers*.

and lieutenants . . . all chosen by the King in hopes that he could trust men who had taken an oath directly to him and were drawing wages from him . . . more than the run-of-the-mill townsmen. . . . On the last day of the month he sent for them to come to the Louvre . . . and told them that he was depending on them to protect his person and state, and their own . . . and urged them to be loyal subjects and guard the city well. . . .

APRIL

ORLÉANS JOINS THE LEAGUE.

Sunday, April 7, the King, wishing to make sure of the town of Orléans, and knowing well that the governor, Entragues, favored the League . . . sent the Duke of Montpensier in haste to take over the citadel. . . . [Some of Montpensier's men were killed in trying to capture the fortress] and the rest returned to Paris . . . leaving Entragues in full possession. . . .

The same day came news that Messières, Dijon, Aussonne, and Macon had been taken over by those of the League . . . each day another town. This increased the opinion that the King and those of the League were in secret agreement, although it was false. The truth is that the King's disposition is such that he will lose part of his power rather than give up the least bit of his leisure and pleasure to retain it whole.

DEATH OF POPE GREGORY XIII.

April 18, a courier from Rome arrived in Paris with the news that Pope Gregory XIII had died on the 10th of the month. . . . This Pope had never given his support to the League, and said to Cardinal d'Este a few days before his death that they would have no bull, nor brief, nor letters from him until he saw through their designs more clearly.

FAILURE OF A GREAT ENTERPRISE BY THE LEAGUE.

April 22 came news of the attempt — and failure — of the League to take over Marseilles. It was disastrous for them; most of them were hanged and strangled, as they well deserved. . . .

SIXTUS V, POPE.

April 24, Brother Felix Perret, formerly called the Cardinal of Montalto, was elected Pope in Rome. He took the name of Sixtus V, and was crowned on the 1st of May following. He began his reign with blood and violence, having had the Count of Tripoli and various other gentlemen put to death because he was offended by them, although the Bishops of the Church of God are not supposed to wield the sword, but on the contrary to forgive, not seven times, but seventy times seven. . . .

MAY

THE DUKE D'AUMALE AND HIS TROOPS.

At this time the Duke d'Aumale, one of the leaders of the League, having raised [a motley army] which he conducted in person . . . ravaged a large part of Picardy, stealing, looting, raping, and killing . . . as many Catholics as others . . . even taking the relics and ornaments of the churches and monasteries. . . .

THE QUEEN OF NAVARRE JOINS THE LEAGUE.*

Toward the end of this month the Queen of Navarre declared herself a member of the Holy League and took over Agen, with the help of the Seigneur Duras. . . .

JUNE

VENETIANS, BAD LIGUEURS.

At the beginning of June the Venetians, fearing the power and ambition of Spain, offered the King assistance on their part to dull the horns of King Philip, in accord with the ancient alliance of the Signory with the crown of France. . . .

THE ACCORD AT ÉPERNAY.

On the 20th day of the month of June, after many difficulties and debates, comings and goings, the treaty was concluded at Épernay between the King and the House of Lorraine. By this it was decided that there should be but one religion in France, and the other exterminated. . . . This was the only subject dealt with, because on the matter of the refor-

---

* This is only one instance, though an extreme and ostentatious one, of the hatred of Marguerite de Valois, wife of Henry of Navarre, for her brother, Henry III.

mation of the kingdom, of which there was some talk before and since, they were afraid that it might have to begin with them. . . .

The worst part of this is that the King is on foot and the League on horseback, as is proved by his Penitent's sack and their cuirasses. . . .

JULY

THE KING AT THE PALAIS FOR THE PUBLICATION OF THE LEAGUE'S EDICT AGAINST THE HUGUENOTS.

Thursday, July 18, the King went to the Palais to have published in his presence the Edict agreed to with the Guises which revokes all previous edicts of pacification with the Huguenots. . . . He made this notable comment to the Cardinal of Bourbon, "My uncle, I made the former edicts of conciliation [with the Huguenots] against my conscience, but willingly, because I knew they would relieve my people. This one is according to my conscience, but I do it most unwillingly, because from it will stem the ruin of my state and my people."

There were cries of *Vive le Roi!* when His Majesty left the Palais, which astounded everyone, as it is a long time since that much favor has been shown him, but it was later discovered that certain partisans of the League . . . had given money to various bums . . . and candy to little children to do it. . . .

HENRI D'ESTIENNE.

At this time Henri d'Estienne had come from Geneva to Paris because the King had promised him 1,000 crowns for his book, *De la Préexcellence du langage françois.* The treasurer [from whom he tried to collect] mocked him, and offered him 600. D'Estienne refused and offered him 50 if he would hand over the rest . . . he ran hither and yon trying to collect . . . had finally to return to the same man, to whom he offered the 400 if he could take the rest . . . but the other laughed at him and . . . the upshot was that he lost everything, and with the rumors of war against those of his religion flying around, and the Edict [Épernay] he was forced to leave the country unsatisfied.

DEPARTURE OF THE GUISES.

July 30, the Guises left Paris . . . they had stayed quite a long time, going every day to the Louvre to the meetings of the Conseil d'État where they were respectfully heard because the Queen Mother was on their side. This was made clear in the agreement between them and the King . . . in which they were granted all their conditions, to the great disadvantage of the King of Navarre, her son-in-law, whom she didn't like because he wouldn't treat her daughter as she wished. It is common talk that they [the Guises] have begun all these recent troubles with her approval . . . and that she favors them as much as possible, in order to deprive those of Bourbon of the crown, and assure that it falls instead to the House of Lorraine, to the children of her daughter Madame Claude. . . . To speak without prejudice, this appears to be the pure truth.* On the last day of the month, the following *pasquil* was found posted on the door of the Queen Mother's apartment at the Louvre:

France to the Queen

You waste your time, Queen, the Lorrainers are hated
As much as the Bourbons highly are rated.
To steal from them the crown don't bother to try,
It is theirs by my laws and those from the sky.

AUGUST

YO-YOS IN STYLE.

At this time the King began to carry around a yo-yo in his hand, even in the streets, and played with it as small children do. Imitating him, the Dukes D'Épernon and Joyeuse took it up . . . they in turn were followed by gentlemen, lackeys, and young men of all sorts . . . so great is the weight of the actions of kings, princes, and lords, especially in the matter of folly. . . .

* A good many of the contemporary writers assert that Catherine de Medici was secretly in league with Guise against her son, Henry III, even at the crisis of his reign, the Day of the Barricades, May 1588. François Miron, royal physician, Villeroy, who played an important part in negotiations between the League and the royalist party, the English ambassador, Stafford, and even De Thou, are among them. The evidence is not altogether clear, however, and one must not discount the intense unpopularity of the Queen Mother and the general tendency to make her the scapegoat for all the ills of the kingdom. Although L'Estoile shares this antipathy and makes many disparaging remarks about Catherine, he does not suggest, in his very full account of the outbreak of the Rebellion in 1588, that Catherine was working against Henry III's interests. In fact, the reader gets the impression that she did everything possible to save the situation.

SEPTEMBER

PAPAL BULL AGAINST THE KING OF NAVARRE AND THE PRINCE OF CONDÉ.

Toward the end of this month the Papal Bull of excommunication against the King of Navarre and Prince of Condé, issued in Rome on the 9th of the present month . . . was published in Paris. [In this Bull] this new Pope, instead of instruction, breathes destruction, exchanges his pastoral lamp for a flaming torch, and loses wholly those whom he ought to be trying to bring into the fold. . . .

THE COURT OPPOSED TO THE BULL.

The Court of Parlement made strong protests against this Bull to the King . . . saying in conclusion . . . that it was far removed from the policy and methods of ancient Popes . . . that the princes of France had never been subject to papal justice . . . that [the Papacy] had no authority over kingdoms established by God before the name of Pope existed in the world . . . and that [it should be] thrown into the flames in the presence of the entire Gallican Church. . . .

OPPOSITION OF THE KING OF NAVARRE AND OF THE PRINCE OF CONDÉ TO THE BULL OF EXCOMMUNICATION OF POPE SIXTUS V.

There was also another expression of opposition, worded as follows, and released at this time:

Henry, by the grace of God, King of Navarre, first Peer and Prince of France, opposes the declaration and excommunication of Sixtus V, so-called Pope of Rome, and maintains that it is false. . . .

As to the crime of heresy, of which he is falsely accused . . . the so-called Pope has lied, and is himself a heretic. This he [Navarre] offers to prove in a full Council freely assembled. . . .

[He further claims that] as, in the past, the Kings his predecessors knew well how to handle the temerity of such gallants as this pretended Pope, when they forgot their duty and confounded temporal and spiritual power, so the said King of Navarre, who is not inferior to them in any respect, trusts that God will give him grace to avenge the insult to his King, his House and his blood, and to all the Parlements of France. . . .

To this effect he begs the help of all true Christian princes, kings, towns, and communities . . . and all allies of this crown to join him in opposition to the tyranny and usurpation of the Pope and the conspirators of the League in France, enemies of God, of the state and their King, and of the peace and welfare of all Christendom.

The above, written by the author of the present memoirs, was sent to Rome from the Palais in Paris, and was included in the *recueils* of our times printed in La Rochelle, so great is the vanity and curiosity of our times.*

OCTOBER

NEW EDICTS CAUSED BY THE LEAGUE.

Tuesday, October 1, an Edict was published in Parlement by which all the offices formerly suppressed and reformed were re-established by the King because of the financial necessity imposed on him by the war. Thus is all war a devouring monster, but worst of all is civil war, which creates new expenses for kings and new sufferings for the people.

THE LEAGUE THROWN OUT OF AGEN, THE QUEEN OF NAVARRE IN DANGER.

At this time the *bourgeois* of the town of Agen in Gascony, being unable to support any longer the tyranny and indignities of the League under the direction of the Queen of Navarre, rose against her, killed or put to flight those who fought for her, and without the intervention of the Marshal de Mattignon they would have thrown her off the ramparts, despite her rank and position, so furious were they at the treatment they had received. . . .

NOVEMBER

On November 1, Day of All Saints, the inhabitants of Aussonne in Burgundy managed by ruse and subtlety to get the Seigneur de Tavannes, governor for the League, out of the fortress and into prison. He was given a trial in which he was accused of planning to turn over the town to the Spaniards. The rumor is that this was done at the secret command of the King, who is outraged in his heart (though he disguises it on

---

* It is possible that L'Estoile merely means that he copied this declaration, but his precision of expression makes it doubtful. He often speaks of "copying" documents. The use of the verb *faire* here suggests composition.

the surface) that the Guises take over more and more leading cities of the kingdom, under pretext of their League, and install governors devoted to them, just as if they were kings and the lawful rulers of these towns. . . .

THE QUADRANGLE OF THE PALAIS FINISHED.

November 18, the quadrangle or courtyard of the clock tower at the Palais was completed. It is an excellent and beautiful work done by Pilon, sculptor to the King, very skilled in his art. It is an ornament to the city. . . .

ATTEMPT OF THE LEAGUE IN SCOTLAND.

Toward the end of the month news was received in Paris that an uprising had been attempted in Scotland by those of the League and the Jesuits, under the pretext of religion. When they found themselves exposed they could scarcely find refuge . . . most of them escaping the kingdom disguised as sailors.*

On this subject the following poem was circulated in Paris by those of the religion:

> Hardly has the Scotchman, to live in liberty
> Thrown off Antichrist's damnable yoke,
> Than Satan, envious, for a damnable joke
> Begins to disturb his quiet felicity.

DECEMBER

CHANGES OF RELIGION IN ORDER TO SAVE ONE'S WORLDLY GOODS . . . DU CERCEAU.

At this time many belonging to the Pretended Reformed Religion abjured it, took instruction, went to Mass and tried to be good Catholics, in order to save their lives and their property. . . .

There were others who stood firm, however, abandoning all, according to the King's Edict, not without great risks. . . .

Du Cerceau, the King's architect, an excellent man and highly skilled

---

* This entry shows the provincialism of L'Estoile. He conceives of any enterprise of ultra-Catholics against the state — in any country — as a work of the League. In the over-all sense he was right, as the Counter Reformation was an international movement.

in his art, was privately entreated by the King . . . and promised great rewards [if he would abjure] . . . but he preferred to give up all his goods, and the King's favor, than go to Mass. . . . He left his new house . . . which was very elegant and expensive. . . . When he went to say farewell to His Majesty he asked him not to hold it against him that he was as faithful to the service of God, his great Master, as he had always been to the King's, and would be to the day he died, saving his honor and his conscience. . . .

THE DEATH OF RONSARD.

On December 28, the first and last of our French poets, M. Pierre de Ronsard, died at the age of sixty-two in his priory of St. Cosme. He had a reputation for excellence as a poet surpassing all others under the Kings Henry II, Francis II, and Charles IX, who loved and honored him; all but Henry III, who never gave him any promotion nor signs of favor.

1586

STRIKE AT THE PALAIS

JANUARY

THE PUBLICATION OF THE DECREES OF THE COUNCIL OF TRENT CONSIDERED;
JUDGMENT SUSPENDED BECAUSE OF THE WISE REMONSTRANCE OF M. FAYE.

On January 10, the King, who has been greatly pressed and importuned by the clergy of France and by the League, as well as by the Papal Nuncio, to receive and publish the decrees of the Council of Trent in his kingdom, asked the advice of M. Jacques Faye, his lawyer in the Parlement de Paris. The latter made a fine and courageous protest, pointing out the wrong that [this policy] would do to the kingdom . . . and gave such good and convincing reasons . . . that the King said to the ecclesiastics that he wished to hear no more of it until the war, just begun, had been settled.

Thereupon the clergy divided into two factions, one favoring the King and the other the Pope.* Everything is at sixes and sevens, the Papists and the Huguenots pillage at will, neither the ecclesiastics nor the nobles nor the people can do anything about it. The King gives benefices to gentlemen and ladies, as before, without consulting the Pope. . . .

FEBRUARY

A MAN WITHOUT ARMS.

On the 10th of this month I saw a man without arms, who could write, wash dishes, take off his hat . . . play cards . . . and shoot . . . he is about forty years old and claims to be a native of Nantes in Brittany.

THE DUKE OF GUISE FRIGHTENS THE KING.

On February 15, the Duke of Guise arrived in Paris, where the King

* The French clergy divided thus into Gallican and ultramontane factions over all of the Counter-Reformation policies and instruments, such as the Inquisition, the Index, and the Society of Jesus; the League clergy following Spain and the Papacy, the royalist clergy opposing them.

had sent for him. He was heavily escorted and had delayed his arrival for several days because of measures which the King had taken, reinforcing the guards of the Louvre and those of the gates of the city . . . and even having houses searched for strangers, not by the captains of the quarters, who did this regularly, but by Knights of the Holy Spirit. Once arrived in Paris, the Duke made himself very popular by flattering and honoring the people . . . which doesn't profit them any.

MARCH

THE KING'S DEVOTIONS AGREEABLE TO THE LEAGUE.

On March 25, Feast of the Annunciation of Our Lady, the King did not go through the city with the procession of the Penitents as usual . . . but the next day . . . he went to Chartres, on foot and dressed as a Penitent, and accompanied by about sixty of the Brotherhood. . . . In the night of Maundy Thursday he did enter into [their] procession . . . through the streets and churches of Paris, and from Good Friday until Easter Tuesday he did not leave the [Monastery of the] Capuchins, doing penance and praying.

Thus does this good prince (to the great satisfaction of Messieurs of the League, his enemies) live more as a Capuchin than as a King . . . the cloister his battlefield, his cuirass exchanged for the robes of a Penitent.*

APRIL

EMBASSY FROM DENMARK.

April 24, the ambassadors from Denmark arrived in Paris. They came to protest to the King about his making war and persecuting those of the [Protestant] religion. The King gave them such an unsatisfactory response that they went home. . . .

THREE PRODIGIOUS DEEDS IN THIS MONTH.

In this month of April, a thirteen-year-old boy . . . a scholar of eight-

* *Politiques* and conservatives like L'Estoile regarded Henry III's demonstrations of piety as overdone and unsuitable, while the "professional" Catholics of the League regarded them as insincere in a King who made concessions to Huguenots and opposed the Papacy.

een . . . and a man of fifty . . . hanged themselves miserably [in different quarters], which seemed to be an augury of some evil hanging over the city of Paris.

MAY

THE DUKE OF GUISE LEAVES PARIS.

May 18, the Duke of Guise left Paris for Châlons. During the three months he was here he did nothing but study how to undermine the foundation of the King's support . . . that is, the good will of his subjects. . . .

HIGH COST OF WHEAT IN PARIS.

In this month of May, wheat was selling at seven or eight crowns a bushel in Paris. There was such a tremendous number of beggars in the streets and knocking at people's doors — coming from all over France and even from foreign countries — that it was necessary to raise a special fund to relieve them. Two men went the rounds in each parish, and everyone gave what seemed suitable to him.

Toward the end of the month La Mersilière, Secretary of the King of Navarre, came to the King at his master's command . . . to try to persuade the King to call off the war [against the Huguenots] . . . and outlining to him some excellent and sure ways to get rid of the League. . . . But one can hardly get the King out of a monk's cell . . . and the more he thinks about the situation the weaker is his side and the stronger is the League. The result was . . . that his heart failed him (as if the Duke of Guise had him already by the neck), and the said La Mersilière returned with an answer as cold as the resolution of the prince was lukewarm.

JUNE

THE PALAIS WITHOUT PROCUREURS, BECAUSE OF THE KING'S EDICT.

Since the 18th day of the present month of June, the *Procureurs* of the Court and the Chastelet have been on strike to a man (as the result of a common resolution) because of the King's Edict . . . that they would have to pay one or two hundred crowns in order to continue in their office. . . .

JULY

SIGNS OF EMOTION IN PARIS.

The 8th day of July, the King returned suddenly to Paris from St. Maur ... fearing an uprising that he had been told was brewing in Paris because of the twenty-seven Edicts. . . . He had also learned that the previous day two very seditious Latin pasquils attacking him had been posted in the streets. . . .

THE PROCUREURS RE-ESTABLISHED, WITHOUT HAVING TO PAY.

Saturday, July 12, the *Procureurs* of the Court, led by some of the most prominent among them, went to the Louvre in large numbers and threw themselves on their knees before the King . . . asking his pardon . . . and asking him to have pity on their poverty. The King replied that if they had made this clear sooner, the course of justice would not have been so long interrupted. . . . He told them to rise, and to resume their offices . . . and to behave like good men . . . that he had pity on them and would revoke the Edict. He asked them to pray for him. The King did this, according to the common rumors, because all the courts, in all the regions of jurisdiction in France, were about to follow the example of Paris. . . .

To tell the truth, the people were to blame for all these evils themselves, because they followed and supported the League, which was the sole cause of their ruin. . . .

In this month of July, a letter was brought to Brother Maurice Poncet, curé of St. Pierre-des-Arts, by an ecclesiastic in a long robe . . . whom no one recognized. The said letter charged Poncet to warn the King that if he did not cease his hypocrisy and oppression of the people (who were laden daily with new financial burdens), there were two hundred people who had sworn to kill him. This letter, given to the Chancellor, was found to be in the same writing as certain evil placards which had appeared throughout the city in mid-June, containing evil and detestable injuries against the King, the Queen, his mother [and others].

This is how, by the devices of *Madame la Ligue*, the love of their King was uprooted from the hearts of the people, who spoke of him only with contempt . . . as a sort of *prince fainéant*. . . .

AUGUST

DRAKE.

About the middle of August, Drake, the great and renowned English captain of the seas, arrived in London after a long and perilous voyage on the great ocean, bringing to the Queen of England, his mistress, bold and beautiful conquests and a fine, rich booty, consisting of gold, silver, pearls, precious stones . . . not to mention artillery and other munitions . . . taken from the Spaniards in the Indies and in the New World. He was welcomed, greeted, caressed, favored, and honored, by the Queen and by all the nobility and people of England, for having made such a hazardous, long, and memorable voyage . . . and for such a bold and fine deed, greater than any other exploit of a maritime nature since the discovery of America and the other lands which are called new. He is called the Terror of the Spaniard and the flail of their King.

. . . [In the month of August] the poor people of the countryside, dying of hunger, went about in gangs and cut the half-ripe grain in the fields, then ate it on the spot . . . in spite of the measures taken by those who owned the fields. Sometimes they threatened to eat [the owners] too, if they would not allow them to eat the grain.

SEPTEMBER

CONSPIRACY DISCOVERED IN ENGLAND.

On September 6 news came to Paris of a conspiracy on the part of English Catholics to kill the Queen and all the members of her council, and to exterminate all Huguenots, native and refugee . . . the chiefs were found to be the Queen of Scots, helped by various lords of her party, and the Jesuits, who killed caution in the assassins by promising them that they would go straight to Paradise wtihout passing through Purgatory. . . .

September 19 . . . an English gentleman arrived in Paris . . . to bring a transcription of the trial of the said Queen to the King and his council. Thereupon His Majesty decided to send M. de Bellièvre to the Queen of England to prevent, if possible, any harm coming to the said

Queen of Scotland, his good and close relative. But those of the League thought this mission was more to hasten her execution than to delay it because of the ill-will they said the King bore to all the House of Lorraine.

OCTOBER

GERMAN AMBASSADORS LEAVE DISSATISFIED.

October 13, the German ambassadors . . . left Paris to return to their country, indignant and annoyed against His Majesty because he will not accord any mercy, nor truce to the [Protestants] of his kingdom. He excuses himself for this by blaming the violence and military power of the League.

COUNTERMEASURES OF THE KING OF NAVARRE.

At this time the King of Navarre . . . knowing that, under the pretext of religion, the attempt was being made to ruin him and rob him of the succession which by right belongs to him, published and spread around a new declaration. In this he said that he did not wish to be stubborn about his religion, but would submit to the judgment of a free national council. . . . At this those of the League took violent alarm, for fear lest he change his religion . . . and published many writings to the effect that he must not be received. . . .*

NOVEMBER

DEATH OF OUR M. PONCET.

Sunday . . . November 23, Brother Maurice Poncet . . . died in Paris. He was a good and learned preacher, greatly honored and esteemed by all the people of Paris because he reproved vice and spared neither great nor small. When he got warmed up . . . he preached with great fire and zeal. He was, in addition, a man of good life and sincere conscience. . . .

* The League pretended that their opposition to Navarre was on religious grounds. Actually they feared nothing so much as his conversion, which would rob them of their role as Defenders of the Faith. This became very obvious in the later stages of the rebellion, when he did, in fact, become a Catholic. See entries for 1593–1594.

DECEMBER

THE KING'S JOY SHORT-LIVED.

At the beginning of December the King . . . gave thanks to God because he thought the Queen was pregnant. . . . This was found to be false in three or four days, to his great regret and the joy of the League, who fear nothing on earth so such.

CONFISCATION OF THE GOODS OF CARDINAL PELLEVÉ.

About the middle of December the King seized all the temporal wealth of the benefices held by Cardinal Pellevé . . . because of the bad services he had done His Majesty in Rome. . . .*

BRIGANDAGE OF LANSSAC.

About this time young Lanssac seized and occupied the Garonne from Bordeaux to the sea, using six vessels. He robbed all indiscriminately, Huguenots and Catholics alike, recognizing neither the King, nor the Guises, nor the King of Navarre, nor any party but his own. . . .

BELLIÈVRE IN ENGLAND.

Toward the end of this year, 1586, M. de Bellièvre arrived in London . . . where he was well received and patiently heard by the Queen. To his remonstrances she replied with her own mouth, sitting in full council, which I have extracted faithfully from the original sent by the ambassador.

SPEECH OF THE QUEEN OF ENGLAND ON THE AFFAIR OF THE QUEEN OF SCOTLAND.

Messieurs Ambassadors, So much do I trust the good will of the King, my good brother, that I am sure that when he has heard what has happened he will not take in bad part what I have done against her [Mary] who has so often conspired against my person and my state. I am distressed that such a person as you, M. de Bellièvre, took pains to come to this kingdom for an affair in which there is no honor, being aware . . . that everyone knows my innocence.

I here call God as witness before you, if ever I have given her any cause

---

* Cardinal Pellevé was one of the most narrow and ferocious of the League leaders. He played a considerable part in the Estates of the League, 1593.

for discontent. Everyone knows how many times she has offended me and how patient I have been. One must weigh how precious is my royal rank. She is my inferior, being in my kingdom. I have done her many offices of friendship, but never have I been so afflicted, not even the death of the King my father, the King my brother, and the Queen my sister, have moved me so much as this subject. I call God to witness if I wished to treat her as she has treated me. I have read as many histories as any prince or princess in Christendom but I never found a thing like this. . . . I heard every word of your discourse, M. de Bellièvre, but it does not change my mind.

I am always in pain, lacking security in my own house and kingdom. I am assaulted and spied upon from all directions. I am not free but captive. I am her prisoner instead of her being mine. She has surrounded me on all sides with so many enemies that I do not know where to turn. I only hope that God will save me and my people. . . . If I accord what you ask I would perjure myself and take His Holy Name in vain.

I would not make such a request [as Henry III was making] to your good master nor to any other prince in Christendom, wanting them to be safe from their enemies. . . . I am a poor woman who must resist many assaults and ambushes.

Following this the death sentence was cried in all the cities of England, and all [Mary's] people dressed in mourning. Well might she say, "Alas, the League which I have loved so well is the cause of my death."

THE CLERICAL OFFENSIVE

JANUARY

SPEECH OF THE KING TO THE PEOPLE OF PARIS.

January 10, the King called to the Louvre [various members] of the Parlement, the Prévost des Marchands and Échevins, and some leading *bourgeois* of his good city of Paris. In the presence of [members of his Conseil] he told them that he was determined to make war to the death on those of the new opinion [Protestants]. . . . When he paused a little, this speech was received with acclamation by all . . . until he said further that he was going to need from them 600,000 crowns . . . that would be raised by a special tax on the richer men of Paris. . . . At this they were at a loss for words and went home much put out. . . .

FEBRUARY

FEAST DAYS.

In the days before Lent the King held masquerades, feasts, and ballets with ladies participating, in his accustomed manner, and enjoyed himself very much . . . continuing his devotions (which many call hypocrisy), he shut himself up with the Capuchins on the first day of Lent, doing or pretending to do penance with his *mignons*. . . .

A PLOT DISCOVERED.

Saturday, February 22, the King was informed of a conspiracy against him and his city of Paris . . . so he reinforced the guards, had the drawbridges raised . . . and had the streets patrolled all night. The following Monday, the Duke of Mayenne complained of this angrily to the King . . . saying [that it had been unfairly attributed to him and his followers] by the heretics and *politiques*, and that they would regret it. The King, however, took prisoner a number of captains . . . and sent the Knights of the Holy Spirit through all the quarters to search for arms. . . . (He didn't believe the Duke at all, and in fact . . . [the conspiracy] was later confessed by one of the archconspirators of the College de Forteret, which is called the cradle of the League. . . .)

SORCERERS EXECUTED IN PARIS.

Thursday, February 26, Dominici Miraille, Italian, an old man of seventy . . . and a bourgeoise of Étampes who was the mother of his second wife . . . were hanged, strangled, and then burned on the Parvis-Notre Dame, convicted of magic and sorcery. . . .

This was remarked as something new in Paris, where these vermin have been allowed freedom, especially at [the King's] court where they are popularly called philosophers and astrologers. In the time of King Charles IX they numbered thirty thousand, as their leader had confessed in 1572. This against the express commandment of God, whose law condemns sorcerers to death. . . .

MARCH

NEWS OF THE EXECUTION OF THE QUEEN OF SCOTS.

On Sunday, the first day of March of the present year, 1587, news came to Paris of the execution of the Queen of Scots, whose head was cut off by the executioner on the 18th day of February, following the death sentence against the said Queen by the Parliament of England several months before, for the crime of lèse-majesté, and for conspiracy against the state and Queen of England. . . .

At eight o'clock in the morning she was led to a scaffold draped in black, in the great hall of the castle of Fotheringay. She mounted it with five ladies of her suite, whom she comforted for their tears, and showed great courage and fortitude, welcoming the end of her long captivity, and embracing death with a generous and masculine resolution. She showed great firmness in her religion and consideration for her son and her servants. She was not willing to have the executioner disrobe her, saying that she was not used to the services of such a gentleman, but undressed herself, and, kneeling on a black cushion, presented her head to the executioner. It was held by his assistant (this is contrary to the privileges of princes) to make the blow more sure. When he showed her head, severed from her body, to the people, they began to shout, "Long live the Queen!"

When her hair fell to the ground it could be seen what suffering had done to her, for, at the age of forty-five, it was entirely white. She was reputed to be one of the most beautiful women in the world.

She was born on the 7th of December, 1542, crowned at eighteen months, brought to France at the age of six, married at fifteen to the Dauphin of France. After his death she returned to Scotland and married Henry Darnley, aged twenty-two, handsome and perfect in every way, who was [later] strangled in the night at Edinburgh, and blown up. . . . Then she married for the third time the Count of Bothwell, suspected of the murder, whereupon her people rose against her, accused this poor Queen of adultery and murder, and took her prisoner. Her husband fled to Denmark, where he died in prison. She escaped, took arms against her rebellious subjects, but was finally forced to flee to England, where she was beheaded after an imprisonment of eighteen years. Here is a truly tragic life and a real mirror of the vanities of the world! . . .

At the news of this death a great show of mourning was put on at the court of France, especially on the part of the members of the Houses of Lorraine and Guise, to whom this Queen was closely related (too close for her good, according to many).

Indeed, on the following Sunday the King and Queen and members of the House of Lorraine all put on deep mourning . . . and on the 13th of this month a solemn service was held in the great church of Paris . . . [with ecclesiastics, nobles, and representatives of the Parlement participating].

Her death was infinitely regretted and mourned by the Catholics, principally by the League, who cried aloud that she was a martyr to the Roman, Catholic and Apostolic religion, and that the Queen had put her to death on this account . . . no matter what the pretext was. In this opinion they were carefully and cleverly supported by the preachers, who canonized her every day in their sermons.

Poems, placards, epitaphs, and all sorts of discourses on this death are circulating in Paris, reflecting the passions of the factions. . . .*

* Thirty-four pages of the *Journal de Henri III* following this entry are filled with L'Estoile's copies of some of the verses, epitaphs, etc. about Mary Stuart, principally those of the League which extol her as a martyr and brand Elizabeth, commonly called "Jezebel," as a tyrant. L'Estoile shows a degree of sympathy for Mary which is surprising in view of his royalist sentiments, but he never accepts the League party line about her martyrdom nor the accusations against Elizabeth.

APRIL

THE KING VENTS HIS ANGER ON THE HUGUENOTS, THOUGH HE IS LESS
OFFENDED BY THEM THAN BY THE LEAGUE.

Thursday, April 23, the King learned that the people of Paris were murmuring loudly — stirred up by those of the League — that he had not carried out the matter of confiscation of the goods of the Huguenots, that the preachers in their pulpits were pecking at him with their beaks, accusing him of secretly favoring heretics. As a result of this all the little people were dragging him in the gutter with their vulgar jokes and libels. . . . [Henry III] thereupon had the Edict published confiscating their goods . . . and complained to the Court at the same time about these defamatory writings . . . which served as kindling for . . . rebellion. . . .

To meet this problem the Court issued a fine ordinance [to control the libels against the King] but it was written in wax, because His Majesty's authority was already so weakened (by his own too great leniency and connivance) that he was spoken of exclusively in contempt and all his actions of devotion condemned publicly as hypocrisy. . . .

THE DUKE D'ÉPERNON.

In this month of April the Duke d'Épernon returned to Paris from Provence . . . in great magnificence, accompanied by three hundred mounted men. He was welcomed by the King but the League took a dim view of him, saying that he was the only one who put courage in the heart of the King, and in truth he was the only servant whom His Majesty could really trust.

THE DUKE OF JOYEUSE.

A little afterward, the Duke of Joyeuse returned to Paris from Normandy . . . he was rebuffed and withdrawn from favors . . . because the King had sure information that he had joined the League, thus showing himself as ungrateful a traitor to his master as D'Épernon had shown himself faithful.

HIGH COST OF WHEAT IN PARIS.

In this same month of April, wheat was selling in the market for 22 francs a bushel. In the suburbs there was frost every day, and hordes of poor beggars invaded the city.

MAY

VINES FROZEN.

Trinity Sunday, May 24, the vines froze in the vicinity of Paris. Three or four days before it snowed heavily near Meaux.

THE COURT'S PROTESTS BADLY RECEIVED BY THE KING.

May 30, a certain number of Présidents and Conseillers of Parlement were deputed to go to the King . . . to protest the seizure of the income of the city bonds, and the suspension of their wages. They said that unless he returned these immediately they were resolved to leave his service and go no more to the Palais. The King, much annoyed, said . . . that they had pressed him to wage war . . . and that he would see that they got justice, but that he understood well enough what they were up to: they were negotiating so that they would not be thrown in the river in sacks. He said this because . . . the majority of the preachers of Paris had violently denounced the men of the Court and said they should be tossed in the water, tied up in sacks. . . .

JUNE

Thursday, June 4, Roland, one of the buttresses and pillars of the Holy League, was arrested and taken to the Conciergerie by the King's command, because two days before he had spoken treasonable words against His Majesty in public, at the Hôtel de Ville. . . . He was a violent man, whose nature was to talk frequently and loudly, above all, lies. . . . Du Bellay of Toulouse was arrested on the same day, but for the opposite reason, that he had defended the King, and the King of Navarre and his family, from the libels and slanders of the League. The next few days showed that [the League] had more concern for its servants, and could take better care of them, than the King for his, when Roland was released . . . and poor Du Bellay held, on the false charge that he was a heretic, that is, that he opposed the Papal bull against the King of Navarre. . . .

Saturday, June 27, the chambers of Parlement were assembled to consider four new Edicts which the King was urging on them in order to raise money. The first was the creation of a sixth chamber in Parlement; the second, a third chamber of Requests; the third, the alienation of the royal domain, to the extent of 300,000 crowns; and the fourth, the creation of a new chamber of Domain. . . . But the Court rejected them all and wrote on them: *denied.* . . .

JULY

THE TABLEAU OF MADAME DE MONTPENSIER.

Thursday, July 9, a picture was removed from the cemetery of St. Séverin, which the *politiques* call "the tableau of Madame de Montpensier," because it was put there by M. Jean Prévost, curé, at her request, so they say . . . and at the urging . . . of some of the asses of the Sorbonne . . . bold councillors of state who spend their entire life locked up in a college, devouring the poor novices with pedantry. . . . Among them are Rose, Boucher . . . Pelletier, the Scotsman Hamilton . . . Ceuilly . . . and many others.* This picture depicted with graphic detail the cruel and inhuman tortures of the Catholics by the Queen of England. . . . It had been put there for the purpose of stirring up the people more and more to make war on the Huguenots . . . and even against the King, who the people (led by the preachers) say favors them secretly. And, in fact, the stupid people of Paris went in great numbers every day to see this beautiful picture and were moved by it, crying out that all *politiques* and heretics must be exterminated. For this reason the King had commanded the Parlement to have it removed, but as quietly as possible . . . to avoid a disturbance. . . .

This same day the chariot of Ste. Geneviève was paraded through the streets, with prayers that the rain might stop . . . but she produced no miracle. . . .

THE ARRIVAL OF THE FEUILLANTS IN PARIS. BROTHER BERNARD.

On this same day there arrived in Paris sixty-two Bernardines from the

* This year, 1587, marks the launching of the clerical offensive under the direction of Madame de Montpensier which was to last till the end of the rebellion in 1594. The Parisian *prédicateurs* were the chief propagandists of the League.

Abbey of Feuillant, near Toulouse. . . . The King lodged them . . . in an edifice he had especially built in the faubourg St. Honoré. . . . But the people of Paris . . . did nothing but mock them, and called them hypocrites. Some of these Feuillants gained quite a following by their preaching, however, among them a young Gascon of twenty-two or twenty-three, Brother Bernard, who, according to rumors, lives very austerely and preaches with miraculous power. He was so favored by the ladies of Paris that they spoiled him . . . and turned his head. They sent him sweets so often that, they say, he developed an appetite for meat.

SCARCITY OF GOOD THEOLOGIANS.

We are not provided with good religious leaders in Paris this season . . . with the exception of seven or eight . . . they are all in the pay of the League, to take advantage of the gullibility of the people and stir up rebellion. . . . Instead of the word of God they preach I don't know what bigotry and hypocrisy . . . following the catechism of the League, which has produced more atheists than Catholics, and instilled superstition and rebellion instead of religion. . . .

RIOTS IN THE MARKETS OF PARIS AGAINST THE BAKERS.

July 22, the people mutinied in the market against the bakers because the price of bread was too high . . . bread was stolen . . . booths overturned . . . and two *bourgeois* were killed . . . the bakers' wagons were burned, and the crowd forced its way into several houses where the bakers had taken refuge. . . .

AUGUST

CHARLES, MONSIEUR, GRAND PRIOR OF FRANCE.

Sunday, August 2, the King conducted Charles, *Monsieur*, bastard son of the late King Charles IX, his brother, to the Augustinians' . . . and there made him Grand Prior of France in the presence of all the Knights of the Order of St. John of Jerusalem, the Queens, and many lords and ladies. He gave him the white cross with all the accustomed ceremony and ritual. Since then the King has kept him at court and shown him great signs of favor and affection.

Sunday, August 9, all the preachers of Paris in their sermons exhorted the people to pray devoutly for the Dukes of Guise and Joyeuse . . . to ask God that in His goodness He would assist them in their just and praiseworthy war against the false and evil fox (this is what they call the King of Navarre). They mentioned the King coldly and in passing. . . .

WEDDING FEAST OF THE DUKE D'ÉPERNON.

Sunday, August 30, a magnificent wedding feast was held for the Duke d'Épernon and the Countess of Candales . . . with the King, the Queens, the princesses . . . present in great pomp. The King seemed to be enjoying himself hugely, though his death's-head was hanging all the while from his belt.* He gave the bride a necklace of a hundred pearls, estimated at 100,000 crowns.

DEATH OF M. MANGOT.

This day there died in the city of Paris, in the prime of life, M. Mangot, Lawyer of the King in the Parlement. He was called the pearl of the Palais because of his singular righteousness, great learning, and other virtues. Like Noah, God took him into the protection of his ark on the eve of a great tempest, when the waters of the wrath of God seemed about to submerge France and ruin her. . . .

SEPTEMBER

THE DAY OF ST. SÉVERIN.

Wednesday, September 2, at six in the evening, great rumors spread through the quarter of the rue St. Jacques, and men rushed into the streets shouting "To arms! To arms! It is time for all good Catholics to show that they know the Huguenots are planning to kill the preachers!" and the bell of St. Benedict began to toll. The foundation of this excitement seemed to be that Rapin, Lieutenant of the short robe, had been told to bring to the Louvre a theologian who had preached seditiously at St. Germain-l'Auxerrois, and the curés of St. Séverin and St. Benedict, whom the King thought too insolent in their sermons. And in truth, these two and

---

* Henry III manifested his religious fervor in a variety of ways offensive to conservatives like L'Estoile. In the months immediately preceding the rebellion he not only encouraged the new Penitent Orders and marched barefoot in their processions, but often wore a large medal with a skull embossed on it, hanging from his belt.

most of the preachers of Paris admitted themselves that they preached only what was in the bulletins sent them by Madame de Montpensier.

A notary named Hatte, very prominent in the quarter, an impudent and violent man, furious *ligueur*, was held to be the instigator of the uprising and [royal officers] went to arrest him at nine that evening, but he was not there. . . .

THE KING GOES OFF TO WAR.

Saturday, September 12, the King left Paris to go to his camp at Gien-sur-Loire, after taking an affectionate farewell of [the Parlement and the officials of the city] in which he charged them with the peace and welfare of the city, and of the Queen, his mother, during his absence. . . .

In the meanwhile Madame de Montpensier is the Governor of Paris for the League, and keeps her brothers in the good graces of the Parisians . . . and does more through the mouths of her preachers (by paying them to build up [her brothers'] reputation with the people at the expense of the King . . .) than they with all their arms and men. . . . She is impudent enough to brag of this out loud, and it comes to the King's ears. . . .

OCTOBER

THE DAY OF COUTRAS.

Tuesday, October 20, occurred the fight and cruel encounter of the King of Navarre and the Duke of Joyeuse at Coutras, which has since been called the day of Coutras, in which the army of the said Duke was entirely defeated and put to rout. He and his brother were killed, and the remains of his army chased three leagues by the King of Navarre. . . . Such a great number of nobles died on the battlefield that . . . the Queen Mother said that in twenty-five years of battles and encounters in France not so many gentlemen had died as on that one day. The King mourned the nobles, not their chief, knowing that he was of the League, that is, bad servant. The reigning Queen (of good blood and incapable of lying) cried for him sincerely, the Queen Mother, as a matter of form, as usual, the Cardinal of Bourbon like a beast. He said . . . *ligueur* that he is . . . that he wished his nephew, the King of Navarre, had been in his place. . . .

NOVEMBER

THE SWISS BROUGHT INTO THE SUBURBS, AGAINST THE QUEEN'S PROMISE.

Friday, November 6, two or three hundred bourgeois of Paris, accompanied by [the officials of the city], went to the Queen, mother of the King, to beg her not to lodge the four thousand Swiss whom the King had sent for in the suburbs . . . for fear of an uprising. She promised to do what she could. In spite of this the said Swiss were brought into the suburbs on the 8th and 9th of the month, to the great discontent of all Parisians.

THE VICTORY AT AUNEAU.

Tuesday, November 24, the Duke of Guise . . . with a few forces . . . managed to get the captain of St. Paul . . . into the citadel of Auneau. It is said that he did this by negotiation with the commander in charge of the defense, who was secretly in his service. . . . It was done so successfully that great numbers of the defenders were killed, the chiefs imprisoned, and much booty taken. All the honor and credit for this signal exploit was given to the Duke of Guise throughout France and especially in Paris, where it caused great rejoicing (and to tell the truth he deserved a large part of the glory).

The King was nevertheless much put out by this, and even more when he heard that the preachers in Paris were saying from the pulpits that Saul had killed his thousands and David his ten thousands. . . .

Thus the victory of Auneau was the theme song of the League, the joy of the clergy . . . and the cause of the King's jealousy. He knew that these laurels were heaped on Guise to diminish his own. A truly miserable thing, for a great king to be jealous of his vassal.

DECEMBER

The preachers cried that without the prowess and constancy of the Duke of Guise the ark would have fallen to the Philistines . . . and heresy triumphed over religion. At this point the Sorbonne, that is, thirty or forty pedants . . . who dispose of scepters and crowns . . . made a secret decision (though not so secret that everyone didn't hear of it, and the King among the first) that one could remove the power of government from the hands of incapable princes . . . these are the exact terms of the decision of the Sorbonne, agreed on in their college, Wednesday, December 16, of the present year, 1587.

THE KING RETURNS TO PARIS FROM THE WARS.

Wednesday, December 23, the King entered Paris, returning from the wars, accompanied by the members of the courts in red robes, the officials of the city, many notable *bourgeois* and various seigneurs. . . . He entered by the St. Jacques gate and rode directly to Notre Dame . . . where a solemn *Te Deum* was sung . . . later he went to the Hôtel de Ville where fireworks and other signs of rejoicing were held. . . . He did all this deliberately because he was envious of the honors that the stupid people heaped on the Duke of Guise . . . for this victory . . . with no mention of the King. . . .

REPRIMAND OF BOUCHER AND OTHER PREACHERS.

December 30, the King sent for the Parlement and the Faculty of Theology to come to the Louvre, and administered a sharp and bitter reprimand to the theologians in the presence of the court for their insolent and unbridled preaching against him . . . even in affairs of State. . . .

He addressed himself particularly to Boucher, curé of St. Benedict . . . the King contented himself, for the moment, with this chastisement in words. . . .

RUMOR OF THE DEATH OF THE KING OF NAVARRE EXPLAINED TO THE DUKE OF GUISE BY THE KING.

At this time there was a great rumor of the death of the King of Navarre, especially in Paris, where it was believed, to the point that none of the great knew what to do, or what would happen. The Duke of Guise, who half believed it because he desired it, went up to the King as he was sitting by the fire and asked him how he was and what was the news? The King began to laugh and replied, "I know the rumor which is about, and why you ask. He is as dead as you are. He's fine and is having fun with his mistress," meaning the Countess of Guiche with whom the said King of Navarre is passing the time. . . .

Toward the end of the year the King was told, by a lady of Paris whom I know, that the Duke of Guise had made a visit to Rome in disguise.

. . . His Majesty heard, about the same time, that the Pope had sent the Duke of Guise a sword engraved with flames and the Duke of Parma had sent him his own coat of arms, saying that of all the princes of Europe, only Henry of Lorraine should have the right to bear them. . . .

GUISE'S TRIUMPH AND
HENRY III's REVENGE

JANUARY

THE KING'S REMARKS TO THE DUCHESS OF MONTPENSIER. PREACHERS.

At this time the King, aware of the machinations of the Duchess of Montpensier, sister of the Duke of Guise, and all that she was planning in his city of Paris against him and his state, told her that he well knew she was playing the Queen in Paris . . . and the sedition she was plotting, and that she was giving money to Boucher, Lincestre, Pigenat, Prévost, Aubry, and other preachers, promising them bishoprics, abbeys, and other benefices for continuing their bloody sermons, and even that he knew she had said that she had advanced the League's cause more by [these means] than her brothers with all their armies.

For this and other good reasons, he ordered her to leave the city of Paris . . . but she avoided it . . . and even had the impudence and shamelessness to say, within three days, that she carried at her belt the scissors which would give the third crown to Brother Henry of Valois.* Her preachers also gave sermons more violent and full of invective than ever, against the authority of the King. . . .

NOTABLE OBSERVATION IN PARIS.

Sunday, January 24, such a great and thick fog descended on this city of Paris and its environs, especially from noontime on, that nothing like it has ever been seen in the memory of man. It was so thick, and the atmosphere so dark, that two people walking in the street together couldn't see each other, and torches were needed at three o'clock. Wild geese and other creatures fell out of the air into the courtyards of houses, suffocated. . . .

* An allusion to the religious excesses of Henry III. The "triple crown" is worn by the Pope.

WEDDING OF THE DAUGHTER OF MARSHAL RETZ.

Monday, January 25, M. Albert de Gondi, Duke of Retz and Marshal of France, held a wedding for his two eldest daughters . . . in the hall of the Bishopric of Paris. It is said that he gave each of them 50,000 crowns as a dot. . . . Fine wedding presents to be given by a man who thirty years ago didn't have a hundred pounds of income. Thus does God raise and cast down, impoverish or enrich, as He pleases.

THE FOUCAUDE GIRLS ARRESTED FOR THEIR RELIGION, INTERROGATED BY THE KING AND QUESTIONED IN HIS PRESENCE BY THEOLOGIANS.

On the last Sunday of this month, the King visited the prisons, accompanied by two doctors of theology. . . . At the Chastelet he interviewed two poor girls of the [Protestant] religion, called the Foucaudes, who were imprisoned for not obeying his Edicts. . . . He talked to them a long time, and urged them not to remain stubbornly in their heresy. He promised them that if they would attend Mass, he would himself release them from prison at once. But they excused themselves on the grounds of conscience, and of the fear of displeasing God. . . . "I see what the story is," said the King, "you are among those obstinates who must be converted by the fire." Then turning to the theologians, Prévost and Benoist, he said, "See what you can do. . . ." So the King listened an hour while a great dispute went on. These poor women responded to the questions and objections of these doctors so resolutely and pertinently, even on the main points of controversy . . . that the King was amazed . . . and it was not possible to vanquish them. . . . The King said that he had never seen women defend themselves so well, nor so well-informed. And the doctors had to agree.

FEBRUARY

THE KING'S PLEASURES.

On February 12, the King prolonged the fair at St. Germain for six more days, at the request of some ladies, and went there every day, seeing and allowing infinite and villainous acts by his *mignons* and courtiers, especially outrages to the women and girls they encountered. Every night he attended parties . . . with girls . . . in various quarters of the city, dancing, laughing . . . and dining sumptuously. . . . He also held masquerades and balls, just as if the times were those of greatest peace, and as if there were no war and no League in France. . . .

MARCH

NEW ATTEMPT OF THE LEAGUE AGAINST THE DUKE D'ÉPERNON.

At this time the Duke d'Aumale planned another attempt on the person of the Duke d'Épernon, mortally hated by all the members of the House of Lorraine and by the zealots of the League. But the plot was discovered, and had to be postponed. The people of France, poisoned by the false words of the League, hated this man to the death, and called him the chief of the Navarrists and *politiques*. . . .

GOOD AND PROMPT JUSTICE.

Thursday, March 3, a young boy from Normandy, about nineteen or twenty years old, was surprised cutting the watchchain of a gentleman . . . in the broad daylight of Parlement. When he confessed to it, he was condemned within the hour to be hanged and strangled in the courtyard of the Palais. This was done immediately.

Wednesday, March 9, the news arrived in Paris of the death of M. Henry of Bourbon, Prince of Condé, on the 5th day of the month . . . and the second of his illness. According to the rumors he had been poisoned by a page at the command of . . . his wife. . . .

This prince was regretted and mourned by all good Frenchmen but especially by those of the [Protestant] religion, who lose in him their greatest support and best captain. The *ligueurs* and the Lorrainers, on the other hand, are holding bonfires for joy, for they have lost their most dangerous enemy . . . for he was always the first to attack and the last to retreat. He never said, "Go there!" but, like Caesar, went himself. For the rest, he was a prince sincere in his religion, *homme de bien* even according to his worst enemies, who feared God and hated vice (a rare thing in a prince). He had a truly royal and heroic heart, very jealous of his honor, and a little too much so of his wife, which cost him his life.

M. le Cardinal de Bourbon, his uncle, said to the King, when he heard the news [of Condé's death], "See, Sire, what it is to be excommunicated! I for one attribute his death to the blow of his excommunication." The King replied to this, laughing, making fun of him, "It is true, my cousin, that it is a danger, but if everyone thus struck were to die, there'd be lots more deaths. I don't think that had anything to do with it, but something else was responsible."

BOLDNESS OF THE DUKE D'AUMALE.

In this month the Duke d'Aumale, accompanied by twelve hundred men of war, seized one of the suburbs of Abbéville . . . and [spoke defiantly to the King's messenger sent to reprove him]. When the King heard his answer, he said, "I can see that if I let these fellows alone, they will soon be not my companions but my masters. It is high time to get them under control." This was indeed the truth but nothing came of it but words. . . .

APRIL

NEW UNDERTAKING OF THE LEAGUE.

Sunday, April 24, the King and the Duke d'Épernon were informed of a plot which those of the League were planning for St. Mark's day. The guards of the Louvre were strengthened and the Forty-five Gascons brought in there at night.* The King also ordered the four thousand Swiss from Lagny to St. Denis for the safety of the person of his *mignon.* The League admit they have it in for him, but deny they have any intentions against the King.

THE DUKE D'ÉPERNON LEAVES PARIS FOR NORMANDY.

Tuesday, April 26, the Duke d'Épernon left Paris [the King accompanying him] to take up his new government of Normandy. . . . He took four companies of armed men . . . to prevent the violence that seemed likely to be attempted, because he was so hated by the lesser and envied by the great, to whom nothing is given but all to him. . . . Friday morning, the 29th, the King left him and retired to Vincennes to the Hieronimites, where he said he wished to spend seven entire days in penance and that no one was to disturb him for any reason.

* The "Forty-five" were the private bodyguard of Henry III.

THE LEAGUE REBELLION
IN PARIS

MAY 1588 — APRIL 1594

1588

GUISE'S TRIUMPH AND
HENRY III's REVENGE

MAY

ARRIVAL OF M. DE GUISE IN PARIS, DESPITE THE KING'S COMMAND.
Thursday, May 5, the Seigneur de Bellièvre returned from Soissons
. . . and reported to the King that he had told the Duke of Guise not to
come to Paris as commanded . . . he brought news of haughty words of
dissatisfaction from the Duke, so that the King sent him back again with
very express orders that he was not to come to Paris, and that if he ever
did come, things being as they are, he would hold him forever guilty and
responsible for any excitement which might ensue. As for the city, warned
that there was an uprising in the making against him and his state, [the
King] to put things in order and forestall the conspirators, strengthened
the guards of both day and night . . . showing his resolution to chastise
some of the League disturbers of the peace. . . .

When those of the League learned of this they sent an urgent message
to Soissons to beg the Duke to come at once and rescue them from the
cruel designs of the King. Brigard was the man they sent, who was called
the "courier of the Union." He explained to M. de Guise the danger the
Paris League would be in if he didn't come . . . using these words, "that
the brothers were very much demoralized, but that his presence would
straighten things out, and that he assured him on his life and honor that
everything would work out if he came." M. de Guise thought this over
. . . and the King's specific prohibition, but nevertheless he mounted his
horse, and left at nine in the evening with eight of his gentlemen, Brigard
making the ninth . . . and they arrived in Paris at noon the next day,
which was Monday, the 9th of May.

Having arrived, [the Duke] went straight to the residence of the
Queen Mother, who, though she was indisposed, had herself carried at once
to the Louvre, with the Duke right at her side, on foot. This arrival when

it was announced to the King, surprised him and was so displeasing that he said to the Seigneur Alphonse Corse, who was with him in his study, "Here is M. de Guise, arrived although I told him not to come. In your opinion, Captain Alphonse, if you were in my place and you had commanded him thus, and he had paid so little attention to your order, what would you do?" This he said sadly and full of indignation. "Sire," [replied the other], "there is only one way to decide that: do you consider M. de Guise your friend or an enemy?" The King made no reply to this except a gesture which the other understood well enough . . . so the Seigneur Alphonse said to him, "I think I understand your Majesty's answer. That being so, if you will honor me with the charge, without bothering further about it, I will bring you his head today and lay it at your feet, or take him to some place which you shall name, so that no one in the world will move, unless it is to his ruin. And I will lay my life and honor on it." But the King said that there was no need for that yet, and that he hoped to manage things by another and shorter means. . . .

Thereupon [Henry III] left his study . . . the Duke made him a very deep bow, but with less assurance than usual. His Majesty acknowledged it perfunctorily and complained that [the Duke] had disobeyed his command. . . .

The Duke excused himself as well as he could, leaving the rest to be said by the Queen, who never ceased trying to appease the prince . . . [notwithstanding] he felt much resentment in his heart, especially because he had heard the cries of reverence and acclaim which the stupid people raised at the Duke's arrival. In the rues St. Denis and St. Honoré they had shouted, *Vive Guise! Vise le pilier de l'église!* and one woman had even shouted, "Good prince, now that you are here we are saved!"

THE KING DEFIES PARIS.

Tuesday, May 10, the King was told that the Duke of Guise had brought his men of war near the city . . . and that his followers were entering Paris in a file, and even that the Archbishop of Lyons, the intellect of his council, was dining at the Hôtel de Guise, [so the King] redoubled his precautions. . . .

Thursday, May 12, in the early morning, the King brought in a company of Swiss and one of French soldiers to the Petit Pont, from St. Séverin to the Hôtel-Dieu; at the Pont St. Michel [he stationed] a French company; at the Marché-Neuf three companies of Swiss and one of French; and in the Place de Grève the same; in the Cimetière des Innocents four Swiss and two French. All the rest . . . [were placed] around the Louvre. By this means the King tried to carry out what he had decided with his council, namely to seize a number of the League *bourgeois*, the most important, and some of the Duke's partisans . . . who had signed the pact which was known to have been made between the Parisians and the Guisards . . . to seize [the King's] person and dispose of the Crown. He hoped to have them executed . . . to make an example to other Guise adherents, who had followed [the Duke] in good faith, deceived by the mask of religion which he used to cover his damnable and ambitious designs.

This was the King's intention. The Président Séguier, quite imprudently for a great courtier, as he is, revealed this to a *ligueur* that morning, when asked what all the preparations were about. He said that it was reasonable for all men to be masters in their own houses, and that the King would show himself master that day, liberating his good servants by showing justice to those who were mutinous and disturbers. But this plan of the King did not succeed, because the people, seeing the troops in the city, began to be stirred up, and feared something worse, saying that no one had ever seen a foreign garrison in Paris.

Immediately all took arms, went into the streets, took the chains and barricaded the corners and intersections. The artisan left his tools, the merchant his deals, the University its books, the procureurs their brief cases, the lawyers their hats, even présidents and conseillers putting their hand to the sword. Everywhere were frightful cries and seditious words to arouse the people to white heat. And as secrets, love, and wine are no good when they are aired, so the Duke of Guise having discovered the King's secret (as conversely the King had discovered his), fearing to be taken, sent various of his partisans *sub rosa* to each quarter, to encourage the people who were rebellious but disorganized . . . to barricade and defend themselves well. The Archbishop had assured the Duke, on the part of the King, that the presence of the troops was not directed against him, if he would confine himself to his own sword.

On the contrary, the King, who up to noon was the stronger, having the means to interrupt the communications and break the barricades of Guise, turned the tables by instructing his men to pull their swords only halfway, on pain of death. He hoped that temporizing, gentleness, and kind words would lessen the fury of the mutineers, and that gradually the people might disarm. But the exact opposite happened . . . [The people] . . . after dinner, assembled and barricaded even more than before, and feeling themselves strong, began to look at the Swiss and French soldiers threateningly and to bait them with words, and [said] that if they did not withdraw they would cut them in pieces.

When the King heard of this he sent the Seigneur D'O, Captain Alphonse, Marshals Biron, Domont, Grillon, and others, to move all the companies . . . as quietly as they could, back to the Louvre, but not before an uprising had begun between the Petit Pont and Marché-Neuf. . . . D'O and Corse started to draw them back, via the Pont Notre Dame, begging the people to let them pass peacefully. The poor Swiss, all the way from the Petit Pont to the Pont Notre Dame, could do nothing but throw down their arms and cry, *Bonne France!* and with hands tied together, "Mercy!" to keep the furious people from killing them with arquebuses, blows, and stones which the women and children threw out of the windows. Other [Swiss] gave themselves up crying *Vive Guise!*; they were disarmed by M. de Brissac and shut up in a butcher's shop . . . and the dead buried in a ditch dug in the middle of the Parvis Notre Dame. The rest of the King's guard got over the bridge with great difficulty, and D'O and Corse, who were leading them, were in great danger of their lives, later confessing that they'd never known such fear as in that hour.

Those of Grève and Innocents, threatened also with being torn in pieces, were saved . . . by the Duke of Guise, who at the request of the King (who sent Marshal Biron to him for the purpose) went himself to conduct them to safety. Without him they would all be dead . . . as they have since admitted, and claimed that they owe their lives to this prince who begged the people to spare them, which they did at once, the fury of the stupid populace being instantly calmed at the mere sound of Guise's voice, so poisoned were they with love of him. He hadn't come out of his house all day [up to then] sitting at the windows of his Hôtel de Guise with a white vest and a big hat, until at four o'clock he did this good service for the King.

When he appeared he heard various hoodlums [*faquins*] gathered to see him pass shout, "We mustn't wait any longer, we must carry Monsieur to Rheims!" Everyone in the streets tried to shout loudest . . . by which [the Duke] pretended to be displeased, lowering his great hat (we don't know if he was laughing under it) and saying to them, "It is enough, Messieurs, it is too much, my friends, cry *Vive le Roi!*"

The other French companies of the King's guard retired to the Louvre without incident, except two or three. . . . Brissac, in the morning, had armed the scholars of the University, and built the first barricades near the juncture of the rue St. Jacques and the Place Maubert, where a lawyer of the Court, named La Rivière, had shown himself active and ardent beyond the others in rousing the people . . . shouting, "Courage, Messieurs! We have been too patient, let us barricade this fool of a King in his Louvre!" . . .

All that night the people were in a state of alarm, and twice during the night Brissac went the rounds to encourage and further animate them, organizing the students . . . to march when it was necessary. Because all the gates except that of St. Honoré had been closed the Day of the Barricades, the next day, Friday, the 13th of May, the gates of St. Jacques, St. Marceau, and St. Antoine were opened and guarded by the League . . . so that the poor King had only the false gate of the Louvre by which to escape his plight, as he did.

The Prévost des Marchands and Échevins, seeing that the people were still armed and mutinous, and that all night they had made a tumult in the streets which was still going on, and threatening even worse, because the Guise partisans were coming into the city in a steady stream, went to the Louvre . . . to speak to the King and warn him that if he couldn't appease the tumult at once, his city of Paris would be lost. To this the King replied . . . that he would do whatever they wished, but that he wanted the people to lift the barricades and put down their arms. He assured them on his honor as King that he would withdraw his forces seven leagues away, even ten, if that were not enough. . . . The Prévost and accompanying captains said that matters were pressing, and that it would be a good idea if His Majesty ordered them out on the hour without waiting any longer, to reduce the fever of the people, that it was the only way to make them put down their arms and destroy the barricades, and that, if he waited longer, they were afraid that it would be too late. So he agreed to act at once, and told them for their part to calm the people.

After these negotiations the Seigneur de Méru, whom the King had sent for, presented himself with his company at the Porte St. Honoré, but the *bourgeois* on guard wouldn't let them pass. The King ordered him to retire . . . fearing an attack. . . . As the tumult grew, the Queen Mother, who had done nothing but cry all during her dinner, went to the Hôtel de Guise to try to pacify the excitement. She could barely get through the streets, so blocked by barricades, and those who guarded them made an opening just big enough for her litter to get through. When she got there she begged the Duke to put out the fires, to go to the King, from whom he would have as much satisfaction as he could hope for, and to show him, at such a critical moment, that he cared rather to serve than to destroy the Crown. But the Duke replied coldly that he was very much put out, and that the people was a bull which it was hard to hold back when it became excited. As for going to the King, he said that he did not trust the Louvre, and that it would show weakness of spirit for him to go there, things being in too deplorable a state to throw himself on the mercy of his ene-mies. Then the Queen, seeing the stubbornness and resolution of the Duke's intentions, sent word to that effect to the King by Pinart.

The King, seeing the people grow more bold from hour to hour, and the Hôtel de Ville and the Arsenal taken by Guise partisans, and that they were even beginning to raise barricades near the Louvre . . . and further informed that at the University Brissac and the preachers were marching at the head of mutineers like colonels and talking of taking Brother Henry in his Louvre (having armed 800 students and 300 monks), with those around him saying that he had better leave at once, or be lost . . . left on foot, a cane in his hand, as if to walk as usual in the Tuileries. He no sooner was outside the door than a bourgeois of Paris, who had saved Biron the day before, advised him to leave at once, as the Duke of Guise was about to capture him with 1,200 men. . . .

Having arrived at his stables in the Tuileries, he mounted on horseback with those of his suite who had any mounts, the others staying behind or going on foot. Du Halde put on his boots. . . . "Never mind," said the King, "I won't go to see my mistress, we have a longer trip to make." When mounted he turned toward the city and cursed it, reproaching it for perfidy and ingratitude for many favors received at his hands, and swore that he would not re-enter except by the breach. He took the road to St. Cloud, accompanied by the Duke of Montpensier, Marshal Biron, the Seigneur D'O, the Chancellor Villeroy, and Brulard, Secretaries of state, Bellièvre, the Cardinal of Lenoncourt, Maistre Jacques Faye, his lawyer in the Parlement, and various others, with his 4,000 French and Swiss guards . . . who escorted him to St. Cloud. . . . He spent the night, still booted, at Trappes, and the next day dined in Chartres, where he was well received by the inhabitants and where he stayed until the last day of May.

This Thursday, the 12th of May, called the Day of the Barricades, was the beginning of the great troubles we have seen since, praised and magnified greatly only by the League and the asses of Paris. The goodness of the King alone saved the day, and not the Duke of Guise, who, thank God, forebore to take his sword against his peers and good friends. . . . They showed such devotion to him that day that there remained for him to do only that which he didn't dare do, the next day. On this subject, a *quidam* spoke well who said that both Henrys made asses of themselves, one for not having courage to carry out what he had undertaken (having the leisure and means to do it until after eleven o'clock), and the other for letting the beast escape the next day when he had already caught him in the net. And the truth is that he who wants to drink the wine of the gods once should never admit he is a man again, for one must be Caesar or nothing at all, which the Duke of Guise finally learned, but too late.

In all this good men who fear God should observe the judgment of God on this murderous house . . . the fathers and the children burning with ambition and daring to advance themselves by the ruin of the [Protestant] religion in France, thus veiling their tyrannical designs. . . . God abandoned them to the desires of their bloated and blinded hearts, to the point where they lost all reason . . . [calling] the Very Christian King, successor of St. Louis, tyrant, hyprocrite, and heretic . . . chasing him ignominiously from his capital city . . . Friday, the 13th of May. Poor condition truly for a King, but worse in the long run for the usurper, on whom God's judgment would fall for this tragic catastrophe.

Saturday, the 14th of May, the fortress of the Bastille was surrendered to the Duke of Guise, who removed the King's captain and put in Master Jean LeClerc, *procureur* in the Parlement, captain of his *dixaine* in the rue des Juifs, who was thought to be a brave soldier for a *procureur*, and very zealous in the League cause . . . and established him governor with the consent of the Parisians, that is, the mutinous *zelés* of the League. . . .

On this same day [May 14] the Duke of Guise sent the Count of Brissac to the English ambassador . . . to offer him a safeguard and promise of protection amid the popular disturbances . . . in the name of M. de Guise. The said Ambassador replied resolutely and generously that since he was in Paris on the part of the Queen his mistress, who was allied with the King in friendship, he neither could nor would accept any safeguard except that of the King. As for being alarmed at the situation, he had means to protect himself, and that where he might have been afraid as a private person, as an ambassador he had his rights and his faith to sustain him.

Sunday, May 15, Hector, Seigneur de Perreuse, Maistre des Requêtes and Prévost des Marchands, was taken prisoner in his house in the rue du Temple by some armed *bourgeois* and captains of the mutineers, who charged him with having known about and consented to "the plot" on the Day of the Barricades. They took him to M. de Guise, who, after talking to him, sent him back to his house. Shortly afterwards Bussi-LeClerc had him seized and taken to the Bastille . . . along with some others suspected of being heretics or *politiques*, that is, good servants of the King. The next day they were all sent home by M. de Guise except [Perreuse] who is extremely hated by the people. . . . The Queen Mother begged M. de Guise to release him, and he replied, "If you want him out, Madame, I'll bring him to you myself, but he is better off there than in his house and safer than anywhere you could put him." . . .

At this time Madame de Montpensier, marvelously happy and unable to hide her joy at the happy outcome of her brother's enterprise, took up her lodging, without a by-your-leave, in the Hôtel de Montmorency . . . when she was reproached by the Queen Mother she replied, "What would you have me do, Madame? I am like brave soldiers whose hearts are swollen with victory."

NEW ELECTIONS OF PRÉVOST, ÉCHEVINS, AND OTHER OFFICERS OF THE CITY.

Tuesday, May 17, the *bourgeois* of Paris, *catholiques zelés* as they are called, assembled at the Hôtel de Ville and proceeded with great heat to elect new officers for the city, naming Clause, Sieur de Marchaumont, as Prévost des Marchands, instead of Perreuse, who is still a prisoner; Compans, *marchand drapier*, Échevin, instead of Lugoli, who left with the King; Cotteblanche, *drapier* . . . instead of the lawyer St. Yon, who is sick; Robert des Près, *marchand teinturier*, Échevin, instead of Bonnard; and M. Jean Brigard, lawyer in the Parlement, as Procureur du Roi at the Hôtel de Ville, instead of Pierre Perrot. . . . Marchaumont . . . wouldn't accept the charge, and excused himself so forcibly that La Chapelle-Marteau, Neuilly's son-in-law, was nominated and elected, and he accepted. A man of wide information, arch-Leaguer, creature of the Duke of Guise. . . .

This day thirty-five Capuchins, preceded by Brother Angel (formerly Sieur de Bouchage), carrying the cross, set out in bare feet for Chartres to see the King. They entered the town singing as if in a procession. This astounded the people of Chartres who were in the streets . . . some finding these new mysteries beautiful, others laughing and making fun of them, and many offended, as if they were taking the ceremonies of the Roman, Catholic, and Apostolic religion as a mask . . .

Monday, May 23, the Président La Guesle, his son the Procureur-Général and the conseillers of the Court chosen as deputies to go to the King at Chartres and receive his instructions, returned to Paris and reported that His Majesty's intention was that the Parlement and all other jurisdictions in the city should continue in their offices. Among other notable things, the King said, "There are some who are covering themselves with the mantle of religion falsely and wickedly. They would do better to follow another course . . . I want you to understand, and they too, that there is no prince in the world more Catholic, nor desiring more the extirpation of heresy than I. . . . I'd give my arm to see the last heretic executed in this chamber." . . .

To the Président Neuilly, who, in making his speech as deputy of the Cour des Aides, cried like a bull, and made excuses for what had happened, the King said, "Fool that you are, do you think that if I had any ill-will toward you and the others of your faction I couldn't have acted on it? . . . No, I love the Parisians in spite of themselves . . . what I did on the Day of the Barricades was with no thought but of their good and conservation, as I hope to prove at a convenient time and place. Go back, continue your office as usual, you and the others, and show yourselves as good subjects as I have shown myself a good King . . . you must show yourselves worthy."

Similar remarks were made by the King to the deputies of the various companies sent from Paris to His Majesty, seeming debonair and gracious, but nevertheless, as noted, showing the indignation of a sovereign offended by his subjects. Indeed it is a terrible blow to a father when he is outraged by the child whom he has loved most and advanced more than his brothers, and an unbearable affliction to a master when he is assailed by the servant to whom he has given most. . . .

BOURGEOIS OF SUBSTANCE UNEASY IN THEIR HOUSES.

Toward the end of this month some captains and armed men of war, calling themselves Guise partisans, went about searching the houses of Paris, and especially searching for money, only going to those they knew to have a good deal. Saying that [the owners] were heretics and *politiques* [they] made them come out of their houses on the pretext that the Duke of Guise wanted to see them. Then they held them for ransom, threatened them with having their throats cut if they didn't hand over promptly whatever sum was asked. When the Duke heard of this he disowned them, and wanted to know their names, and if possible to catch them, so as to make an example of them by punishment. . .

Tuesday, the last day of May, thirteen mules bearing . . . the principal furnishings of the Duke d'Épernon was seized by the *bourgeois* guarding the Porte St. Jacques; they were taken to the Hôtel de Ville in spite of the Queen's passport and the covers of the mules which were hers (to give the impression that the goods were hers also) . . . so bold and insolent were the Parisians with the support of the Duke of Guise. . . .

JUNE

VILLEROY, FOR PEACE.

The 15th of the present month, M. de Villeroy left Paris to go to the King at Rouen, and took with him the articles of the Treaty which is in the making between the King and those of Guise. . . .

CITY ASSEMBLES TO REMOVE CAPTAINS UNDER SUSPICION, THAT IS, GOOD SERVANTS OF THE KING.

Saturday, the 25th of this month of June, an assembly was held . . . in which the Prévost des Marchands proposed new means for the security of the city of Paris. Among others . . . to depose old captains (at least those suspect) and put in others who were known to be zealous for the Holy Union . . . he made this beautiful proposition at the express wish of the Duke of Guise, who, seeing a treaty about to be made, wanted to be sure, before anything was decided, that his authority was so well established in Paris that that of the King could never overthrow it.

THE FOUCAUDES BURNED AS HERETICS.

Tuesday, June 28, two Parisian sisters, daughters of the late Master Jacques Foucaud . . . were hanged and burned in the Place de Grève . . . as stubborn heretics . . . one of them was burned while still alive, because the furious people cut the cord before she was dead and she fell thus into the fire.

JULY

[Thursday, July 7] the Cardinal of Bourbon and the Duke of Guise had gone to the Parlement . . . to discuss the murmur and tumult that was in the making on account of the dismissal of the captains and the majority of royal officers . . . all loyal servants of the King. . . . In this assembly the Premier Président spoke long, loud and freely for the maintenance of the old officers and the abolition of the new ones, and he was seconded by various members of the company. The Cardinal . . . spoke little, and through the Duke of Guise he decided that the new ones should remain and the old ones yield. The Duke . . . with very few words, but showing sufficiently the annoyance he would feel if they decided otherwise, begged the Court to give a little more time to the public [temper], that is, to his ambitions and private interests, which the Court understood very well, in spite of his appearance of reverence. They knew that force was on his side, and were constrained to obey and oblige this iniquitous demand, for fear of worse.

JEAN GUITEL, ANGEVIN.

Saturday, July 16, a certain Guitel, an Angevin, was hanged and strangled, and his body reduced to ashes, in the Place de Grève in Paris . . . for the abominable heretic he was. . . . The people believed and said that he was a Calvinist (as they were told to), but on the contrary, he was a real atheist, as he showed on the scaffold, where he blasphemed horribly against God, the Holy Trinity, and other articles of the Christian faith, which Calvinists believe in common with Roman Catholics. The tragedy of the times is such and the minds of the simple people so poisoned with the sorceries of the League that all criminals are Calvinists, heretics, *politiques*, or Navarrists.

THE SECOND EDICT OF JULY FOR THE LEAGUE.

Thursday, the 21st of July, the Edict of Union, made not so much against the religion of the King of Navarre as to take from him what no one but God can take, was published in the Parlement de Paris, sitting in red robes. Afterward a solemn *Te Deum* was sung with all the courts and corporations, princes, princesses, and queens attending. . . . The next day bonfires were held in the Place de Grève . . . with little or no support from the people, who murmured that the princes had made an accommodation with the King, leaving the people in the lurch. This is news only to ignorant idiots, as the people are, because the great never do anything else. The King . . . was seen to cry when he signed it, regretting, poor, good prince, that to save his person he must risk his crown.

THE LEAGUE ON HORSEBACK.

Friday, July 29, the Prévost des Marchands, accompanied by Compans and Cotteblanche, Échevins, Captain Bussi-LeClerc, and others, went to see the King at Chartres, on the advice of the Queen Mother, to offer their services, receive his commands, and beg him very humbly to return to his good town of Paris.

The next day . . . the Queen Mother and the Duke of Guise, accompanied by eighty horsemen, the Cardinal of Bourbon, preceded by fifty archers of his guard, dressed in velvet embroidered with gold, the Archbishop of Lyons, and other seigneurs, left Paris for Chartres where they arrived Monday, the first day of August. . . . [They all urged the King to return to the capital] but he responded very firmly that that was something he would not consent to, and that they might ask anything they wanted but that. . . . [Catherine], having recourse to tears, which she always could produce at a moment, said, "My son, what will people think of me? and what attention will they give me when they see me, whom God gave you as a mother, held in so little account by you? Is it possible that your nature has changed? For I have always known you to be good-natured, prompt and quick to forgive." "What you say is true, Madame," replied the King, "but what will you? It is that wicked D'Épernon," he said laughing, "who has spoiled me and entirely changed my nature." . . .

PARIS: VUE DU LOUVRE

PARIS: LA TOUR DE NESLE

THE DUKE OF NEVERS RECEIVING A BOOK

HENRY · IIII · ROY · DE · FRANCE · ET · DE · NAVARRE ·

Ce monarque francois tout graue de victoire,
Apres auoir chasse l'ennemy de chez-Soy)
Donne la paix au peuple et puis haussautsa gloire
Vray Phœnix, de son san, fait naistre vn aultre Roy.

Thomas de Leuse
F. Quinct pinxit.

HENRY IV

AUGUST

LAUGHING ATTACK OF THE KING ON THE DUKE OF GUISE.

Tuesday, August 2 . . . the King entertained the Duke at dinner. When asked by the King to whom they should drink, "To whomever you please, Sire," replied the Duke, "it is up to Your Majesty to choose." "My cousin," said the King, "let us drink to our good friends the Huguenots." "Well said, Sire," responded M. de Guise. "And now to our good Paris barricaders, let us drink to them and let us not forget them!" The Duke laughed at this (with a laugh that couldn't get through the lump in his throat), and withdrew shortly afterward . . . very much annoyed at this coupling made by the King of the Huguenots with the builders of the barricades. . . .

THE DUKE OF GUISE LIEUTENANT OF THE KING.

Friday, August 26, letters patent of the King were published in the Parlement declaring the Duke of Guise, his dear and beloved cousin, his Lieutenant-General in all armies and military matters, with a magnificent eulogy of his virtues, generosity, fidelity, and ability, and thus [he] gives him without the title the office of Constable; in brief he gives him of the rays of his splendor, an arm of his power, a live reproduction of his majesty.

To the Cardinal of Bourbon, by other letters . . . he gave authority to designate a chief of each *métier* in each city of the kingdom . . . and by this ratifies the first and prime article of the League . . . which is to exclude the King of Navarre from the throne . . . giving to a King of thirty-six years a successor who has passed sixty-three. . . .

GREAT AND IMPOSING SPANISH ARMY, CALLED INVINCIBLE, BLESSED BY THE POPE AND CURSED BY GOD.

At the same time, the great and formidable naval army of Spain, menacing England with horrible ruin and desolation, and regarding France at the same time, already so afflicted, with an evil eye (if God had permitted it to accomplish its purpose) was miraculously ruined and defeated, and reduced to nothing, not so much by the English (though they are given the credit for this victory which belongs to God alone) as by a contrary wind which entirely submerged it and threw the remains on such distant coasts that it is still not known what became of it. In this we must recognize the finger of God. . . .

This army was called the Invincible, the Pride of the World, and the Terror of the Isles . . . which the Holy Father of Rome has blessed. But all these great and proud designs were only stuff for the glory of God, and the wind of their vain attempts . . . dissipated in three days by the God of sea and earth.*

DAUGHTER OF THE POPE.

It is said that the Pope called this army his daughter . . . because he had a great hope of accomplishing by it his long-time desire to re-establish his domination over England. . . . And in truth this army was magnificently outfitted, the result of seven years' preparation, which could well frighten a stronger country than England. . . .

Also the displeasure of the Pope at this defeat was so great that a *pasquil* about it appeared in Rome:

If there is anyone who has news of the Spanish army, lost at sea about three weeks ago, who can tell anything about what has become of it, let him go to the Palace of St. Peter, where the Holy Father will give him some wine.

TESTU.

In this same month of August, the King tried to put Testu back in his offices of Chevalier of the Guard and Captain of the Bastille (which the League had taken away from him). . . . although the said Testu is more fitted to guard a bottle and a ham than a place like the Bastille . . . the King wanted to use him to get rid of Jean LeClerc, arch-*ligueur*, which was not possible to accomplish, any more than he could get the 4,000 crowns he asked of Paris to recompense the said Testu.

SEPTEMBER

THE CHANCELLOR AND SECRETARIES OF STATE CHANGED BY THE KING, M. DE
MONTHELON GIVEN THE SEALS.

Wednesday, the first day of September, the King arrived at Blois. . . .
Several days later he sent . . . individual letters to Hurault, Chancellor,

* There follows a long Latin poem of Theodore Beza on the defeat of the Armada.

Villeroy, Brulart, and Pinart, Secretaries of state, and Bellièvre, conseiller of state, dismissing them from their offices. It is said that he did this on his own, with no prompting, which astonished all the world, as did the fact that he then sent for M. François de Monthelon to give him the seals, a simple lawyer in the Parlement de Paris, but one of the oldest, most learned, most honest, and wholehearted Catholics of the Palais, though little versed in affairs of state, and still less in those of finance. . . .

DEATH OF THE CURÉ OF ST. NICHOLAS DES CHAMPS IN PARIS.

September 25, M. Jean de Ferrières, *curé* of St. Nicholas des Champs, died. Le Geay, theologian of Navarre, to whom he had left his cure before his death, was prevented from taking possession by some men, allegedly of the parish, saying that they wanted a good *curé*, devoted to the League. Instead they chased him out rudely, calling him a Huguenot, along with the late incumbent, and named [instead] Pigenat, one of the six paid preachers of the League and Madame de Montpensier whom the Cardinal of Guise had sent them. . . .

They did as much at St. Gervais . . . making a scandalous tumult on Sunday after vespers, crying that Du Buisson was not wise enough to preach and that they wanted [one] of the League. . . . In fact they installed Lincestre, a Gascon doctor of theology, whose conscience didn't prevent him taking over the benefice of a living man . . . showing himself as good a man as Pigenat. . . . The King, hearing of these fine events, said aloud that the Parisians were become Kings and Popes, and that they would dispose in time of all the temporal and spiritual [substance] of his kingdom.

OCTOBER

OPENING OF THE ESTATES.

Sunday, October 16, the King opened the Estates at Blois and made his proposals. After him the Sieur de Monthelon, Garde des Sceaux, spoke, praising the King, and his good intentions to reform abuses . . . and to relieve his subjects. Then the Archbishop of Bourges spoke for the clergy, the Seigneur de Senneçay for the nobility, and La Chapelle-Marteau, Prévost des Marchands, for the Third Estate. But the remarks of these latter were short and badly pronounced. . . .

The King's speech, which he pronounced with great eloquence and

159

majesty, was not agreeable to those of the League, because the prince, dissimulating though he was, gave them sufficiently to understand that their actions did not please him, and that he had an infinite desire to avenge himself for the injury the Parisians (at the instigation of the Duke of Guise) had done to him on the Day of the Barricades. [The Duke] was so put out that he changed color and lost his composure, and the Cardinal, his brother, even more. He [the Cardinal] made the clergy complain of it to the King the next day . . . and [Henry III] was so menaced by them, and principally by the Cardinal, that he allowed him to change the speech and have it printed quite otherwise, according to the retraction which they imposed on the poor prince, in their presence. The Cardinal was presumptuous enough to say to his brother that he never did things by halves, and that if [the Duke] had taken his advice he wouldn't be in the fix he was in. When these words were reported to the King they did not help the situation of the Lorrainers. It was noted that during the retraction a great dark cloud and fog appeared that made lights necessary in the middle of the day. Someone said that it was the last testament of the King and of France that was being written and that a candle had been lighted to witness the last breath.

SENAULT USED AS A ROYAL MESSENGER TO PARIS.

Thursday, October 20, the King sent orders to his Court of Parlement and his city of Paris to have a *Te Deum* sung at Notre Dame and fireworks set off in front of the Hôtel de Ville . . . to give thanks to God that . . . the Edict of Union had been solemnly confirmed. . . . He had this letter carried by Pierre Senault, *clerc de greffe*, whom he knew to be one of the worst *ligueurs* of Paris and most partisan of all the Sixteen. He honored him with this commission especially to please the League, who recognized the said Senault for the worst servant the King had in Paris.

NOVEMBER

THE SEIZURE OF THE MARQUISATE OF SALUCES EMBITTERS THE KING STILL MORE AGAINST THE DUKE OF GUISE.

In this month the seizure of the Marquisate of Saluces * increased the

---

* Fief brought under the French crown by Francis I. Henry IV exchanged it for Bresse in 1601 following his brief successful war with Charles Emanuel of Savoy.

delight of the Barricaders of Paris, and marvelously embittered the King against the Duke of Guise . . . knowing well that his ambition . . . was behind this enterprise . . . a little princeling daring to oust a King of France from his remaining foothold in Italy. . . . This was the final straw in determining him to get rid of the Duke, and of the domination of all these mayors of the palace, who wanted to despoil him. . . .

DECEMBER

THE KING CONSTRAINED TO DISMISS HIS IMMEDIATE SERVANTS.

Sunday, December 4, the King dismissed the Seigneurs d'O, Miron-Chenailles, and the other Miron, his first physician, claiming that he was much importuned to do it by the deputies of the Estates, that is, by the Duke of Guise, who knew them to be devoted to the King rather than to him. [They each made submission to the Duke and were thereupon permitted to return.]

PRETENDED RECONCILIATION.

This done . . . the King swore . . . and promised perfect reconciliation and friendship with the Duke, which he did freely and frankly on the surface, even, to satisfy them, or rather, to make fun of them more, [said] that he was determined to put the government and conduct of all the affairs of the kingdom in the hands of his cousin of Guise and his mother. . . . But he was thinking of something quite different (as the issue was to prove) and as the Duke sensed and remarked to the Queen. She assured him of the contrary, and promised to guarantee all his enterprises. This made him disregard all the warnings that were given to him; [he thought] that the King was too soft a prince to carry out vengeance, with too little courage to risk the execution of a violent thought.

THE VAIN PROJECT OF THE CONDEMNATION OF THE KING OF NAVARRE; AND THE TRUE EXECUTION OF THE CONDEMNER INSTEAD, WORK OF GOD, NOT MAN.

Friday, December 9, the condemnation of the King of Navarre was put on the agenda of the Estates, with the consent of the King, to appease the insatiable appetite of the League . . . who daily importuned His Majesty on this matter. . . . [Henry III] declared that he thought it neither just nor reasonable to condemn him without a hearing . . . and

urged . . . that he be summoned one last time to declare himself Catholic
and sign [the articles of] the Union. . . .

But the League, which could not accomplish its aims unless the line of
St. Louis was first degraded, decided that the King of Navarre was incapable of all succession, crowns, and royal dignity, as a chief of heretics
and personally apostate. . . .

While the King was weighing what to do, balancing his craving for
revenge against his natural leniency, those close to him began warning
him of an approaching attempt on his person . . . thereupon this prince,
filled with a just wrath, determined to kill the Duke of Guise, who, on
his side, having crossed the Rubicon, prepared to take over the kingdom,
after knocking down its pillars. But the great God, Whose judgment is
quite other than that of man, entered the theatre of events, and with His
will eternally working toward His glory, lighted the King's heart (which
He holds in His hand) with a new force, and armed him with a new
courage, to attack Guise, believing that [the Duke's] longer life would
mean his own death.

Having assembled various of his close associates [the King made clear]
that he was determined to carry out [his plan to kill the Duke] at whatever price. One or two of them suggested imprisonment as more sure,
and that [the Duke] should have a trial, but all the others were of the
opposite opinion, that in the crime of *lèse-majesté*, the punishment should
precede the judgment. . . . This advice was followed by the King, who
said these words: "To put the Guisard in prison would be to catch a boar
in the net who might prove stronger than our cords; if he is dead, he
won't give us any more trouble — a dead man can't go to war." . . . His
Majesty deferred the execution to the following Wednesday . . . when
he was advised to postpone it still further.

Thursday, the 22nd of this month, as the Duke of Guise sat down to
dinner, he found a note under his napkin in which it was written that
he should watch out, that a bad turn was about to come to him. Having
read it he wrote on it, "They wouldn't dare," and threw it under the
table. The same day the Duke d'Elboeuf, his cousin, warned him . . .
that an attempt would be made on his life, to which he replied laughing
that he saw that [D'Elboeuf] had been reading the almanacs . . . which
were full of such warnings.

DEATH OF THE DUKE OF GUISE.

Friday, the 23rd of December, the King sent for the Duke of Guise early in the morning, and for the Cardinal his brother, to come and discuss affairs of importance. . . . As they entered the Château they saw that there were more guards than usual. . . . Although the Duke had been advised from various quarters that something was afoot against him . . . even that morning he put [a note] in his pocket, saying, "This is the ninth, today" — but still [he] didn't think that the King could or would do him a bad turn, so he was blinded . . . the good Lord having bound his eyes, as he usually does to those he wishes to chastise and punish. He went to the Council dressed in a new suit of grey, very light for the season. The eye on the side of his scar seemed to weep, his nose was bleeding a little, so he sent a page for a handkerchief. In it they say there was a folded note warning him to leave before he was killed, but that the note was removed by the page. Afterward he had a pain in his heart and a moment of weakness, which many interpreted as more of a result of excesses with a woman the night before than as a sign of apprehension. (This last was a common saying, but false according to those who were acquainted with his private life.)

The King sent for him by Revol, one of the Secretaries of state, who came to him as he was taking a silver-coated pill and some raisins or prunes for his pain. He left the Council to go to the King, and instantly as he entered the royal chambers one of the guards trod on his foot. Although he knew what it meant he pursued his way, because he could not escape. Suddenly he was seized by ten or twelve of the Forty-five, who took him by his arms and legs, and ran him through with poniards from behind a tapestry. Among other cries these were clearly heard, "My God, I am killed, have pity on me! My sins are the cause of it." A . . . rug was thrown over his poor dead body, and it was left there for some time exposed to the mockery of the court, who called him the fine King of Paris, a name the King had given him.

The Cardinal of Guise, seated at the council table with M. de Lyons, hearing the noise and his brother's voice crying for God's mercy between the blows . . . pushed back his chair to get up, saying, "They are killing my brother!" When he and M. de Lyons tried to leave they were stopped, and the Marshals Domont and Metz, holding their naked swords in their hands, shouted, "Let no man move unless he wants to die!"

Immediately the Cardinal and the Archbishop were sent for by the King and imprisoned in a barracks. . . .

Saturday, the 24th, the King was informed by M. Claude d'Angennes, Bishop of Mans, that the clergy had resolved to ask the King to release the Cardinal of Guise, their president, to them . . . so they could finish their *cahier* with the benefit of his advice. His Majesty had resolved to have him follow the Duke . . . but he was hesitant because of his quality of prelate, and needed a word of advice. . . . [It was decided that] the crime of *lèse-majesté* was a worse example and more punishable in a cardinal than in a simple priest, and that the King would have accomplished nothing if he didn't rid himself of this one as well as the other, even though it was more dangerous, and the method of his execution more important than that of the Duke, because of his quality and title of Cardinal.

This was the reason that the King at once commanded Captain du Gast to kill him . . . but he excused himself . . . finally four men were found at a cost of 400 crowns. . . . These mounted to the barracks where [the Cardinal] was locked up with the Archbishop of Lyons (who threw himself at the foot of a crucifix, thinking they would deal with him next) and pretended they were taking him to the King, then fell upon him with daggers, halberds, and other weapons.

This was the end of the Cardinal, who breathed only war and massacre and inhaled blood, who was brought to earth by a just judgment of God, and was drowned this day in his own blood. As soon as His Majesty was informed that this had been done he went to Mass accompanied by the Cardinal of Vendôme and other seigneurs, and found at his feet the Baron of Lux, who offered his head to save the Archbishop of Lyons, his uncle. [The King] assured him, not of his uncle's liberty — the King saying he wanted to pull the quintessence of the League out of him — but of his life, which he gave him.

On the evening of this day the bodies of the Duke and Cardinal of Guise were cut in pieces by the King's command in a lower room of the Château, and burned to ashes, which were then thrown to the winds so that no relic or memory would remain. A sepulcher worthy of their ambition, though it seems at first glance iniquitous, and even tyrannical, is nevertheless God's secret judgment . . . and we should receive it as such. It is also certain, as is seen in all history, that in all great examples there is something of evil, which is even so compensated for by some public utility.

MUTINOUS PARIS IN REBELLION AGAINST HER KING.

The news of these murders and imprisonments arrived in Paris, Saturday, December 24, Christmas Eve, and "disturbed the feast-day," as it was said. The people were strangely moved; they seized arms at once and began to keep a stringent guard night and day. The Sixteen unfurled their flags and began to shout, "Murder! Fire! Blood! Vengeance!" as usually happens in revolts and seditions — the most wicked make the most of the mutiny. The captains assembled the *bourgeois* in their *dixaines* . . . and everyone said that for vengeance on the tyrant — for thus was Paris beginning to describe the King — the last bit of money and the last drop of blood ought to be used. Although many good men were of the opposite opinion . . . even including those of the courts, who still had force on their side if they had cared to use it, they were seized with apprehension and fear, their hearts failing them in their need, as the saying goes, and they allowed themselves to be carried along with the mutinous and wicked. These latter, seeing that the others were afraid, jumped at their throats, having seized arms while the others were debating . . . took the advantage and so the victory, which in all revolts and seditions goes to those who act first.

The Duke d'Aumale . . . was declared governor of the city, and then began the war on the pocketbook and the houses of royalists and *politiques* by the Sixteen.* Mine was so searched, the first of the quarter, by Messieurs Pierre Senault and La Rue, Wednesday, the 28th of this month, Day of Innocents. Other [*politiques*] were imprisoned to get money out of them, and orders were given to the *curés* to get as much money from each parishioner as they could for the war and the defense of the city.

Thursday, the 29th of December, the people who had heard the afternoon sermon of Doctor Lincestre at St. Barthélemy tore down the arms of the King which were on the portals of the church by force . . . dismembered them, and threw them in the river, or trampled them with their feet, animated by what the preacher had said . . . that *vilain Herodes*

---

* L'Estoile uses the word "Sixteen" to refer to the extreme (clerical-Spanish) faction of the League, as opposed to the Mayennistes, or French, or moderate faction, regardless of number.

(for thus have the preachers anagrammed the name of Henri de Valois) was no longer their King because of perjury, disloyalty, barbarous murders, unworthy imprisonments, and terrible assassinations which he had committed on the persons of the protectors and defenders of the Roman, Catholic, and Apostolic religion, and that they owed him no further obedience.

1589

LEAGUE MURDERS HENRY III
AND DEFIES HENRY IV

JANUARY

TRUE CATHOLIC AND CHRISTIAN OATH, AT THE END OF A SERMON, WORTHY
OF THE PULPIT OF TRUTH.

The first day of the year 1589, at the end of his sermon at St. Barthélemy, Lincestre extracted from all of his listeners (making them raise
their hand as a sign of consent) an oath that they would employ all
means to avenge the two Catholic princes, even to the last sou in their
purses and their last drop of blood. . . . And he extracted a particular
oath of the Premier Président de Harlay, seated right in front of him . . .
interpolating at various times, "Raise your hand, M. le Président, raise
it good and high, still higher, if you please, so that the people can see it."
[De Harlay] was forced to do it, but not without some scandalized mur-
murs from the people, who had been given to understand that [he]
had . . . given his consent to the death of the two Lorraine princes whom
Paris adored like tutelary gods. . . .

NEWS OF THE DEATH OF THE QUEEN MOTHER.

Saturday, January 7, the news of the death of the Queen Mother
arrived in Paris . . . [she] died in the Château of Blois the preceding
Thursday, January 5th. She was 71 years old, and carried it well, for a
plain, fat woman. She ate well, but did not understand matters of state,
although she had as great importance in them as any Queen in the world
in the thirty years since her husband died. She died in debt 800,000 crowns,
being very extravagant and generous beyond any prince or princes in
Christendom, a trait she inherited from her family. She was already sick
when the executions of December took place. And when the King her
son came to see her, saying, "Madame, I am now sole King of France, I
have no more partner," she replied . . . "What do you think you have

167

done? God will you come out all right. You have killed two men who leave many friends behind them. But at least, my son, have you given orders [for control] of the cities, especially Orléans? If you haven't, do it as soon as you can, otherwise it will go badly for you, and don't fail to notify the Papal Legate, by Cardinal Gondi."

After saying this, and after the King . . . had begged her to take care of herself, assuring her that everything would be all right . . . she had herself carried, sick as she was, to M. le Cardinal de Bourbon, who was also sick and a prisoner. . . . When he saw her he cried, with tears in his eyes, "Ah Madame, Madame, these are your acts . . . you will be the death of us all." She was terribly moved by these words, and replied that she wished God would damn her if, on the contrary, she were not terribly upset . . . with such regret in her soul that she would die of it. She left at once, saying, "I can do no more, I must go to bed," as she did, and never got up again, dying January 5, the day of Kings, fatal to her house. Alexander de Medici was killed that day, and Lorenzo de Medici, and others in the history of Florence. She was mourned by some of her domestics, and a little by the King, her son, who still had some dealings with her.

Those closest to her were of the opinion that her displeasure at what [the King] had done shortened her days, not for friendship to the fallen princes (whom she loved *à la Florentine*, that is, to use them) but because by [the act] she saw her son-in-law the King of Navarre established, which is what she least wanted in the world, having sworn his ruin by all means.

All the same, the people of Paris thought that she had consented to the death of the two Lorraine princes. And the Sixteen said that if her body were brought to Paris, to be buried in the magnificent sepulcher she had had built for her late husband and herself in St. Denis, they would . . . throw it in the river. So much for the feeling of Paris. As for Blois, where she had been revered and adored as the Juno of the court, she had no sooner rendered her last breath than they took no more notice of her than if she had been a dead doe. . . .

THE WAR ON THE PURSE.

January 8, the Prévost des Marchands and Échevins, by command of their governor the Duke d'Aumale, sent orders to the captains of the *dixaines* to raise a new levy . . . on the inhabitants, as the first, done by the *curés* . . . was not sufficient to make the fund they want. . . . This second levy, following so closely on the first, wasn't very agreeable to many people, even the most Catholic, who suspected that [the Sixteen] wanted to loot their pocketbooks under this pretext, as has since become obvious.

This day the Little Feuillant in his sermon apostrophized the late Duke of Guise with these words, "O Holy and Glorious Martyr of God, blessed be the womb which carried and the breasts which nursed thee!"

THE COURT OF PARLEMENT IMPRISONED BY THE PROCUREUR LECLERC, ONE OF ITS VALETS.

Monday, the 16th of January, Master Jean LeClerc, formerly *procureur*, now captain of his quarter and governor of the Bastille, accompanied by twenty-five or thirty scoundrels like himself, armed with cuirasses and pistols in their hands . . . went to the Palais, and into the Grand'Chambre with a list, and said loudly (the chambers being assembled), "You, so and so" (he named them), "we have something to say to you." And to the question of the Premier Président . . . as to by what authority he was acting, he replied "that they should hurry up and follow him, and that if they forced him to use his authority it might be too bad for them." So the Premier Président and Présidents Potier and De Thou got ready to follow him. After them went voluntarily fifty or sixty conseillers . . . many who were not on the list . . . saying that they could not do less than follow their leaders. Walking ahead [Bussi] led them, at six in the morning, as if in triumph, to the Place de Grève via the Pont-au-Change . . . to the Bastille . . . with the streets full of people with drawn arms (their shops closed) to watch them pass and cover them with a thousand taunts and villainies.

This is how, by a just judgment of God, the first court in Europe was led in triumph and imprisoned by a little armed *procureur* . . . who, entering into the Chamber of Peers of this kingdom, where the great leave their swords at the door out of respect to justice, carried the sword to the throat of the Parlement, and took them to the Bastille . . . where they were rudely treated by him, some [held] for a longer and some for a shorter time, depending on the ways and means they could find to get out.

He went to take others from their houses. . . . Indeed the face of

Paris was miserable, unless one could say that it was being punished by the hand of God. Whoever has heard or read in Joseph of the actions of John, of Simon, and other hangmen and brigands who, under the veil of religion, sacked and pillaged the city of Jerusalem, would have seen something similar in Paris at this time, because he would have seen a Louchard, a Senault, a La Morlière . . . looting the best houses of the city . . . but above all M. Bussi-LeClerc, as he calls himself, was powerful, since although orders might be given that certain prisoners should be released, they didn't get out until it pleased Monseigneur Bussi, to whom (beyond the three to five crowns he took for their keep per day, which was wretched) it was necessary to make some present of pearls or gold chains for Madame [Bussi], or vessels of silver filled with money for Monsieur, before they could get out. . . .

All day long on this day, the 16th of January, the 6th of the ancient calendar, day of Kings and unlucky, the gates and shops of Paris were closed, and guards set up in the quarters. . . .

THE COURT MEETS TUESDAY, AS USUAL.

Tuesday, the 17th, the Grand'Chambre held session . . . notwithstanding the absence of the best and sanest part of the Court. Brisson [presided] . . . by some ruse and promise of the Sixteen . . . exercising the office of Premier Président. . . .

FORETHOUGHT OF PRÉSIDENT BRISSON, WHICH IN THE END DID NO GOOD.

Today [January 21] Barnabé Brisson, Premier Président of the League, fearing a tragic catastrophe tending to his ruin and that of his house, because he is forced every day to do and allow iniquitous and detestable things against the authority of his King, and desiring that none of it should be blamed on him in the future (having always had the fleur-de-lis in his heart) and so that all should know that it was done against his will . . . wrote the following protestation and signed it, had it witnessed the next day by two notaries, as his last will. It follows, in the exact words of the original:

I, the undersigned, declare that having looked into all methods of escape from this city, in order to avoid saying or doing anything that might offend my King, whom I desire to serve, obey, and respect all my life . . . hating all rebellion against him, I have found it impossible to get out because every move is observed. . . .

So, being constrained to stay in the city, and to join in the deliberations which the people force upon us, I protest that everything I have done, said and deliberated in the Court of Parlement, and whatever I shall do, say, judge or sign from here on, is against my free will, done by force and violence . . . which reign at present in this city, and also [done] by the advice of good men, faithful servants of the King, exposed to the same evils, who advise me to temporize and accommodate myself to the desires and wishes of the people, unjust though they are. [I do this] as much to save my life and those of my wife and children . . . as to try, in time, to accomplish something toward the reconciliation . . . of these people with the King. . . . At present one does not dare speak on this subject for fear of one's life.

I call God to witness that I am not to blame, so that no one will hold against me my continued residence and my actions here [God], who knows the content of my heart and the candor, purity and sincerity of my conscience. . . . In order that this may be so I have written and signed the present protestation . . . Paris, the 21st of January, 1589.

[Signed] Barnabé Brisson

(Witnessed the next day by Lusson and LeNoir.)

RECEPTION OF THE ROYAL HERALDS IN PARIS.

Thursday, the 26th of January, the herald Auvergne, sent by the King, arrived in Paris, bringing to the Duke d'Aumale, who called himself governor, a command to give up the office, and prohibitions to the Parlement, the Chambre des Comptes, the Cour des Aides . . . and all royal officers to continue their charges. He was not heard — nor the letter read — but [was] imprisoned — he was in great danger of being hanged — and finally sent off with no reply but with calumny and injuries, so insolent and aroused were the Parisians against the King. His name is so odious to the people that to mention it is to endanger one's life. Everyone in the city calls him Henri de Valois, son of a prostitute, tyrant . . . of which the vile pictures and libels distributed in the streets by the errand boys of Madame de Montpensier, printed with the privilege of the Holy Union, are ample evidence.

At this same time the Sorbonne and the Faculty of Theology (the trumpets of sedition) declared and published in Paris that all the subjects of the kingdom were absolved of their oath of fidelity and obedience to

Henri de Valois, formerly their King. They removed his name from the prayers offered in the churches, and gave the stupid people to understand that with a clear conscience they could unite, arm themselves, and raise money to make war on him, as on an execrable tyrant who had violated the public faith to the notorious prejudice of their Holy Roman Catholic faith, and of the Estates of the Realm.

On the other hand the preachers, instead of preaching the Gospel to the people, applied themselves to vomiting an Iliad of injuries against the King, lighting the fires of revolt and sedition in the hearts of the people (who wouldn't do much without this urging), so much so that they never came out of a sermon without hot heads and hands ready to attack the *politiques*, as they call them, that is, the best men of the town, enemies of sedition and tyranny.

SERVICES HELD FOR THE GUISES IN PARIS.

Monday, the 30th, a solemn service was held in the Cathedral of Notre Dame for the late Duke and Cardinal of Guise . . . being martyrs as the League and the preachers say, deified and canonized by the Holy Union. . . . There was a tremendous crowd of people as if it were the funeral of a King of France, and the obsequies were magnificent. The Bishop of Rennes read the service; Pigenat, of St. Nicholas des Champs, gave the sermon. The Duke d'Aumale, all the courts, and the Bureau, attended. . . .

In the following days and months, solemn and devout services . . . were held in all the churches and monasteries of Paris, with great lamentations of the people who attended. And it can be said that since France was France, no Kings nor princes, however great and powerful they were, have ever been so honored, mourned and cried over after their death as these two Lorraine princes.

At the end of the month little children of the city, boys and girls, began to hold processions, going from one church to the other in bands, walking two by two with lighted candles in their hands, singing litanies . . . and psalms, hymns, and prayers dictated by the *curés*. Other processions followed . . . by the Parlement . . . as well as by the monks . . . and parishioners from all over Paris followed them, of all ages, sexes, and qualities, marching in pairs, mostly in open shirts with bare feet, although it was very cold, singing with great devotion and carrying candles. . . .

THE KING MAKES FUN OF THE PARISIANS, ALTHOUGH THERE'S NOT MUCH TO LAUGH AT.

At this time the King . . . knowing that he was called nothing but Henri de Valois in Paris . . . when he heard that a craftsman from the capital was in Blois, sent for him to come to him at the Château . . . in the morning when he was still in bed with the Queen. . .

The King asked him, "Do you recognize me?" "Yes, Sire," said this man, "I recognize you as my King." "And this lady beside me, who do you think she is?" "It is the Queen," said the poor man. "That's right, my friend," said the King. "And in Paris, isn't it so that I am called Henri de Valois?" "Yes, Sire.". . . "All right, friend, when you get back to Paris don't fail to tell them that you found Henri de Valois in bed with the Queen!"

FEBRUARY

THE DUKE OF NEMOURS IN PARIS.

On the first of February, at ten in the evening, the Duke of Nemours, having by stealth escaped from the Château of Blois where he had been held prisoner, arrived in Paris where he was received with great joy. . . . "God be praised" (said this stupid mob), "here is one of our best princes escaped from the claws of the tyrant!" . . .

BAPTISM OF THE DAUPHIN IN PARIS.

Wednesday, February 7, the posthumous son of the late Duke of Guise, whom the Duchess bore in Paris since the death of her husband, was carried from the Hôtel de Guise to St. Jean-en-Grève to be baptised. He was held at the font by the governor of the city of Paris, who christened him François, for his grandfather. . . . There was magnificent ceremony in this baptism, most of the captains of the *dixaines* marching in pairs carrying white, lighted candles, followed by archers. . . . A great banquet was given in the Hôtel de Ville following the ceremony . . . and the artillery was fired as a sign of joy. The people of Paris gathered in great numbers in the streets, blessing the child and mourning the father with great sorrow and lamentations. . . .

February 14, Mardi gras, all day long fine devout processions were held in Paris, instead of the masquerades of other years. Among others, there was one in which about six hundred scholars of all the colleges of the University (most of them ten to twelve years old) marched naked or in shirts, with bare feet, carrying lighted candles, and singing devoutly, though sometimes discordantly, in the streets as well as in the churches. . . .

The people were so heated and enraged . . . after these beautful processions that they often got up during the night to rout out their *curés* to lead them in more. It happened to the *curé* of St. Eustache. Some of his parishioners went to him in the night, forced him to get out of bed and lead them. When he tried to remonstrate with them they called him heretic and *politique*, and he had to give in. In truth this good *curé*, with three or four others, and no more, condemned these nocturnal outings, which continued all during Lent, and which brought about many other things under the cover of devotion. For men and women, boys and girls, marched together naked, and produced other fruits than those which had been intended. A daughter of a hatter near the Montmartre gate produced [some] at the end of nine months, and a *curé* of Paris, who had preached that women in these processions were agreeable to God, planted another, which matured at the proper time. . . .

ESTABLISHMENT OF A COUNCIL OF THE UNION.

February 16, a general assembly was held at the Hôtel de Ville to consult on the establishment of a general council for the Holy Union, which was attended by all the Catholic princes and seigneurs then in Paris . . . the Échevins, conseillers of the city, the *quarteniers*, and four *bourgeois* . . . of each quarter. The plan was advanced by the Duke of Mayenne . . . concerning the proper people to be on such a council. He used the list which had been drawn up by Master Pierre Senault and other members of the Council of Sixteen, who on their own authority ordained and disposed of things as they pleased, and treated affairs of state like the great personages they were, so worthy of these responsibilities of which they understood nothing. They took this power to themselves by the favor of a stupid people, a beast of many heads, of which they had gained control.

The next day . . . the persons chosen were read out. The list, drawn by Senault, was printed by Nicholas Nivelle, printer for Senault under the title of the Union. The said Senault has since taken off some names and added others, according to his own wishes. Because, although he is supposed to be only the secretary of this council, actually he is its Premier Président and nothing happens except as he wishes it. He ordered himself 1,600 crowns of wages (from the *deniers* taken daily from the inhabitants for the expense of the war, as they are given to understand) in addition to the other emoluments he gets. For a clerk he has a marvelous authority . . . more than all the rest of the council together. . . . For when something is proposed that he doesn't like, and he sees that it is likely to pass by a majority, M. le Greffier gets up and says loudly, "Messieurs, I oppose and prevent (veto) this in the name of forty thousand men." At his voice they lower their heads . . . and say no more of it. . . .

MARCH

THE DUKE OF MAYENNE MADE LIEUTENANT-GENERAL OF THE STATE AND CROWN OF FRANCE.

Monday, March 3, the Duke of Mayenne took the oath, in court, as Lieutenant-General of the Royal State and Crown of France. This ambitious and ridiculous title was accorded him by fifteen or sixteen good-for-nothings, and confirmed by this imaginary Parlement, the real Parlement being miserable in the various prisons of the city. It is to be noted that . . . there are to be two new seals on the arms of France, a large one for the council, a smaller one for the Parlements and Chancelleries, bearing the inscription, "The seal of the kingdom of France." Those of the League hold the King in such horror that they refuse to have his name on any of their deeds . . . and to give color to their infamous usurpations and rebellions, have themselves authorized an assembly of slaves of a prostituted mob, which they call Parlement. . . .

PRISONERS RELEASED.

Saturday, the 18th of March, [various members of the Parlement] were released from the Bastille . . . having been locked up without any accusation but the suspicion of favoring the King in their consciences. . . . The reputation of being rich was one of the worst things against one, although everything was concealed under the specious name of religion. It was very hard to get these few out . . . others remained prisoners although they were no more guilty than those who were let out, and although their wives, relatives, and friends did everything they could, even to bribing the worst scoundrels in the city, who had the most credit with the council and princes and princesses . . . the League rejoiced in the ruin and triumphed over the misery of France.*

APRIL

AGREEMENT OF THE KING WITH THE KING OF NAVARRE, AND THEIR MEETING AT PLESSIS-LES-TOURS.

About this time the King and the King of Navarre made a treaty and pact declaring themselves friends, and enemies of each other's enemies . . . and they united their forces and councils, and joined to bring to an end the Guisards and those leagued with them . . . who had sworn their death and were making open war on them.

At the beginning the King of Navarre made great difficulty, not daring to trust the King's promises, which for four years he hasn't kept . . . and feared that at the first chance he would share the same fate as the Guises, knowing that it wasn't so much a matter of love as of need . . . and that Henry III might gladly send [Navarre's] head to the Parisians if he wanted to make a peace with the League. Finally . . . remembering the old saying that two heads are better than one, and thinking that . . . the war was really his own . . . [he agreed] especially with the added security that those who were most against him, and particularly his mother-in-law, had fallen . . . he felt adequate assurance. . . .

Having taken this resolution, he crossed the river [Loire] Sunday, the last day of April, and went to His Majesty at Plessis-les-Tours. It was incredible with what joy this interview was received . . . for there was such a crowd of people . . . that the two Kings spent a quarter of an hour . . . holding out their hands without being able to join them, the press was so great and the voices of the people resounding exultantly, *Vive le Roi! Vive le Roi de Navarre! Vivent les Rois!* Finally meeting, they embraced very affectionately with tears, especially the King of Navarre, from whose eyes they fell as big as peas from the great joy he

---

* Following this entry there are ten pages of satirical verses against the League which appeared in March 1589, some by Rapin, later co-author of the *Satyre Menipée*. "I copied them myself, in the evening, in my study, and let them fall in many good hands, more boldly than prudently."

had in seeing the King. He said that evening, "I'll die content with today, whatever death I die, because God has granted me to see the face of my King. . . ."

It came about that the King, who had fought him for so long, and even furnished the League the means to do so, was the one who took him by the hand to install him, so that he would get his great heritage, promised him by God . . . so also it was the Pope, it was the Spaniard, it was the Lorrainer, it was the Savoyard, it was the League, it was the Sixteen — in brief it was by his greatest enemies that he was carried, on their shoulders, to the royal throne. Miracle of miracles in truth, which we have seen with our own eyes.

THE GOSPEL OF PARIS.

The Parisians and those of the League published [*in re* this association of the two Kings] and by those trumpets of sedition the preachers of Madame de Montpensier, they preached, that the mask was now off, the tyrant had lifted the veil of his hypocrisy and openly declared himself the partisan of the heretic . . . there was no doubt that by this war he hoped to exterminate and banish the Catholic religion from France . . . for its defense one must be more resolute than ever and spare neither life nor goods. No other gospel was preached in Paris at this time . . . and it was better received than the true Gospel of peace. . . . The preachers called the King dog, tiger, heretic, tyrant . . . and wouldn't allow him to be spoken of otherwise. There was no little preacher who couldn't find a place in his sermon for a list of injuries against the King, no pedant so obscure that he didn't write a couple of sonnets on the subject, no minor printer who couldn't find a way to roll some new libelous and defamatory discourse off the press every day . . . with all the atrocities one could invent, even borrowing from old memoirs of ruffians and no-goods of the Petit-Pont. I was curious enough about these to acquire about three hundred different ones, all published in Paris and peddled in the streets; they fill four large volumes . . . besides a great folio of pictures and placards . . . which I should have thrown in the fire, as they deserved, except that they may serve in some way to show and expose the abuses, impostures, vanities, and furies of this great monster of the League. . . .*

* *Les Belles Figures et Drolleries de la Ligue* is L'Estoile's own title for this collection contained in vol. IV of the Brunet edition.

MAY

Friday, May 12, was a holiday all day long in Paris, being the anniversary of the Barricades; the Parisians consider this day a solemn and remarkable one. They held a great procession in which was included the chariot of Ste. Geneviève.

THE SIEGE OF SENLIS LIFTED; THE BEGINNING OF THE RUIN OF THE LEAGUE.
Wednesday, May 17, M. le Duc de Longueville, the Seigneur de la Noue . . . and other captains . . . came to the rescue of those besieged in Senlis [which thus fell into the hands of the royalists].

It was dangerous to laugh in Paris at this time, for any reason whatever. Those whose faces looked at all cheerful were taken for *politiques* and royalists, and risked their lives, because the *curés* and preachers were warning the people to be on guard [against them] and saying that all who were seen to laugh or rejoice should be seized. . . . One honorable house was nearly sacked on the report of a servant who said that her master and mistress had smiled and seemed happy that day. . . .

NEWS OF THE DEFEAT OF SAVEUSE.
Wednesday, May 24, news came to Paris of the defeat of the troops of the Seigneur de Saveuse, Picards, the best of the Union, at Bonneval, by M. de Châtillon, on Thursday, the 18th of this month. . . . These were the first laurels of victory against the League, taken by M. de Châtillon to the King at Tours. The King was so pleased that he embraced M. de Châtillon on both cheeks and kept him with him alone in his study for two hours . . . which was the reason that he was much afflicted by the death of the King [August 1589], saying that he had lost his good master. . . . When he was reproached one day by someone reminding him that [Henry III] had killed his father the Admiral [Coligny], he said, "What you say is true, but remember that he recognized when one had done him a service. . . ."

RETURN OF THE DUKE OF MAYENNE.
Tuesday, May 30, the Duke of Mayenne, returning from Normandy, dined in St. Cloud and spent the night in St. Denis. . . . [L'Estoile's entries for the month of June 1589 are missing.]

JULY

PREPARATIONS OF PARIS.

Sunday, July 2, [the League] began to send 1,500 or 2,000 *bourgeois* to the trenches to stay for twenty-four hours on guard duty, each *dixaine* in turn, with the soldiers lodged in the *faubourgs* . . . nevertheless the poor people of the villages near Paris, very much upset, began to flee in great desolation, chasing their cows, sheep, horses, and asses before them, and taking as many of their possessions as they could. The nuns of the neighboring convents did likewise.

PASTIMES OF MONKS.

This day [July 5] the Cordeliers took the head off the King's picture that is set above their high altar — where he is painted on his knees praying beside his wife the Queen. And at the Jacobins', where he is painted the same way, they disfigured his face. A fine occupation and amusement for those who have nothing to do, and work, as they say, worthy of monks.

DISCIPLINE OF THE ARMY OF THE DUKE OF MAYENNE.

Friday, July 7, some troops of the army of the League took Villeneuve-St.-George by force, where they killed, pillaged, ravaged, violated women, and behaved as if they were conquerors in a foreign country . . . which was why the people said that they were much better treated by the enemy than by those of the Duke, in whose army there is no order, no military discipline, nor respect for religion even, though they call themselves Catholics, but nevertheless eat meat on Fridays. To prove their total lack of religion, they forced the priests of the parishes, with the sword at their throats, to baptize (they actually used this word) cattle, sheep, hogs, hares, chickens . . . and when complaint was made to the Duke . . . he could make no better response than that he must use any means to defeat the tyrant. . . .

THE FALL OF PONTOISE; THE HUMANE TREATMENT OF THE VANQUISHED BY THE KING OF NAVARRE.

Wednesday, July 26, Pontoise, attacked on all sides, gave itself up, by agreement, to the King of Navarre. Because of this composition, which left gentlemen mounted on their horses, soldiers with their swords, *bour-*

geois not pillaged . . . [people said] as much good of this prince as formerly of bad, even the Sixteen of Paris and Boucher, who said aloud that if it were necessary to make a compositon, he would always recommend that one treat with the King of Navarre, because he would do what he said, which the tyrant wouldn't do, and that, heretic that he was, he was better than Henri de Valois.

POLITIQUES IMPRISONED AS THE WAGES OF A JACOBIN.

Monday, the last day of July, the Parisians, astounded to see themselves so tightly surrounded, heard that the King (whom they call Henri de Valois) was seated at the window in the house of Gondi in St. Cloud, looking from time to time toward Paris and saying, "It would be too bad to ruin and lose such a good and beautiful city, but I must teach reason to the mutineers and rebels within, who chased me [out] ignominiously, supported by the Guisards. I am avenged in part, but am resolved to have all my revenge. I shall enter the city sooner than they think."

When they were told of this, the Sixteen had about three hundred *bourgeois* locked up in the various prisons, including the most notable and prominent, whom they suspected of favoring the King in their hearts. They called them Huguenots and *politiques*. . . . They did this, they said, so that when the armies of the two Kings tried to come into the city these alleged royalists would find themselves unable to move, and so [the opposite party] would find itself blocked within and without.*

AUGUST

THE KING KILLED BY A MONK.

Tuesday, the first day of August, a young monk, priest of the order of St. Dominic, called Jacobins, or Preaching Brothers, a native of the village of Sorbonne in Burgundy, twenty-three or twenty-four years old, resolved to do what he did . . . had himself taken to the house of Gondi in St. Cloud to see the King through [the agency of] M. La Guesle, Procureur-Général in the Parlement de Paris. (He had left Paris the day before, the same day the *politiques* were shut up as hostages.)

At eight in the morning the King was informed, as he sat in his bathrobe in his chamber, that a monk wanted to speak to him . . . and hear-

* L'Estoile was one of those locked in the Bastille. See above, p. 18.

ing that the guards were making it difficult, he told them to let him in or else they would say in Paris that he refused to associate with monks.

The Jacobin came in with his naked knife in his sleeve. As the King rose (he didn't have his pants on yet) he made him a deep bow and gave him letters from the Count of Brienne, then a prisoner in Paris, saying that when he had finished the letter he had something of importance to communicate further, in secret. The King, not thinking that any harm could come from this little monk, told those who were near to retire, and opened the letter and began to read. When the monk saw him absorbed in reading, he pulled the knife from his sleeve and struck him right below the navel. . . . The King reeling from the blow, struck the monk on his left side and cried, "Ah the wicked monk, he has killed me! Someone kill him!" At this cry the guards rushed in, those who were nearest massacring the little Jacobin at the King's feet. He was at once removed and carried to the King's chamber, and stripped naked, because some thought he must be a soldier in disguise, as it was too bold an act for a monk. But he was soon seen to be just what he was, a real monk, from whom one must guard oneself on all sides as from a mad animal.

Wednesday, the 2nd of August, two hours after midnight, the King died. Opening his body, the surgeons found that the wound was such that he couldn't have survived, as the veins were cut, from which he lost so much blood at the time of the attack. . . . His body was carried to the Abbey of St. Cornille in Compiègne by order of the King of Navarre, who was proclaimed King of France in the army, as the real successor and legitimate heir to the crown. (They had no access to St. Denis which was held by the League.) [Henry III's] intestines were buried beside the great altar in the church of St. Cloud; his epitaph can be seen there in letters of gold on black marble. . . .

This King, when he died, left the kingdom of France and all his subjects so poor and debilitated that one would sooner have expected their ruin than hoped for any recovery. And this as much or more by their [the people's] fault and rebellion, as through any fault of their King, who would have been a very good prince if he had met with a good century.

The King of Navarre, after [Henry III's] death, which he didn't weep over though he swore to avenge him, took the title of King of France and Navarre . . . carried out the plans of the late King, which were to make himself master of Paris, and consequently of the other towns of the kingdom. (All the Huguenots and associated Catholics together, in fifty years, couldn't have done as much good service to his cause as the League did, without meaning to, in a quarter of an hour through this silly little monk with his wicked little knife.)

The city of Paris and other cities of the League gave the title of King to the Cardinal of Bourbon, holding him legitimate successor because nearer in blood . . . so that the war was fiercer than before.

The dead body of the Jacobin was drawn and quartered, and burned in the square in front of the church of St. Cloud, by command of Henri de Bourbon, fourth of that name, King of France and Navarre, whose reign began Wednesday, August 2, 1589 — ending the line of Valois who had reigned in France since 1515 — at the death of Henry III, King of France and of Poland, last of the said race of Valois, by an accident so remarkable that the more one knows about it the more amazing it seems . . . to see a King, in the flower of his age, in the middle of his camp, surrounded by guards on all sides . . . and warned of what might happen . . . so poorly and miserably assassinated by a little cavalier of a monk, giving him a blow with a vile little knife . . . and dying so soon with no way to remedy it.

It is strange and unheard of that a Frenchman, and especially a man of the church, who is supposed to serve as an example to the people in obedience to his superiors, should be so suddenly changed into a bloody murderer of his prince. A case which certainly shows the absence of the spirit of God, which we have forfeited by our enormous sins, and a sign of the ruin of the state, if God hadn't chosen to pity us and lift us up with His strong arm, and give us back that spirit. Under its guidance, the people, recognizing their sins, received the King whom God had miraculously chosen and elected in the eyes of all Europe to succeed to this crown, which He gave him . . . by the very hand of his enemies, to use him as an instrument of His Glory and re-establish this poor desolated Kingdom of France . . . so be it.

The news of the King's death was known in Paris early in the morning of August 2, and divulged to the people in the afternoon. To show the joy it gave them they put on green mourning [livery of the house of Lorraine-Guise], livery of the insane. At once Madame de Montpensier, transported with an insolent fury and ostentation, distributed green hats to all the conspirators. She threw her arms around the man who brought the news and kissed him, saying, "Welcome, my friend! But is it really true? Is the wicked, perfidious tyrant dead? God! but you give me pleasure! It is marred by only one thing, and that is that he didn't know before he died that it was I who had it done." Turning to her ladies she said, "What do you think, don't I look better this morning?" . . . Her mother, Madame de Nemours, was equally happy; both of them promenaded through the streets in their carriages, crying, "Good news, friends! The tyrant is dead! There is no more Henri de Valois in France!"

Madame de Nemours betook herself to the Cordeliers', mounted the high altar, and from there harangued the people on the death of the tyrant, showing thereby great immodesty for a woman, especially in libeling the dead.

They both had bonfires built everywhere, and showed in general the joy they felt in their actions, words, and festivities. Those who didn't laugh, and who bore any trace of sorrow in their faces, were considered *politiques* and heretics.

Elsewhere the theologians and preachers . . . cried to the people that this good religous [Clément] who endured death so heroically to deliver France from the tyranny of the dog Henri de Valois, was a real martyr . . . called this assassination and detestable treason a great work of God, a miracle, a pure exploit of Providence, and even compared it with the mysteries of the Incarnation and the Resurrection!

Thus the jurisprudence of the monks and preachers of these times, to whom the parricides and most deplorable murders are miracles and works of God. There is no better proof of this than the libelous writings published and shouted against the memory of this poor prince. Those that follow. are among them, printed with the privilege of the Holy Union, signed Senault, reviewed and approved by the Faculty of Theology. . . . I have extracted them and keep them to witness to posterity their doctrine, in which they sell places in paradise to assassins. . . .*

Monday, the 7th of August 1589, those who had been imprisoned in Paris the Monday before were released and set at liberty, because with the King's death their retention seemed to have lost its excuse. Shortly afterwards all the others who had been for a long time in the Bastille

---

* Libels against Henry III are included with other examples of League propaganda in vol. IV of the Brunet edition.

were released, after paying a good ransom. The oath which they had taken as officers had expired at the death of their master the King, who was succeeded by Henry IV, to whom the League . . . gave the crown and sceptre . . . through the ministrations of their Jacobin saint.

Thursday, the 24th of August, a band of Paris *ligueurs*, both men and women, who had gone to St. Cloud to show their devotion and veneration of the ashes of the Jacobin . . . as they were coming back in a boat, bringing the ashes of the said saint and martyr, the boat sank . . . and not a single one of the eight persons in it escaped. This is the great and remarkable judgment of God on these idolatries, as, to make a man [like this] both saint and martyr is indeed to make Heaven a refuge for tyrants. . . .

SEPTEMBER

Thursday, September 21, occurred the encounter at Arques, in which God visibly aided and favored the King, showing that it is not the number of soldiers . . . but His will alone which gives victories. . . . In this fight 500 horse, 1,200 French infantry and 2,500 Swiss put to rout the great and powerful army of the League, which numbered between 25,000 and 30,000 men. To God alone belongs the glory . . . and not those whom He used, for this took more than human power. . . .

NOVEMBER

Wednesday, the first of November, All Saints' Day, with the help of a fog which miraculously appeared at six in the morning . . . there was an attack near the Pré aux Clercs . . . principally by the troops of M. de Châtillon, accompanied by great desolation . . . they say that he was remembering the massacre of his father and other Huguenots by the Parisians, as he cried, "St. Bartholomew!" His Majesty appeared in the Faubourg St. Jacques at seven or eight. . . . This All Saints' Day the King, having a desire to see his city of Paris, climbed to the top of the tower of St. Germain des Prés, where a monk conducted him. When he got down he confessed to Marshal Biron that an apprehension had seized him, alone up there with the monk, remembering the knife of Brother Clément, and that never again would he do such a thing without having the monk searched for weapons beforehand.

Thursday, the 2nd of November, the Duke of Mayenne arrived in Paris at ten in the morning, and reassured the great city, which saw itself within two fingers of ruin. . . . Friday, the 3rd, the King withdrew his troops and left the city free, having tried in vain to engage the Duke in battle. . . .

Friday, the 17th, a search was made in all the houses of Paris for old pots and pans of iron or brass, to melt them down, it is said, for bullets.

Saturday, November 25, Louis de l'Estoile, my son, left Paris to go to war. I was forced to permit it, to avoid worse. The tragedy of the century is such that a good man cannot stay here safely unless he connives in the rebellion against the King.

DECEMBER

Toward the end of this year 1589, God added to the victories of the King . . . various good towns fell into his hand, including Vendôme, of his ancient patrimony . . . Mans . . . and Falaise. . . .

At this time there circulated in Paris a piece of advice from M. de Villeroy to the Duke of Mayenne (it was not printed) . . . in which he counselled that he deal with the King rather than the Spaniards, on condition that the King become a Catholic.

In this same year . . . one of the Sixteen . . . killed with his own hands a good woman, widow of the clockmaker Greban, accusing her of being a Huguenot. No pursuit nor attempt at justice followed this murder; on the contrary, he was held to be the better Catholic for it and his *curé*, of St. André, said that he was the best Catholic and one of the best men in the parish.

At the same time another of the Sixteen, named Emmonot, killed a good Catholic named Minterne, whom he accused of being a *politique* in order to rob him of 400 crowns he had on him. . . . His companions beat up and threw in the river a certain Cabri . . . all these attacks were not only not punished in Paris, but were praised and hailed as great signs of zeal for the Catholic religion.

1590

THE GREAT SIEGE OF PARIS

JANUARY

Saturday, January 20, 1590, Cardinal Cajetan . . . [Papal] Legate, arrived at St. Jacques . . . the next day he entered the city, where his mule and dais were taken from him, as is customary at the entrance of a Legate. After a solemn *Te Deum* at Notre Dame he was conducted to the Palace of the Bishop of Paris, which had been magnificently prepared for him to live in during his stay in the city. . . .

FEBRUARY

February 10, the Faculty of Theology at the Sorbonne held a solemn assembly to confirm and strengthen the Holy Union. Their conclusions and resolutions were shown to the Legate, and after he had approved them as tending to the total extermination of heretics and the complete exclusion [from the throne] of the King of Navarre — whether he became Catholic or not — they were sworn on the Gospels, registered, and signed by the body of the Faculty. . . .

Friday, February 23, the Prior of the Jacobins, Bourgoing, was executed at Tours, and drawn by four horses, as an accomplice and collaborator in the death of the late King, and even accused of having urged Brother Clément to do it. He denied this to the end . . . and died bravely, making a beautiful prayer as he died for the conversion of the present King. This is very praiseworthy in a man of his profession and sort, but not enough to make him a saint and a martyr, as the Paris League has done. . . .

MARCH

Sunday, March 11, 1590, the oath of the Union was solemnly and publicly resworn in the church of the Augustinians, between the hands of the Legate. Various bishops and prelates attended, as well as the officials of the city, and colonels and captains of all the quarters of Paris. This was the order of events: after Mass, and a sermon in which they were all exhorted to stand firm for the Holy Union, they went one by one to swear on the Gospels, which were open before the Legate, sitting in his pontifical robes, to dedicate their lives to the preservation of the Roman, Catholic, and Apostolic religion . . . and never to give obedience to a heretic King, under any circumstances whatever . . . a similar form of oath, in writing, was circulated for the people to sign, by the captains in their quarters.

On Wednesday, March 14, the battle took place at Ivry . . . in which the King was victorious, God giving him this sign of His favor. If he had followed this victory by coming at once to Paris, as he could have and should have, many think that the League, frightened and unprepared, would have opened the gates to him, and thus put an end to the miseries we have suffered since. But God's will was otherwise, because of our sins, which divide Him from us. There is no other explanation for this signal mistake. How little even the most powerful princes can avail when God wishes to chastise them, which is plainly seen in history. . . .

Joking in his accustomed manner, [the King] said that one thing the League said was true, that he must be King because he had cured various Spaniards with "the King's touch," and that he had known it all along. . . .

APRIL

Sunday, April 1, the King entered Corbeil, which freely recognized His Majesty, who promised them not only to help them maintain the Catholic religion, but also to favor them as much or more than any of his predecessors.

Saturday, the 17th, the town of Melun fell to the King by negotiation . . . the taking of this town, together with Corbeil, Montereau, Lagny, and other passages of the rivers which were the keys of Paris greatly advanced the King's plan, which was to starve out those of Paris and thus temper the ardor of their rebellion.

MAY

Monday, May 7, the troops of the King began to advance on Paris. . . .
Monday, May 14, the Feuillants, Capuchins, and other monks appeared in arms, led by the Bishop of Senlis (who is crazy in the head

according to the *politiques*), with the *curés* of St. Cosme and St. Jacques
. . . and others . . . they were accompanied by many citizens as they
marched around the city carrying a crucifix and an image of the Holy
Virgin as their banners. Armed as they were, they asked the benediction
of the Legate, and he called them real Maccabees . . . some were not
pleased, and killed one of his men, and wounded a servant of the Spanish
ambassador. . . .

Saturday, May 26, the police reported on the investigation into the
grain supply, which had been made at the order of the governor . . . the
word was that for the number of people there were in the city there was
enough wheat for about a month, if it were carefully rationed; beyond
that, there was . . . barley, which could be used for bread when the
wheat gave out. There were said to be more than 220,000 souls in Paris.

In this month of May the Cardinal of Bourbon, whom the League call
their King without a crown, died a prisoner in Poitou. . . . At the end
of his days this good prince . . . said that he knew well what [the Guises]
intended toward the house of Bourbon, and called his nephew King.
"What I have done, I have done for the King, my nephew, and my other
nephews. The late King and Queen knew very well my intentions."

JUNE

Friday, June 1, 1590 . . . it was decided in the Council to take all the
silver ornaments from the churches, except those that were necessary for
divine service, and melt them down to coin, to pay the men of war in the
service of the Union.

Friday, June 15, Don Bernardino Mendoza, Spanish Ambassador . . .
in an assembly called to find a way to deal with the famine which was
growing from day to day in Paris . . . made a strange proposal, the like
of which had never been heard . . . namely, to put through the mill the
bones of the dead in the [cemetery of the] Innocents, to reduce them to
powder, which could be mixed with water and used for nourishment for
those who had no grain and no way to get any . . . not a man in the
assembly was found to oppose this suggestion.

Saturday, June 16, royal soldiers fired [artillery] which they had placed
on the Mount of Martyrs in Montmartre. One of the bullets hit the Président Rebours and broke his leg . . . and because the said Rebours was

said to be a royalist and *politique* the preachers joked about this in their pulpits, saying that the blows of the King were all boomerangs [*à rebours*].

Saturday, June 23, Noret, public crier, was hanged and strangled for having brought letters to the King's camp from various men in the town who are considered royalists.

JULY

On Sunday, the first day of July, in the great church of Notre Dame in Paris, a solemn vow was taken in the name of the whole city, to Notre Dame de Lorette, that if the city were delivered from the siege, they would present a silver lamp, and other ornaments. . . . There was such a crowd at this occasion that a poor pregnant woman was suffocated in the mob, with her child.

Thursday, July 5, La Chapelle-Marteau, Prévost des Marchands, assembled the city [officials], read to them letters which the Duke of Mayenne had written to the Parisians, in which he exhorted them to hold fast and to cheer up, promising aid at the end of the month at the latest, and if he should fail, he gave them his wife and children to do with what they would. These beautiful words served the people for bread . . . although Boucher . . . and others have assured them of deliverance in two weeks, they were content to settle for a month, so anxious are they to gain that wonderful paradise which the preachers assure them will be gained by dying of hunger.

Monday, July 9, the town of St. Denis fell to the King . . . the settlement was one of the finest and most honorable that one could hope to see, especially for men drawn by hunger and necessity, as they were, for they could get what they wanted, import what they needed, horses were even given to them to move their artillery — not a usual way to treat the vanquished. But the King held this town to be so important, both as a foothold for himself and as a threat to Paris, that he didn't care what price he paid. . . . He called it the citadel of Paris. . . .

When a monk . . . asked him to maintain the church, he said he would, on condition that they pray for him, "otherwise, I will take you for *ligueurs*." When he looked at the royal ornaments and saw that the main stones had been removed from the crown, he asked what had become of them. "M. de Mayenne took them." "So he has the stones [*pierre*] and I the earth [*terre*]," he laughed. . . . Coming to the sepulcher of the late King, "*Voilà mon bon frère*, I want to lie there next to him."

Immediately after the fall of this town . . . stews of the meat of horses, asses, and mules began to be sold in stalls on the street corners; people fought to get them. . . .

The great majority of people are beginning to eat barley bread, and to weigh it out in small amounts. This is true even in the best houses in Paris, which are giving only half a pound a day to their servants. Horse meat is so expensive that the poor can't buy it; they chase dogs, and [eat] grass that grows in the streets, which is a hideous and pitiable sight.

The only thing that is cheap in Paris is the sermons, where the preachers fill the poor people up with wind . . . lies, and stupidities, giving them to understand that it will endear them to God if they die of hunger. They even say that it is better to kill one's own children . . . than to receive a heretic King. They all try to excuse the long delay in the promised aid of M. de Mayenne, and give the people pleasure with the bulletins of Madame de Montpensier. This is the Gospel that is preached in Paris, following the instructions of the said lady.

Saturday, July 28, I saw a poor man near the Cordeliers', who was eating grease, the kind candles are made of. When I asked him if he didn't have something else to eat he said no, that for more than a week that was all the food he and his wife and three children had had. He said that the poor of the city were eating it in place of bread, and this more than a month before the end of the siege, which shows the great necessity of Paris.

Tuesday, the last day of the present month of July, M. Gohorri, Secretary of the King, showed me a little piece of white bread which he got for a sick friend; he swore that it cost him a crown for a pound. This same day I bought a bushel of inferior grain for eight crowns, which I hid in the false bottom of the gallery.

AUGUST

Wednesday, the first day of August, as I was going through the Square by St. Séverin, I read the following words written in charcoal on the wall: "Death to the Judaic Society [Jesuits] and the Iberian nation!"

Saturday, August 4, my wife bought some salted butter from Madame de Bellemanière, one crown for a pound, usually four sous. . . . Eggs are selling at eight francs for four.

Monday, August 6, following the decision of the meeting . . . in the Salle St. Louis, deputies from Paris left the city, with the benediction of M. le Legat, to go to the King [to ask him to provide for relief]. He received them courteously and well, but accorded them nothing of their demands. . . .

Over the portals of the butcher shops, where there are only pieces of old cow, mule, and cat, instead of the usual mutton and beef, I found the following written, in capital letters: "These are the rewards of those who pour out their lifeblood for Philip."

Wednesday, August 8, there was a tumult at the Palais, by a whole crowd of people whom hunger drove — as the wolf drives animals from the woods — armed, and demanding peace or bread. This was undertaken by a large number of *bourgeois* of the city, including some of the most prominent, who would have been glad to see the King in the city as they had nothing to cook in their houses, any more than the poorest have. So great is the poverty and misery to which they are reduced that they ask nothing but a change of masters and conditions. But the plan was noised about too much, and being conducted more by passion than by reason, was revealed to M. de Nemours the day before. Late that night M. Molé found this out and told M. le Président Brisson . . . to warn him of the inevitable dangerous consequences . . . and to beg him (as he was one of the chiefs) at least to put it off for another day. But Brisson paid no attention, and thought it better to gamble everything, and only said to him, *Brute, times?* This stubborn opinion might have ruined the best men in Paris and the Court for the second time, for the next day when the seekers of peace were assembled at the Palais they were broken in an instant, and scattered, and worse might have followed if they had not been so poorly organized and led that they did not recognize each other as fellows. Instead of bread they got blows, as *politiques*, seditious men, heretics and makers of heresy. Instead of peace they got the gallows. Many were imprisoned and ransomed, others beaten or chased out, and some hanged.

It must be confessed that without the wisdom and moderation of M. de Nemours (who pays as little attention as Demetrius to the voices of the people, whether from those who are high or those who are low) very few of the great number involved would have escaped . . . because the Sixteen wanted to massacre the *politiques* . . . some bought their lives. . . .

Master Jean Prévost, *curé* of St. Séverin, was rescued from the crush by Senault, and conducted safely home, after being exhorted to return to the party of the League, which he has left. This *curé* is popularly called by them "Le Politique," as [the *curé*] of St. Sulpice [is called] "Le Ministre," and as [the *curé*] of St. Eustache [is called] "The Pope of the Markets," they being the only ones in Paris who don't preach according to League instructions. . . .

Tuesday, August 14, Eve of the Assumption, my wife, who will soon have a child, left this city of Paris, taking with her Anne de l'Estoile and my little Mathieu, with his nurse, and stayed with my mother in Corbeil. This was very expensive, but nevertheless necessary, on account of the great famine.

Wednesday, August 15, I went to my door at five in the afternoon and saw a poor man dying of hunger, with a child in his arms about five years old, whom I saw die in his father's arms. . . . It was three days since either of them had eaten anything, and more than two weeks since they had seen bread. This filled me with so great a pity (I always had a little bread during the hard times, for which I humbly give glory to God) that I gave him some, with a piece of money. God made use of me to save, or at least prolong, his life, which I would gladly have done also for the child, if God had addressed Himself to me sooner, but when they got to my door the poor child was breathing his last.

Thursday, August 16, it was announced that anyone could leave the city, because hunger was so acute. The bread made of the bones of our fathers, called the bread of Madame de Montpensier, began to be used. (She praised this invention highly though she was unwilling to try it). But it didn't last long because those who ate it died; some said that was the intention of its inventors.

Friday, August 17, there circulated a rumor of peace, based on the general desire, and also because Messieurs de Gondi and Lyons left Paris that day to seek the King [again]. The Sixteen . . . took alarm at this and were reduced to the barbarity of saying that it was better to kill one's own children, and even to eat them raw, than to give in to a heretic. . . .

Monday, August 20, when the extreme poverty and misery of the people of Paris had been explained to the King, and he learned that the streets began to be paved with dead, His Majesty, preferring to break the rules of war rather than those of humanity . . . broke the military custom and regarded the people as his subjects. [He] granted safe conduct to all women, children, and scholars who wished to leave [Paris]. He finally extended [this right] to everyone, including his bitterest enemies. He even enjoined the towns to which they might go to receive them well. Further, he permitted, against the rules of war, that supplies he brought in to the princes and princesses in the city. This was ungratefully accepted. Such [humanity] was one of the principal causes why the siege did not have the success it might have had.

During this time, which was six days before the lifting of the siege of Paris, and up to the end of it, you could see the poor, dying, eating dead dogs on the street; others ate garbage that had been thrown in the river, or rats, or meal made of bones. . . . Because the meat of asses and mules was all gone, their hides were sold for food and were eaten with a very good appetite by the poor. What I record about this I either saw with my own eyes or I have it on the word of men of good faith, including a poor man who, for a piece of bread, brought me news of everything phenomenal or interesting. . . .

Toward the end . . . the most barbarous . . . began to chase children on the streets as well as dogs . . . and three were actually eaten. . . .

I personally heard the proposition made and defended by a well-known Catholic . . . that there was less danger [in the hereafter] by eating a child, in such circumstances, than by recognizing . . . a heretic . . . and that all the best theologians of the University were of this opinion, including his *curé*, of St. André-des-Arts.

On August 29, M. Cotton, M. des Fournaux, and I obtained permission to depart from the city with our retinue, because we were at end of our bread . . . but the siege was lifted next day, Tuesday, August 30, having lasted since the 7th of May.

After the lifting of the siege it was called the greatest of God's miracles since the Creation. It was said by others, "We are saved, although led by a blind man (Mendoza), governed by a child (Nemours), and advised by a priest (the Legate), none of whom knew a thing about war." Another . . . said "that a one-eyed man, meaning our M. Boucher, governed Paris,

193

like a little king." To which the answer is, "This is not surprising, since in the kingdom of the blind the one-eyed is king."

Friday, the last day of August 1590, the King wrote with his own hand the following letter to Madame de la Rocheguyon:

My Mistress, I write you this word on the eve of battle. The issue is in the hand of God, who has already ordained the outcome according to what is best for His glory and the welfare of my people. If I lose it, you will never see me again, for I am not a man to flee or retreat. I can assure you that if I did, my next-to-last thought will be of you, and my last of God. In whose hands I leave you, and myself too.

This last day of August 1590,
From the hand that kisses yours, and which is your servant,
Henri

This letter . . . [was intended to tell] Madame de la Rocheguyon that His Majesty was determined to give battle to the Prince of Parma the next day, the Prince having forced him to raise the siege of Paris. . . . In this we can see that the destiny of men, even of great kings and princes, is very uncertain, and depends on One higher, who holds the outcome in His hand, and often ordains an opposite outcome from that intended. There is also no doubt that the advice given to the King to lift the siege entirely, and not keep the suburbs blocked, as he could have, was very pernicious and disadvantageous for him. He wouldn't listen to the good advice of . . . M. de la Noue, one of the oldest and most experienced captains in France, and one of his most faithful servants . . . who predicted . . . just what happened, namely that he would lose Paris, and wouldn't be able to engage in battle. . . .

SEPTEMBER

Friday, September 7, 1590, the Duke of Mayenne and the Prince of Parma took Lagny from under the beard of the King. . . .

Saturday, September 15, 1590, it was learned in Paris that the Pope had died on August 28 . . . and the next day, Sunday, the 16th, I heard our *curé*, at St. André, preach that this was one of the greatest miracles — together with the lifting of the siege — that God had made — that God had delivered us from a wicked and *politique* Pope. . . .

Monday, September 24, the Legate Cajetan left Paris to return to Rome, where he found his master the Pope dead, and a good thing for him. He ought to have had his head cut off, because he had stirred up the fires of sedition, instead of putting them out, which had been his orders.

This same day General Benoist died in Paris. He was buried the next day with no ceremony and no candles. He was the greatest *politique* in Paris, but because he was poor, the Sixteen . . . said this was a false rumor. . . .

Take note (said a bad *politique* of Paris) that in this state one thing is sure, where there is a Catholic, there is a Spaniard.

OCTOBER

Thursday, October 11, 1590, word came to Paris from Rome that the Cardinal Joannes Baptista Cattaneo . . . had been elected Pope and had taken the name of Urban VII.*

This same day came news of the death of Jacques Cujas in Bourges . . . which was a great loss, for he was the toast of good wits and the light of the law. . . .

Today a false rumor was noised about in Paris that Beza was dead . . . there was no other news at this time but deaths and sicknesses.

Monday, October 15, news came . . . that Pope Urban VII, elected September 16, had died September 27, having been Pope for eleven days. . . .

Monday, October 22, I had a letter from my wife, saying that she had been held up for 75 crowns of ransom by the Spaniards, which Mademoiselle Miron had paid for her. . . .

Wednesday, the last day of October . . . my wife returned to Paris and to her own house, by the grace of God, who preserved her in as great hazards as a woman has experienced in a long time. Which boon I pray God she may use to advantage, and I also.

At this same time there died in the town of Tours M. François de Monthelon, my uncle, Garde des Sceaux of France, without seals, however, because he had resigned them (a thing so rare that it is without precedent) because of an overscrupulous conscience, and of an excessive zeal for the Roman, Catholic, and Apostolic religion. He was a person

* Urban VII died fourteen days after becoming Pope.

to be forever mourned, however, for his singular uprightness, learning, and courage.

When the Duke of Mayenne came to make his farewells to his Excellency, the Duke of Parma, he [Parma] advised him to distract the King (whom he called the Prince of Béarn) with truces of peace and constant sorties and overtures, "because time and temporizing will sooner ruin that prince than force, this Béarnais uses his boots more than his shoes."

DECEMBER

Monday, December 10, the King, at St. Quentin, learned that the town of Corbie had returned to its obedience. This was very good news, because it is one of the strongest places in Picardy, well supplied with food and arms.

Tuesday, the 18th of December, the Duke of Nemours left Paris to resume his government. He left the [Parlement] well content with him because he had always treated them with respect; likewise the fanatical Catholics because he had held [the city] so well against the King. . . .

Wednesday, December 26, 1590 . . . news came that Nicholas Sphondrat, of Milan, Bishop of Cremona . . . was elected Pope and took the name of Gregory XIV. . . .

Sunday, December 30, the sellers of horse meat opened their doors again in Paris. . . .

At the end of this year, since the lifting of the siege, there were so many deaths in Paris that the doctors said that the plague of 1580 hadn't killed in six months . . . as many as malnutrition and its fevers did in these four, because of the famine. Death took the good and the bad, even the zealous Catholics . . . many who had imprisoned the Court. . . . In truth sickness killed more than fell by the enemy's hand. . . . The number of *procureurs* of the Parlement alone who died between Easter and Christmas was sixty-two, of whom I have a list, with their names and surnames.

Thursday, December 20, 1590, Ambrose Paré, surgeon to the King, died in his house in Paris, at the age of eighty. He was a learned man, foremost in his art, who, despite the times, spoke freely for peace and for the public welfare, which made him as much loved by good men as hated and feared by the wicked — which latter far outnumber the others, especially in Paris, where the rebels have all the authority. . . .

In this same year Master Bernard Palissy died in Bussi's dungeons in the Bastille. He was held prisoner because of his religion, and was eighty years old. He died of misery, need, and ill treatment. At the same time three women died of hunger and vermin, who were held for the same reason.

This good man, when he died, left me a stone which he called his philosopher's stone, which he assured me was a skull which had long since turned to stone, with another which he used in his craft [pottery]. These two stones are in my study; I love them and treasure them in memory of this good old man, whom I loved and helped in his necessity, not as I would have liked to, but as much as I could.

This good man's aunt, who brought me the stones, returning to see how he was, found that he had died. Bussi told her that if she wanted to see him, she would find him with the dogs on the ramparts, he had had him put there like the dog that he was.

In this same year, to keep the people busy at their devotions, and comfort them in their miseries, M. le Legat left Panigarole, Bishop of Ast, an Italian, a learned and persuasive man. He [preached] in Notre Dame before great crowds of people . . . combating heresy and heretics with fine, subtle arguments . . . all tending to turn the people more against the King. . . . He said that he never would have thought that Frenchmen could be so vindictive . . . even if [Henry III] had been the worst tyrant in the world, with death, anger and abuse should cease, if men had a grain of decency . . . and that in this respect Frenchmen were worse than Italians, considered vengeful, who nevertheless with death ceased to attack even their bitterest private enemies.

L'AFFAIRE BRISSON

FEBRUARY

Tuesday, February 12, the Spaniards and Neapolitans [troops] arrived in Paris and were installed in the houses of the absent. . . .

Friday, February 22, a general procession of thanks to God for the money promised by the Pope [Gregory XIV] was held. . . .

MARCH

Sunday, March 3, solemn processions and prayers were held in Paris to celebrate in all the parishes the deliverance of the town of Chartres, which is pictured as very much in distress, although the siege has just begun.

Sunday, the 10th of the present month of March, a false rumor circulated in Paris that the King had raised the siege of Chartres and that he was wounded. This false rumor was denied . . . by the *politiques* to spite the *ligueurs* (who had spread it) and . . . another started . . . that Chartres had been taken . . . each trying to insist that what they wished was happening . . . showing themselves equally wise. . . .

Wednesday, March 13, our Master Boucher, who is preaching this Lenten season at St. Germain l'Auxerrois, attacked the Béarnais and the *politiques*. . . . His sermons were even worse than the others, containing blood and murder, even against the Court, whom he discounted as no good. He excited the people by his atrocious gestures and exhortations to chase them and get rid of them. One of the conseillers of the Court, a friend of mine, told me the next day that if the crowd hadn't been so thick around him he would have left, for fear that in his rage [Boucher] would come down from the pulpit, jump on some *politique* and eat him raw with his teeth. [Boucher] also said that he wished he could strangle the dog of a Béarnais with his own hands, which would be the most welcome sacrifice one could make to God.

Sunday, March 24, the *billets* of the preachers instructed them to keep the people from accepting [the idea of] the King's conversion. . . . What they said was that an excommunicate and relapser couldn't be received no matter what face he put upon it. The result of this was a bunch of injuries and vomit against the King. The *curé* of St. André called him son of a prostitute and bastard, Boucher called him the red dragon of the Apocalypse, and [said] that his mother was an old wolf . . . Commolet said that only heretics and *politiques* wanted to see him go to Mass. He further said that to call him either King or King of Navarre was a real mark of *politique*: there was no such thing as a kingdom of Navarre, which was ruled by the King of Spain, and as for France, he was only king of some mud in the Beauce. They called him dog, tyrant, heretic, wicked. . . . Our master Cueilly called him a stinking goat and alleged ulterior motives for his [supposed] desire to attend Mass, the said *curé* not having enough brains in his head to fry an egg. These were the beautiful Lenten sermons preached in Paris.

Monday, March 25, Boucher preached that the *politiques* should be proscribed, and the Parlement too. . . . But God prevented the Duke of Mayenne from heeding this bloody counsel, and he contented himself with exiling them. . . .

APRIL

Friday, April 5, a false rumor went around that aid had come to Chartres. Commolet, preaching about it, stamping his feet and banging the pulpit for joy with his hands, [said,] "Go hang yourself, go hang yourself, *politique!* There is good news from Chartres. Your Béarnais is routed . . . despite his mustache and his teeth!" The truth was quite the reverse; this whole story was invented to amuse the populace.

Saturday, April 6 . . . Brigard, *Procureur* of the city of Paris, who had done so many services for the Union, as one of the main pillars of the same, was arrested and imprisoned by Bussi-LeClerc, his cousin . . . who took him to the Bastille, notwithstanding their kinship and friendship. He was charged, they say, with intelligence with certain leaders of the King's party, with treasonable designs.

Easter Day, the 14th of the present month of April . . . in the Queen's chapel, the Spaniards made three bundles of straw into the likenesses of girls, gave them buttons for eyes, dressed them in taffeta . . . and placed them in front of the great altar, beside the Holy Sacrament. The people of Paris (although they are the most stupid and easily imposed on in the world in matters of religion) were so scandalized at this that they had to be removed. A *quidam* . . . said . . . on leaving the church . . . that the religion of Spaniards was all masquerades and plaster.

The day after Easter . . . all the *curés* of Paris exhorted the people to pray for Chartres, which was not yet taken although the *politiques* claimed that it was, [and said] that God should be asked to move the good people of the town to ignore the treaty which had been made with the heretic. . . .

Only Chavagnac, at St. Sulpice . . . preached that day [April 16] without mention of Chartres. . . . He is more liberal than ever, though under constant threat, with the rumors that are flying around. Among other things he said that he had been reproached for not preaching against the heretics, which was true, because he didn't know any . . . but that he saw good-for-nothings who were considered good Catholics, but whose religion consisted of brigandage and robbery . . . that one recognizes trees by their fruit. . . . Returning to the subject of heresy, he said that one who asked for instructions was not a heretic, but one who refused it was . . . this proposition offended the zealous very much.

The next day [April 17] Paris was full of processions to pray God to bless this imaginary aid . . . a friend and I counted 5,074, someone else counted 5,112 . . . the confusion making it hard to count them exactly. Indeed it can be said that there is no sort of devotion . . . which wasn't used by the people of Paris for the deliverance of Chartres . . . nothing was omitted, including prayers, offerings, and vows to the Virgin to keep her in the party. But whether she was indifferent, or what, it was all to no avail, because Friday, April 19 . . . Chartres was reduced to the King's obedience. . . . The news came to Paris on April 20. . . .

All the preachers cried out against it . . . made the ladies cry hot tears by the beautiful apostrophes they made to Our Lady . . . reproaching her for deserting them in their hour of need. . . . In the end they turned to fury against the *politiques* who were said to be the cause of this disaster.

Boucher said that they should be killed; Rose, that a bloodletting was necessary, and that the cure was to cut the throat; Commolet, that the death of the *politiques* was the only way to assure the lives of good

Catholics. The *curé* of St. André said that he would lead the procession
. . . The *curé* of St. Germain l'Auxerrois, in the most sublime advice of
all, said to seize anyone who laughed, as they would be *politiques*, and
throw them in the river. . . .

The common people . . . seeing that the promised aid had come to
nothing, spoke out against the Duke of Mayenne, telling him to go to the
devil. . . . The preachers . . . also sniped at him . . . from their pulpits,
and said privately that he was a great hog, sleeping with his sow . . .
and that he could only carry on war with a bottle.

Monday, April 29 . . . when it was rumored that crosses were appearing in various places, I went to St. Bartholomew out of curiosity to see
the miracle . . . there I saw a churchman passing a great piece of linen
to be kissed, on which people said there was a cross, although I didn't see
a trace of one. It might be that it had been rubbed out by the multitude
of kisses. . . . I passed up the privilege, having seen nothing on that
handkerchief which was any different from my own.

MAY

This day, May 8, there was a great rumor in Paris of the death of the
King of Spain, who is killed and resurrected again three or four times
every year . . . it was believed by many people because . . .various members of the royalist party [outside Paris] had said so in letters to friends
in the city. Those of the League, who feared it as much as the others
wanted it, had it from friends of theirs. . . . This false news circulated
for one week in Paris, and two in Chartres, where it was printed. . . .

Wednesday, the 22nd of the present month of May, an assembly was
held at the Bishopric of Paris to name the deputies to Estates [General]
announced by public crier, for the last of this month at Rheims . . . it
was beginning to be said that we must have a King, as we couldn't get
on without one. When it came to finding delegates from the nobility,
only two gentlemen of the Union appeared from the whole *prevoté* and
vicomté of Paris, Messieurs de Vitry and Chevrières, of which it is said,
"we can't find a gentleman, but we expect to make a King!"

Thursday, the 30th of this month of May, the Briefs and Excommunications of the Pope against those who adhere to the King, especially the

Ecclesiastics, were brought to Paris. The Chapter of Notre Dame, having received theirs . . . appointed [deputies] to go to the Parlement and read [the documents] the next day.

JUNE

Saturday, June 1, 1591, Eve of Pentecost, Seigneur Alexander, Colonel of the Neapolitans, sent some of them to St. Denis to ask M. de Vicq to release several tons of clothes and other equipment belonging to them, which had been seized. . . . M. de Vicq . . . having received them most graciously, kept them there over Sunday. . . . After having heard Mass, which was very devoutly performed, he gave them dinner, and showed them all over the tombs and beautiful objects of the great church . . . this astonished them greatly, because they were given to understand in Paris that in the towns held by the King no religious services were held. . . . The next day, when they went to make their farewells . . . with infinite thanks to M. de Vicq, he, seeing them in a good humor, asked them, "Messieurs, before you go I want to ask you something. I see that you are men of understanding — tell me, what do you think of the people of Paris?" "By God! Monsieur," replied one, "they are the stupidest and least openhearted people I have ever known. Since we have been in Paris not one of them has had the courtesy to offer us so much as a glass of water. When they look at us it is with such an eye that you would think they were looking at dogs. They speak of others, but we think they are all Lutherans there." "Yes," said M. de Vicq, "but that's not so here, as you have seen." "Ah no, no, you are good Catholics and good men, may God give you long life!" they replied. Then they left, leaving M. de Vicq as pleased with them as they were with him. He was still enjoying this story three months later, and amused the King with it, they say, when he told him this fine story. . . .

[June 15] They say in Paris that M. de Nevers and Cardinal Lenoncourt, with many other great seigneurs and ecclesiastics, have left the party of the King, fearing the excommunication of the Pope. Much of this was false, and said merely to entertain the people. . . . This rumor lasted three weeks, so vouched for and colored that one didn't know what to believe. All the time one heard from people who came and went from St. Denis that the King's party were making fun of it, saying when they met each other, "No, not I but *you* are a damned soul" — having fun at the expense of the Bull and the Pope.

In this month of June 1591 the Parlement of Châlons * gave a decision against the Papal Bull . . . which had been accepted by the Parlement de Paris, and ordered that the said Bull be torn and destroyed, which was done in Châlons in the session of Monday, June 10 . . . and later in all jurisdictions loyal to the King.

When this decision was known in Paris the zealous were scandalized, and the preachers had new material for their cries, though they were already making enough noise without it. . . .

JULY

Monday, the 8th of July, the Palais was closed for eight days because of the rumor that the King was approaching. This was done at the request of Messieurs the Sixteen, who open and close the Palais as it suits them.

At this time the river Seine is as high as in winter, is flooding, in fact, although we've had little rain, a sure sign of the flood of the wrath of God, which we well deserve.

Wednesday, July 17 . . . the Parlement de Paris . . . decided . . . that the decision of those in Châlons, who call themselves Parlement, is null and void . . . that it should be torn apart and burned on the marble table . . . which was done the next day, Thursday, July 18.

Sunday, July 21, the preachers of Paris declared unanimously against the decision of the Châlons Parlement, praising and raising to the third Heaven the present Pope, consigning his predecessor to the deepest Hell . . . falling on those of Châlons . . . avoiding no sort of injury which would make them odious. Boucher, most violent and injurious of all . . . called De Thou a mad bull, Agenous an old drunken Huguenot . . . giving each member of the Châlons Parlement a soubriquet, and declared that there were seventeen heresies in their declaration.

The *curé* of St. André vomited his rage against the King: one should no longer call him Henri de Bourbon, as the excommunication deprived

---

* In 1588, following the uprising in the League cities, Henry III had established Parlements loyal to the crown in other cities, of which those of Châlons and Tours were the most active in the royalist cause. Royalist members of the Parlement de Paris who remained in the capital under the League were much criticized for doing so, though they were able to serve Henry IV well in 1593 and 1594, and were later rewarded by him. See March and April, 1594.

him of that name; if it was necessary to speak of him he should be called "heretic, relapser, excommunicate, villain, son of a prostitute, devil" . . . and said that the Parlements of Tours and Châlons should be burned alive with their decisions.

Rose, Commolet, Ceuilly, Guarinus, Lincestre, Martin, and all the others treated the same subject, in their well-known way. . . .

AUGUST

Thursday, August 1, 1591, the Sixteen held a meeting at the Jacobins', where they held a solemn memorial service for their late brother of sainted memory, Jacques Clément. Following that they all dined together . . . at a cost of 45 crowns.

Thursday, August 8, a Mass and *Te Deum* were sung at the Sainte Chapelle, at the command of the Sixteen, to celebrate the end of a whole year since God had saved them from the *politiques* asking for bread at the Palais.

Thursday, August 15, Boucher preached against Brigard, because of the rumor that Brigard would not be put to death. He said that either Brigard should be hanged, or he [Boucher] should. Some said that it would be better put that he *and* Brigard should be hanged.*

SEPTEMBER

Sunday, September 29, Président Brisson received letters from Rheims, in which he was warned to watch out for the Sixteen, who had in mind to do him a bad turn. He told the man who brought the letters (a friend of mine and worthy to be believed) that he was on guard.

This day Commolet preached that the *politiques* of the Court should be purged again. So did Doctor Martin. A little while before the *curé* of St. André-des-Arts publicly preached against Tardif, his parishioner, as a *politique* and traitor, saying that he was forming . . . conspiracies . . . under color of playing darts in his garden. These words, although false, were partly the cause of the downfall of this poor man, one of the best men and Catholics in the parish.

* Brigard, formerly of the League, accused of conspiracy with royalists in April, had been acquitted by the supposedly *ligueur* Parlement. Out of this acquittal grew the violence of the extreme faction known as *L'Affaire Brisson*.

OCTOBER

Wednesday, October 9, *M. le Président* Brisson was warned again
. . . but he paid no more attention than to the others. . . .

NOVEMBER

Friday, November 1, 1591, All Saints' Day, M. Cotton, my father-in-
law, met by chance Mathieu Launay, ex-minister and now priest, who
ordinarily presides over the Sixteen. The said Launay asked him what he
thought about the acquittal of Brigard. Cotton replied that, knowing no
details, he hadn't any opinion, but that the Justices judged according to
their consciences, presumably, being good men. "Such good men!" replied
Launay. "There was never so great an outrage. But, by God, they'll die
for it." Cotton knew enough to keep still . . . came quickly to me, and I
sent word of it to Brisson by a mutual friend. . . . Two days before,
Cromé, conseiller in their Council, had used almost identical words,
saying that these times call for a St. Bartholomew . . . and that the judges
of Brigard should die.

Saturday, November 2, after dinner, the Sixteen assembled in the
house of Boursier . . . Launay presided. . . .

Tuesday, November 5, the assembly of the Sixteen was held at the
house of La Bruyère Senior, where Launay presided over a very large
company.

Wednesday, November 6, they met *chez* Boursier; Launay and Martin
took turns presiding. [There the ten men whose names follow] were
chosen to be a secret council: Acarie, Le Goix, Ameline, Louchard, Thuaut,
Barderet, Rosni, Du Rideau, Rainssant and Bezancon. . . . There was
also set forth the injustice which all felt to be in the judgment of Brigard.
Brisson was informed of all this that evening by Rabusseau, the glove-
maker, whom he called his "supervisor of the Sixteen."

Friday, the 8th of the month, at eight in the morning, the Sixteen met
at the house of La Bruyère. The *curé* of St. Cosme [Hamilton] and Bussi
were there too. The latter, proposing a new form of oath to the Union,
made several of them sign a blank paper, saying that he would write in
the form of the oath afterward. La Bruyère put a Missal on the table to
be sworn on.

Sunday, November 10, the company of the Sixteen met at the house of Sanguin, Chanoine de Notre Dame. Bussi was there with his paper, on which he had still written nothing. This scandalized several, that they had signed a paper without knowing what it was.

That same day the new Council of Ten assembled *chez* Launay after dinner, and he made excuses for the blank paper, swearing to them on his oath as a priest that nothing would be put on it which was not good and holy and for the advancement of religion.

Tuesday, November 12, the Sixteen met at La Bruyère's . . . when many of them objected to signing the paper; Launay repeated his oath, and assured them that it was a matter of importance concerning the conservation of the faith; to these men brigandage, hangings, murder, assassinations, and all sorts of wickedness serve the conservation of religion.

Wednesday, November 13, the secret Council of Ten met, morning and evening, at de Launay's. Bussi, Cromé, and Hamilton were also present.

A good many people of Paris, hearing about these meetings, and so many comings and goings of Bussi and Cromé, thought some evil was in the making, but they couldn't discover what it was. Of course it was known that it was against the *politiques*, that is, the best men of the city, and especially the Justices and Brisson, who every day had two or three warnings. He was on the point of leaving, but he didn't know how . . . and the irresolution and ambition which had kept him there till now continued. He tried to keep in the good graces of the Sixteen on the one hand, and at the same time to work for the royalists. But he fell between the two, as usually happens to those of his kind who, in great civil troubles like ours, try to be neutral, or to get advantage from each side for themselves, deciding nothing except in the last minute, which makes it impossible for them to save themselves.

Thursday, November 14, the secret Council met in the morning *chez* Launay, where the pitiful tragedy of the next day was concluded . . . to send to the scaffold a good number of the most important men of Paris of the quality of Brisson and his companions, and to rouse the people with blood to purge the *politiques* of Paris. But God, who is good and just, made them fall into the pit they prepared for others.

This day Salé, *procureur* in the Parlement, brought an honest man who had been spying on the Sixteen to Brisson . . . he warned him to look out, as he knew that in their latest meeting they had resolved to get even with the injustice done to Brigard, and had talked of seizing the judges, particularly Brisson, whom they hated above the others, and [he said] that the project was ready for execution. To this Président Brisson responded, "My friend, I don't doubt that all you say is true, and worse too. But it is too late to do anything about it. I am like those dogs which go too far into the water, and feeling that they are drowning, would like to get out if they could, but they can't, because the water is too strong for them . . . in the end they drown. To speak frankly, I do what I can in this tempest. . . . I know that I will drown and can't be saved except by a special miracle of God."

M. Poussemouthe, lawyer in the Parlement, went to warn him also on the same day. Brisson thanked him. . . . Finally, in the evening, Jean Prévost, *curé* of St. Séverin, his good friend, went to see him and told him that the Sixteen had armed themselves and were talking not only of arresting but also of hanging the *politiques* . . . responsible for the trial of Brigard. . . .

"I know they have it in for me," said Brisson, "I am too much warned. But they'll think twice before going in for large-scale attacks . . . their hearts will fail them before they carry it all through. One can't thus imprison the Court every year, and they are not so united as you may think, there are always a few false brothers who let the cat out of the bag. I don't say that the fury of these men, and especially of the most desperate of them, is not to be feared . . . I confess I wish I were out of here . . . but it is not possible. God will keep me if it please Him, and dispose of me as He wishes."

Then M. de St. Séverin said to him, "I pray to God, every day, especially for you, to keep and deliver you, and all of us, from the hand of the wicked, and more, to have pity on the poor afflicted people. These are the best weapons for our times. Just the same, Monsieur, I don't think God has forbidden us to use material weapons . . . when with them one may serve the public welfare . . . if these people aren't resisted at all, they'll hang us all or cut our throats in the end. I hold them wicked . . . and able to carry it out, but a time will come to settle with them."

"But how can we settle with them?" asked Brisson. "Don't you realize that our hands are tied? And he who commands us, though he likes them as little as we do (and they love him little), has forbidden us to raise a hand against them. . . . We can do nothing, we are only judges of what pleases the Duke of Mayenne . . . but God will work it all out in time. . . ." "God will it!" said M. de St. Séverin. . . . "I wanted to warn you, or I couldn't have slept tonight." Brisson thanked him, and said that the next day they would hold a meeting and try to settle things, and do what they could to prevent the evil designs, "which I am sure are afoot . . . there can't be so much smoke without fire. . . ." Thus they parted from each other, because it was very late.

I wrote this all down word for word, as a friend told me, as being worthy of the judgment of God, which made itself known the next day in the death of this great man, without preventing it. . . .

Friday, November 15, 1591, M. le Président Brisson, Larcher, Conseiller in the Grand'Chambre, and Tardif, Conseiller at the Chastelet, were taken prisoner in the morning, strangled and hanged that afternoon in prison.

Brisson was the first to go. He talked a long time and tried to save his life, begging them to confine him between four walls on a diet of bread and water, until he had finished the book he was writing for the instruction of the young, as very necessary and useful for the public good. At last, seeing that he couldn't abate the cruelty of these tigers who were killing him, he cried with great vehemence, "O God, Thy judgments are great!" and repeated it in Latin. . . . Before dying he was taken with such a great sweat and shudder that his shirt looked as if he had plunged into the river. . . . Thus was hanged this day a first Président of the Court, by a clerk.

> A great clerk was Brisson
> But he was taught his lesson
> By a little clerk of the school
> Who treated him *à l'éspagnole*.

After him Larcher was brought to be hanged. He, seeing the Président hanging, cried, "Ah, Monsieur, are you there? I have no further regret in dying, when I see the cruelty to so good and worthy a man."

Tardif, brought last, saw the other two on the gibbet, fainted, as much from fear, one assumes, as from the open place in his arm. (He had just been bled when they took him prisoner at his house.) They carried this half-dead man to the scaffold.

At seven in the morning this same day, while these fine things were going on, the *curé* of St. Jacques, accompanied by La Bruyère and three others, took the paper signed by Bussi, Louchard, Crucé, Soli, and others to the captain of the Spaniards. It contained the reasons for their actions. A similar one was taken to Dom Alexander, Colonel of the Neapolitans, by the *curé* of St Cosme, who walked around Paris that day armed to the teeth and accompanied by various satellites.

This day the Sixteen lost LaRue, who said he was no longer one of them because of this barbarous execution, which he hated, wicked and seditious as he was. In fact, he went to the Bailli de Rochefort, who didn't want to let him in, until he told him what had happened and swore that he would never more have anything to do with the Sixteen, having vowed himself their mortal enemy. . . .

Saturday, November 16, the bodies of Brisson, Larcher, and Tardif were attached to a fence in the Place de Grève with these inscriptions:

Barnabé Brisson: one of the chiefs of the traitors and of the heretic

Claude Larcher: one of the makers of traitors, and *politique*

Tardif: one of the enemies of God and the Catholic princes

It was Cromé, conseiller in the great council, who, having judged them and having had them hanged, conducted the bodies himself to the Grève . . . with a lantern in his hand.

When day came Bussi went to the Place, accompanied by many mutinous and wicked good-for-nothings of the city . . . and when he saw the crowd gathered to see this sad and strange spectacle, he began to cry, "Get the traitors! Get the *politiques* who have sold the city to the heretic. . . ." He and his friends shouted these things to move the mob to blood and pillage. Bussi shouted that if they would follow him, by evening . . . Paris would be cleansed of traitors . . . [of whom] he had a list. . . . "If not," he cried, seeing that no one was showing any interest, "I warn you they will cut your throats . . . we would have all been dead if we hadn't taken their chiefs, whom you see here, and hadn't prevented them [from acting] today."

To these words the populace, instead of being moved to arm, as Bussi intended . . . said no word . . . regarding the poor bodies with pity; they pressed close together, being more filled with mercy than with sedition. There were even some poor folk beaten by Bussi's men for saying aloud that it was a great pity. In which a Christian sees a singular work of God.

Sunday, November 17, the two Rollands left Paris to go to the Duke of Mayenne at Laon. They were sent by Messieurs the Sixteen to explain to the Duke the reasons for the executions. . . .

The lawyer D'Orléans * . . . although one of the foremost of the League, said to [the Sixteen] that he thought the deed so wicked and reprehensible that it could be expiated only by the death of the perpetrators, and he called them wicked men and murderers. M. Le Maistre said virtuously that he would never return to the Palais except to hang those who had killed Brisson . . . he further called the *curé* of St. André bloodthirsty, and blamed him for being the death of the best man and Catholic in his parish. . . .

[Friday, November 22] I saw letters which Rolland had sent to a friend of his in Paris, in which he reported that the Duke of Mayenne was very much displeased with what had occurred, that he was not on good terms with the Sixteen, and that his anger was growing every day . . . and that, when he came to Paris . . . he was resolved to make a great change. This letter came from Laon, and was written on November 20.

This day a good friend of mine showed me . . . a letter from his brother, who is with the King, in which, among other news, he told in cipher how the King, during dinner, was talking of the murder of Brisson in Paris, and joking in his accustomed manner said "that he had no better servants than the Sixteen, that they served him better than they did their master [Mayenne], and it didn't cost him any doubloons." This letter was written November 19th.

Monday, November 25, I was shown the list of the *politiques* of our quarter, called "the red paper," in which I was much interested because my name was on it, and most of those I know. This . . . was a roll which the Sixteen had prepared for each quarter . . . of all the *politiques* of Paris, as they are called, of all those held to be for the King in their hearts, adherents of his party, or who do not approve of the robbery, brigandage, and cruelty which they call the zeal of God. . . . On this list they put all

---

* Often called "the best pen of the League," D'Orléans had written many pamphlets against the Huguenots and the Valois, advocating regicide. His best-known book is *Le Catholique Anglais* about the supposed persecutions of Catholics in England.

those (however devout Catholics they are) who, as true Frenchmen, refuse to submit to Spanish domination.

They had resolved to hang or stab some and exile others of these . . .
and it was designated which fate was in store by the letters P.D.C. [by
their names], meaning *pendu, dagué,* or *chassé.* I found myself under
the letter D . . . Monsieur Cotton, my father-in-law, under P . . . Monsieur le Président Le Maistre likewise . . . Monsieur Désiré, my neighbor,
under C . . . and so forth. It was the *commissaire* Bazin who had drawn
it up, with the *curé* of St. André, his vicar, and Pierre Senault the [chief]
Sixteen of our quarter. In the whole street on which my mother lives,
only the Monthelons were missing. But God didn't allow these bloody
plans to prevail . . . for the Spaniards and Neapolitans wouldn't use
their forces, no matter what great promises and exhortations were made
to them. Abhorring the enterprise as cruel and unnatural, and rejecting
the plan as pernicious, [they] said that they could not lay hands on anyone not condemned in the courts, nor kill men in their beds who could
not defend themselves, because that was contrary to their profession . . .
for the execution of something of such great consequence they would
have to have orders from their superiors, which were not forthcoming.
. . . [They also said] that it was the business of the Duke of Mayenne
to take cognizance of crimes, and not up to them. . . .

Dom Alexander, Colonel of the Neapolitans, said to the *curé* of St.
Jacques that he wished all the heretics and *politiques* were in Spain where
the Inquisition would deal with them, and all the traitors in Paris in the
river . . . but to take arms against them was a different thing.

[Madame de Nemours] sent a gentleman . . . to her son . . . with
letters . . . in which she told him what was going on, and how much his
presence was needed, as much to forestall the evil designs as to deliver
her, and her children and all good men, from the tyranny and servitude
to which they had been reduced by these men of no principle. She
charged the messenger to tell him by word of mouth to remember that
she was his mother. . . . These words touched the Duke's heart deeply,
as was seen in his hastening his trip and strengthening his resolution.

[Wednesday, November 27] I saw the letter the Sixteen had written
to the King of Spain . . . dated November 20, 1591, headed, "The Rev-
erend Father in God, bearer of this letter, is well informed of our affairs,
and will supplement our letters to Your Catholic Majesty, we beg you to

listen to what he says." And it was signed your humble servants, the Council of the Sixteen Quarters: Martin, *docteur*; Genébrard, *docteur et professeur du Roi*; Sanguin, *l'Un des capitaines*; Turquet, *Colonel*; Mesnager, Rainssant, Ameline, Louchard, Marin-Cromé, *Conseiller au Grand Conseil*; Ysoart Capel, J. Hamilton, *curé de* St. Cosme; Crucé, Acarie, M. de Launay, *l'Un des Présidents du Conseil*; La Bruyère.

Thursday, November 28, 1591, the Duke of Mayenne arrived in Paris . . . and went to the lodging of the Queen, called l'Hôtel des Princesses, because the names King and Queen were odious in Paris. M. de Belin and others went to greet him outside the city. Bussi-LeClerc didn't want to leave his Bastille, and remained inside all day without firing a single cannon shot (as is customary) to welcome him, which was remarked upon. Some of the Sixteen went before the Duke, among others Louchard and Senault . . . and, excusing their companions in the matter of the execution of Brisson and the others, said that [the Duke] would realize in the end that what they had done was for the public good, the conservation of the Church, and the advancement of his service.

The Duke replied to this that as for his service . . . it was identical with that of the public . . . and that he would do justice to all on both sides, and would settle things so that good men would be satisfied. He said this in an aloof fashion, looking at Senault with a disgusted eye for getting too near his horse . . . he said, "You'll get hurt, I beg you stand back." Senault was annoyed . . . he told his *curé* . . . that he knew . . . the Duke had some bad intention toward him. . . .

(Senault hadn't been in Paris at the time of the executions, but had returned that day three or four hours after the game was over. He was angry, and told the Sixteen that they had lost all by what they had done, not that it shouldn't have been done, but in an entirely different way.) . . . The said Senault is of all the Sixteen the most evil, but the best advised and most subtle. . . .

November 30 . . . some of the Sixteen went to the Duke of Mayenne . . . and stormed about without showing any respect, in their usual way. One of them, named Le Normant, said, so that the Duke could hear it, that the Sixteen had put him where he was, and could remove him when they felt like it. The Duke let it pass, and contented himself with learning his name. But M. de Vitry . . . said that the Sixteen were the curse of Paris, and that if the Duke would only say the word he would have them all hanged by evening, and would do it with his own two hands. In truth this gentleman strengthened the Duke's hand and put courage into him. . . .

DECEMBER

Sunday, the first day of December, the Bastille was surrendered to the Duke of Mayenne by Bussi, who left with great regret, on condition that his life and rings should be granted him. . . . In his place was a most honest gentleman named DuBourg, a faithful and good servant of the Duke, if ever there was one.

Monday, December 2, M. de Mayenne went to the Palais and in his presence four présidents were added to the Court . . . Chartier, De Hacqueville, Neuilly, and Le Maistre. . . . On the same day [he learned] of further evil designs of the Sixteen, of whom three hundred were holding a meeting at the Cordeliers', and that there was danger of still worse to come if something weren't done to prevent it. . . .

Wednesday, December 4, Ameline, lawyer of the Chastelet, Louchard, *commissaire*, and Emmonot, *procureur*, were hanged and strangled at the Louvre as punishment for the deaths of Brisson, Larcher, and Tardif. The same day at five in the evening Anroux was hanged, about four hours after the others.

Ameline was, for a Sixteen, a man of understanding and ability, who from the start of the League had roused many of the towns of France against the King . . . which he did sometimes disguised as a Cordelier, sometimes as a Jesuit, another time as a merchant, another as a courtier, depending on the men with whom he was dealing. When the late King learned of it, he decided to hang him, as the most pernicious of all the League members to the state. . . .

As for Louchard, he was a presumptuous fool and good-for-nothing, advancing his own designs under the mask and veil of religion, and had acquired a great reputation in the party for being one of the most audacious and desperate of all. He preferred to be hanged than to renounce the Sixteen and leave their fellowship. When the Duke . . . offered him the post of supply officer in his army, and even to cancel his debts, if he would leave Paris and follow him, and promised him that the past would be canceled out . . . instead of accepting these fine offers he sent the reply . . . that for all the goods in the world he would never abandon his party, nor leave Paris, and that the Sixteen were not so easily disposed of as the Duke thought. . . . When this audacious answer was brought to the Duke . . . he said, "He wants to be hanged then? He shall be, and within twenty-four hours. . . ."

Emmonot was a criminal and murderer who, on All Saints' Day when the King was in the suburbs, had killed M. Minterne, a retainer of the late Cardinal of Bourbon, and universally thought to be a good man and devout Catholic . . . some alleged that he was in no way responsible for Brisson's death, but the Duke said that he was satisfied that he deserved hanging as much or more than the others. . . .

Anroux, who was left to the last, was supposed to surpass all the others in cruelty . . . a list of all sorts of Parisians whom he and his friends proposed to assassinate was found in one of the pockets of his trousers.

When the news of these executions was brought to the King he said his cousin had done well, but had failed in four degrees, meaning that if he had hanged four more, it would have been half of Sixteen.

The *curés* and preachers cried out . . . that religion was lost, and recommended the new martyrs-saints to the people . . . [but] D'Orléans . . . said that he was no *Béarniste* or *politique*, but a true son of the Church, as everyone knew, but that [the murder of Brisson] was so barbarous an act that M. de Mayenne could not be blamed, except for his mildness . . . and that no well-informed person, however Catholic, could think otherwise.

Friday, December 6, LaRue, metamorphosed from Sixteen to *politique* attacked Launay at the door of his house . . . hearing the noise I went out with lots of others, and heard Launay call LaRue a drunkard, LaRue called him an apostate . . . the sign of a great war in which the wolves eat each other. . . .

Monday, December 9, the Duke assembled the Sorbonne . . . [who] were scandalized at what he had done. . . .

Tuesday, December 10, M. le Duc went to the Palais and excused all but three men from blame in the Brisson murder . . . that is Marin-Cromé . . . Gaucheri . . . and the man who served as clerk [at the mock trial].

Wednesday, December 11, the Duke of Mayenne left Paris, taking with him Bussi . . . Launay . . . and all sorts of others of the faction, having been implored to do so by many good men, the best Catholics in Paris. . . .

In this year of 1591, shortly after the reduction of Chartres, M. de Châtillon, Colonel-General of the French Infantry, eldest son of . . . the Admiral of France killed on St. Bartholomew, 1572 . . . died, on his estate, of a fever, proceeding, it is said, from disappointment and melancholy. When the King received word of the death of this young lord, who equaled in wisdom and valor the greatest captains in Europe, and who had done him great services . . . the emotion . . . he felt brought tears to his eyes. . . .

The King . . . pressed [the messenger] for the cause of the fever, and said that he should speak the truth boldly, for there was a rumor that it was annoyance and disappointment. . . . "It seemed to him, Sire," [replied the other] "that for some time his services have not been pleasing to you . . . and the last time he came to kiss your hand you gave him no orders . . . this happened twice, and he had to retreat unsatisfied." . . . "It was that I loved him so much . . . I should have given him a command and satisfied him." This is the usual way with kings: they always mourn the deaths of servants whose lives they could not bear.

THE CRUMBLING OF
THE LEAGUE

JANUARY

Sunday, January 5, Boucher, in his sermon, called Louchard and his companions saints and martyrs . . . and the *curé* of St. Germain l'Auxerrois made a panegyric on Ameline, called him his good friend, and made a new saint out of this deplorable murderer, the worst of them all. . . .

The beginning of this month of January, up to the 9th, was very cold and raw, but the rest of it windy, humid, and too mild for the season.

At the beginning of this year died Elizabeth of Austria, Queen Dowager of France, daughter of the Emperor Maximilian, and widow of King Charles IX, an example to all of piety and charity in her time.

About the same time Duke John Casimir, of the House of the Counts Palatine, also died, very ardent in the Huguenot religion and one of its chief protectors. . . .

MARCH

Tuesday, March 31, an attempted armed uprising of the Sixteen was discovered during the night, but Messieurs de Belin and du Bourg, having been warned, were able to prevent anything happening.

This month of March was hot and humid, which was the cause of much contagious sickness in Paris, and many of the sick developed the plague, especially on this [left] side of the bridges. The parishes of St. Séverin and St. André were much afflicted.

APRIL

Friday, April 17, 1592, the Parlement declared against the authorization of power given to the Sixteen by the Council of State. . . .

Sunday, April 19, the preachers of Paris, annoyed at the Court on this account, preached against them as members of the Béarniste party and makers of heresy. . . .

Tuesday, April 21 . . . M. de Vitry, being temporarily in Paris, told of a parrot . . . who [would speak] if he were shown money. . . . Vitry, to try it out, had pulled a piece of money from his pocket, and seeing that at the sight of it speech returned to the bird, he said, laughing aloud, "By God . . . the preachers of this town must have instructed this parrot, he does just what they do: for money one can make them babble and cry whatever one pleases, but if they don't see any, they won't say a word any more than he will." [In this month, Chicot], the King's fool, died. He was a good soldier . . . but died, not of his wound . . . but of intemperance and drunkenness. The King loved this man, fool though he was, and didn't find fault with anything he said, which is why he got away with so much.

When the Prince of Parma came to France for the second time, in this year 1592, [Chicot] said to the King, before all the world, "Monsieur, my friend, I see that everything else you do will be of no avail, unless you turn Catholic. You must go to Rome, play up to the Pope for all to see, otherwise no one will ever believe you are a Catholic, then take a big beaker of holy water and wash away the rest of your sins."

MAY

Friday, May 1, the *curé* of St. André said that if one could open the stomachs of many in the parish, one would find a big Béarnais inside. . . .

Saturday, May 6, the Duke of Parma, having crossed the water at Caudebec, arrived with his army outside the city of Paris. His son, the Prince of Parma, and M. de Guise . . . dined the next day with Madame de Nemours. . . . The day after that . . . the whole army, much driven and tired, passed by in full sight of the city, which astonished the people more than it pleased them. It also accomplished the ruination of the suburbs, where an infinity of murders, robberies, and extortions were committed and [went] unpunished.

It is usually said, "cool May, hot June," but this year it is just the other way — May was hot and June cold.

JUNE

Monday, the 18th of June, news of two deaths came to Paris. One of these, the worse, proved to be true, that is, the death of M. de Montpensier. The other, that of Bussi-LeClerc, was false. Still it is a lot in Paris for one of two pieces of news to be true. . . .

Tuesday, the 30th of this month, a tinsmith named Poccard, who used to belong to the Sixteen but no longer does, died the day after he had dined with our Master Senault. It is said that the joking words, running down the Holy Brotherhood, which he said to Senault . . . had cost him his life. In this one can see the just judgment of God, who struck down this man through his own buddies, and punished him for the murder of the good Mercier, teacher, the day after Pentecost, in the year 1588, when he was a member of the Sixteen.

JULY

Friday, July 3, 1592, the people of Paris were forbidden to go to St. Denis, to trade or for any other reason, on pain of imprisonment. An injunction was also issued for all those of the opposite party to leave the city within twenty-four hours or be declared prisoners of war. All passports were revoked, which was a measure to raise money by the renewal of them, as was evident the next day, when one got a renewal by paying.

Sunday, July 5, the *curé* of St. André cried out loudly in his sermon against the peace that was being drawn up, supposedly. . . . He also said that those who were with the Béarnais were all damned, no matter how much they protested that they were Catholic; he also said that the *politiques*, of which Paris was full . . . were a hundred times worse than the Béarnais. . . .

Commolet made even more fuss than the others that day, even to speaking by name against three *politiques* he saw leaving during the sermon . . . but not a soul moved . . . [against them]. . . . He laughed uproariously like a circus performer and made grotesque faces.

The *curé* of St. Jacques . . . "excommunicated" all those who talked of peace, or thought trade should be resumed [with the royalist towns]. . . .

Rose, Ceuilly, Martin, Guarinus, Feuardant, and all the others preached in the same way, saying that they were of the opinion, if the Holy Father approved, of receiving the Béarnais in the Church as a Capuchin but not as a King. They attacked those who favored trade between Paris and St. Denis . . . claimed that there were more than 3,000 *politiques* who plotted under cover of trade. They complained that those who should have controlled these things did nothing about it. This caused M. de Belin to have a general check made at all the gates the next day . . . but no one was found who was not armed with a passport and safe-conduct, nor was anyone discovered who declared himself a *politique*.

On Monday, the 27th of the month, a *commissaire* of the Chastelet who is not among the pensioners of Spain, said to another who is one (and who thought the first was likewise), "I have some money at the moment, thank God! Here it is," and he made some coins jingle in his pocket. Lowering his voice he said, "It is my Spanish wages that I've finally gotten." The other, not realizing that he was being made fun of, replied, "You're damn lucky! For over three months I've tagged after Senault for mine, but I haven't got them yet."

During this month of July the news of Paris was all about the alleged impending arrival of the Duke of Mayenne, which everyone wanted except the Sixteen, who feared he would come only to hang them.

AUGUST

In this month [when] our Master Ceuilly had abandoned to the lock-breakers of Paris the houses of the *politiques* (in his sermons) . . . the lock-breakers were offended . . . and sent him an amusing letter . . . which they nailed up on his church . . . this is the gist:

M. de Ceuilly, We find it very odd that you call on us in your sermons to help you to rob and kill so many good and honorable men. Although we are poor and simple men, we know that this is contrary to the laws of God, which you ignore in your preaching. To believe you, one finds the road to Paradise by the scaffold, like your four martyrs of the Louvre [Louchard, etc.] who are doing the cooking in Hell, waiting for you and your fellows. These are the fruits and rewards of your Spanish wages. . . . In sum, don't drag us into your wicked faction. . . . [Signed] Your good friends, The Lock-Breakers.

OCTOBER

Saturday, October 10, 1592, it was rumored that a peace had been concluded which would be made public the next day. A week ago people
thought that they were dying of hunger, today all sorts of abundance is
about to be ours. The inconsistency of minds is as great as that of the
weather this year. . . .

Friday, October 16, assemblies began to be held in all the quarters and
corporations of Paris to make a plan to relieve the necessity of the people.
Among other things, many good *bourgeois* proposed to send the King
an invitation to become Catholic; these have since been christened *Les
Semmoneux* [the inviters]. This was a proceeding of good intention but
without discretion or common sense. Thinking to remedy the evils they
increased them, having no leader, nor forces in hand to carry it out. The
Duke of Mayenne, when he was informed, was very much displeased with
this enterprise and returned to Paris to put a stop to it, which he did with
no difficulty.

Friday, the 23rd, I returned . . . from St. Denis, where I did more
business in one afternoon than I did on my last trip in seventeen days,
because I was able, under the name of Bellemanière, to get hold of part
of my revenues from Orléans. This was because M. du Four, Governor of
Gergeau, who can do anything, promised to back me against those who
treat me as a *ligueur* there — as here I am treated as a *politique* — a fine
way to get things done!

Tuesday, October 27, in spite of the presence of the Duke of Mayenne,
the Chambre des Comptes voted unanimously for peace, and to send to
the King the invitation to become Catholic. The Président d'Ormesson
. . . took news of this to the Duke, and, as all but four had agreed
(L'Huilier, Hotteman, Dalesseau, and Acarie), he begged him to consider
it . . . in view of the necessity of the people . . . and the fact that peace
was the only remedy. He spoke as the representative of the company. . . .
The Duke hardly replied to this embassy, wishing to render their plans
nil without saying so, which he did.

Friday, October 30, the Duke of Mayenne went to the Parlement,
where D'Orléans spoke freely against the Sixteen, calling them no-goods
who were impudent enough to presume to dispose of the state and the
crown, and even to put a Spaniard in charge, as if there were no brave

and powerful princes in France . . . and [said] that they had done injury to all the princes, and particularly to [Mayenne] and his house. He scorned their religion, under which they hid everything, daring to honor with the name of martyr those who had murdered the royal justices . . . spoke also against the clergy, and [said] that their tongues should be bridled for libeling the princes and for meddling in affairs of state, of which they understood nothing.

When the preachers heard this they rushed to the Duke and demanded that D'Orléans be exiled as a mutinous enemy of God's Church and his priests. The Duke replied calmly that he would settle it to everyone's satisfaction. They were not satisfied, and insisted loudly that it was an affront to religion, and that the state would be undone by the injuries of D'Orléans. . . . Then the Duke said to them, "As far as religion goes, I know D'Orléans to be so good a Catholic that none of you can touch him. As for matters of state, I'll take care of [them], it is not your affair. Keep yourselves busy preaching the Gospel, that is your business and nothing else." Nevertheless they continued to attack [D'Orléans] as an apostate.

Thus the Duke . . . gives the Sixteen and the *politiques* something in common, in that they are both very much opposed to him. Formerly there was no mother's son who didn't wish him here; today he is here and they wish him away. So vain and lacking in sensible foundation are the minds of men in these times.

NOVEMBER

Sunday, November 1, our Master Boucher excommunicated the *Semmoneux* of his parish and forbade them the Mass. . . .

The next day he said that there were asses who were of a mind to send to the Béarnais and accept him if he were a Catholic. . . . As for him, he thought that it would be all right for the Béarnais to conquer the Kingdom of Heaven, because he couldn't deceive anybody there, but the kingdom of France, no, he could deceive too many.

The next day . . . the King . . . was told that some wanted to send from Paris to ask him to become a Catholic. "Catholic!" said the King, "I'll be Catholic before the men of Paris are good men, tell them so for me in no uncertain terms."

Wednesday, November 4, the Duke of Mayenne went to an assembly of the city. The loudest *Semmoneux* were brought like lambs to the slaughter, or like little scholars who, in their teacher's absence, have done something foolish, and hide when they hear him coming . . . thus the stupid *manants* lost heart in the Duke's presence, and had nothing to say but to beg for the pardon that was given them, along with a warning not to repeat the offense. The Duke said, "I will forgive the past . . . but I warn you that in the future, if any man, of no matter what quality, dares to do it again . . . I will treat him as an enemy. You have asked for the resumption of trade — you shall have it, and for a session of the Estates which will remedy your necessity and establish order." Turning to La Chapelle-Marteau he asked, "What more do the people want?" "Monsieur," he replied, "they want a King and will have one." M. de Mayenne then said, "The Estates will give them one, but when they have him what can he do that I can't do?"

Monday, the 9th of November, the election of a Prévost des Marchands took place, in which . . . the Duke of Mayenne . . . undertaking something which no King has ever done, abolished the choice of the people [for Échevins] . . . and canceled the votes given [to men] who were held to be honest but a little inclined to be *politiques*, and put in their place Pichonnat, the soul of the Sixteen, who hadn't a single vote, and Neret, who had very few, but who is held to be a good man and *politique* . . . the Sixteen and the *politique* . . . to balance the two forces. . . .

DECEMBER

Saturday, the 5th of the month, a young boy of seventeen years was burned in the Place de Grève, for having impregnated a cow, from which had emerged a monster, half-man, half-cow. . . .

The same day, two Spaniards were hanged and strangled for having robbed two ladies who were leaving Paris with passports . . . the other Spaniards complained loudly, and said that if men were to be hanged for stealing, half of Paris would be hanged. . . .

Monday, the 7th of this month of December, news came to Paris of the death of the Duke of Parma in Arras on the 2nd of the month, at the age of fifty. He had the reputation of being one of the best captains in Europe. He was loved by the Italians, hated and feared by the Spaniards, followed by the Walloons . . . very wise opportunist . . . whose jealousy of his master [Philip II] . . . shortened his days, according to the common rumor.

Wednesday, the 9th of December, after dinner, as I was warming myself at the fire, I was nearly killed by two great stones which fell from the mantel, from under which my children, by the grace of God, had just moved. After that, moving into the hall, the ceiling fell on me, and I was buried up to the belt. God held me by the hand, I believe, in that I was not injured. . . .

Friday, December 18, the Estates, set for the 20th . . . were postponed to January 17th, at which the people murmur and the priests cry out. Doctor Martin says, "Let each man hold them in his own house, there won't be any others." *

Wednesday, the 23rd of the month, there was an alarm during the night in various quarters of Paris, because of a false rumor that the *Semmoneux* were to have their throats cut. . . .

Toward the end of this year, 1592, the King lost the flower of his nobility in M. de la Noue, killed before the town of Amballe in Brittany. He was a gentleman to be forever regetted by all good Frenchmen, as much for his great valor, wise counsel, and upright conduct, as for the great goodness and fear of God in him, rare virtues in captains of this century.

In this year 1592, these things tried the patience of the poor people of Paris and interested them, in the hopes that some of them might cure their troubles: peace, commerce, the trip to Rome, the conversion of the King, the Estates, and the election of a Catholic King.

---

* These Estates, promised by Mayenne since 1590, were finally opened in January 1593. They are called "The Estates of the League" by royalist writers.

CONVERSION OF HENRY IV

JANUARY

Saturday, January 2, 1593, Master Marin-Cromé, Conseiller in the Great Council, and principal instigator, author and executor of the hanging of the late Président Brisson . . . was discovered in Paris by LaRue and Rainsseau, who were prevented from laying hands on him . . . by the Duke of Mayenne, who told them to be quiet about it and not to touch him.

Monday, the 4th of the month, Messieurs de Mayenne and Guise left Paris, to pursue . . . the King. His Majesty was informed of this, and took to laughing. He said, "My cousin Mayenne is a great captain, but I get up earlier in the morning than he does." . . .

Today [January 11] there was an assembly of the city, to discuss the *cahiers* of the Estates, which were full of beautiful propositions and hopes and promises . . . of which our Master Guarinus . . . said in his sermon that there were a lot of fine promises but that there was no meat on the fire.

[January 14] Cardinal Pellevé said to the Council, in regard to the *politiques* of Paris, that the biggest ones should be chased out, the middle-sized ones hanged or drowned, but as for the little ones, they should be pardoned, because when they saw what happened to the others they would be quiet. . . .

Saturday, January 23, the *curé* of St. Jacques attacked a poor boy held to be an idiot . . . with his cutlass . . . and wounded him so seriously that for a long time he was thought dead. When the Duke of Mayenne heard of this he said that it was the third time that he had had complaints of similar follies of the said *curé*, who deserved to be punished, but the times were not right. Two-thirds of his parishioners absented themselves from Mass, even Des Près, the greatest Catholic in the Parish, who said out loud that [the *curé*] was not worthy of performing it, having been party to the death of Président Brisson, against the oath of his office. . . .

[In the Estates] Cardinal Pellevé spoke for the Legate and the King of Spain, although it had been decided that, as a foreigner, he should not take part. Among other points . . . he said that St. Paul was a nobleman . . . which caused someone to remark . . . that these Estates had great need of some nobility, of which there are almost none. . . .

In this month of January there was rumored great activity in France by the Third Party. . . .

The design of this Third Party was to kill the King, the Prince of Conti and M. de Montpensier. Cardinal Bourbon was then supposed to be King. . . . The enterprise was postponed but not abandoned, and the Cardinal was sick with regret. The King teased him about this, in his usual way, "Take heart, cousin, it is true that you are not King now, but you might be yet, after me."

In this month a soup-carrier . . . was beaten . . . for having driven his ass to the Estates, and for making fun of them. And another, called Big Jacques . . . was beaten for the same offense . . . talking to his ass, as he drove him, saying, "Come along, big Jean, let's go to the Estates." This gave rise to the following quatrain:

> Come on my ass! through the gates
> To M. de Mayenne's Estates;
> So you can turn, without a wrench
> Into Spaniard, instead of French!

From the 8th to the 16th of this month of January it was cold with a sharp frost; from then to the end, very rainy and windy, with lots of grippe and pox. The river was very high, rising as one watched it, and frightened those who live on the Pont des Musniers.

FEBRUARY

Monday, February 1, the Council met to deliberate on the letters brought to Paris from the King. Cardinal Pellevé said that they should be burned, but Villeroy contradicted this . . . and it was said that no man of sense was of the same mind as the Cardinal.

[February 4] the sister of the *curé* of St. Jacques . . . was delivered of two children: one beautiful and well-formed, and the other a real monster with no arms or legs, but a tremendous nose . . . and a male organ the size of that of a man of thirty. Immediately this monster became the subject of the sermons . . . as being a replica of the Béarnais. . . . Feuardant said in public that this was the Béarnais, who had no arms or legs, that is to say, no force, that all his power was in his male member, which was very active everywhere, every day, or in his long nose. . . .

Friday, the 19th of the month, the Duke of Mayenne wrote letters to the citizens of Paris, begging them to receive the Duke of Feria, Spaniard, and to honor him as if he were the Duke himself.

Sunday, February 21, the Legate gave communion to about a hundred deputies to the Estates from different provinces, in the great church of Notre Dame. M. Genébrard preached, his sermon being full of the Béarnais, the *politiques*, and all sorts of invective, which is called the gospel of the Sixteen.

Thursday, February 25 . . . M. Le Maistre and Bernard, lawyer in the Dijon Parlement, spoke virtuously to the Estates. Among other points . . . they said that it was necessary to enter into conference with those of the opposite party who were not heretics . . . that it was not forbidden, as some said, but, on the contrary, was enjoined by holy canon. . . . "Is it not a holy and Christian work to embrace them, and to try to persuade them, rather than to reject them?" M. de Lyons was also for the conference, and it was voted by a plurality, in spite of the objections of the Legate and the actions of the preachers and the Sixteen.

This day Messieurs the Présidents d'Orsé and Videville left to treat with those of the King concerning commerce and labor. For this reason they were attacked by the Sixteen and the Sorbonne, and called *politiques* from the pulpit by the preachers of Paris.

Saturday, the 20th of the present month of February, a writer named Constant, a good old man of eighty, died in Paris, poor in the goods of this world, but rich in God, whom he feared, which was the reason I helped him as much as I could.

This month of February was terribly cold; the first part snowy, the rest dry, with very sharp frost.

MARCH

Tuesday, March 8, 1593, the Duke of Feria arrived in Paris . . . he was dressed in green with a little black hat. The son of the Duke of Mayenne, with M. de Belin [Governor of Paris] and Admiral de Villars, marched ahead of him . . . [the officials of the city] waited upon him . . . a whole crowd of people were gathered, but few saluted him. In the rue St. Antoine when he went by, not a soul raised his hat, which was remarked upon.

Thursday, March 11, the Prévost des Marchands went to the Duke of Feria to complain of the insolence of his men, who were ravaging the suburbs . . . saying that if the Duke couldn't discipline them he [the Prévost] would not be able to restrain the people from cutting them to pieces. The Duke . . . thanked him, and promised to see that justice was done. . . .

This day 30,000 crowns of Spanish gold in doubloons arrived in Paris, for the purpose of corrupting as many people as possible in the city, especially the captains and colonels, and others in authority.

Saturday, March 13, some *bourgeois* of the Sixteen went to the Prévost des Marchands to ask him to get the Duke of Feria to put up money for the income of the bonds [*rentes*] of the city. But the Prévost replied that he was no Spaniard, and he would not have it said that while Prévost he had mortgaged the city to a foreigner.

Monday, March 15, M. le Doyen Séguier refused to take money from the Duke of Feria, who offered it for the necessity of the chapter, and said most virtuously that [the Duke] had nothing to do with the chapter, and that when they needed money, they knew where to go.

Wednesday, March 17 . . . the *curé* of St. André said that he couldn't see why people made such a fuss [about accepting Spanish money], that he had never been offered any, but if he were, he might accept it. To say that it placed one under an obligation was true, but only a good one . . . that he would prefer a Spanish Catholic as King to the heretic Béarnais, and that those who thought otherwise were heretics and *politiques*. The soldiers, on the other hand, complained bitterly that the private Spanish pensions were paid to the Parisians and their wages were not. Dom Alexander, captain of the Neapolitans, said it right in public. . . .

The 22nd, 23rd, 24th and 25th of this month great rumors in Paris of a siege. The preachers said that to save ourselves we must break the communications of those in the city with the Béarnais, purge the *politiques* and the "inviters" — or Paris would be lost.

In this year of 1593, March 2, Mardi gras . . . one of my friends saw a Conseiller in the Court, with his wife and five little children, reduced to such necessity that they lived on milk and meager bread . . . and it was thirteen days since they had had any fuel (the weather was bitter cold). . . . Such is the poverty and need of Paris, even in the best houses. Such cases make me lift my heart and my eyes to the sky, to thank God and adore his providence, so great for me and mine.

APRIL

Friday, April 2, the Duke of Feria went to the Estates, made a speech, and presented credentials from his master. Cardinal Pellevé was charged with the reply, which he made in Latin, with many incongruous words. The deputies of Burgundy called him "the red ass."

Today, April 4, Colonel Passart, accompanied by those who are thought to be *politiques*, walking on the Quai St. Germain, refused to speak to Senault, Sanguin, and two others, because they were of the party of the Sixteen, told them to go to the devil . . . the others said that [Passart *et al.*] were more excommunicated than the Huguenots because they used to belong to the Sixteen. No less than 10,000 in Paris have renounced [the faction] since the death of Brisson.

This day [April 6] Madame [Catherine of Bourbon, sister of Henry IV] arrived in Mantes, where she presided over the council and had [Protestant] services held in public. When the preachers heard this they called her the French Jezebel in their sermons, and said that she was playing the Queen Mother [Catherine de Medici] and had at her tail and heels a dozen little devils, running after her all the time like dogs. . . .

Tuesday, April 20, the last day of Easter, the Estates met to name deputies to the conference which was to be held [with those of the King's party] from Thursday, the 22nd, to Thursday, the 29th. . . .

Monday, April 26, placards were posted all over the city against those who went to the conference, or who thought it good . . . called them traitors, *politiques*, heretics . . . [and said] that good Catholics would never recognize the Béarnais, whether he were converted or not, because he was excommunicate and a relapser, that they wanted a real King and true Catholic. . . . One LaRiche, after reading one of these fine placards . . . said that it was the son of a prostitute who had written it. . . . Some of the Sixteen overheard this and started to strangle him. . . .

Tuesday, the 27th, the Estates complained of these placards as injurious to their honor, and required that justice be done to their authors, or they would adjourn.

[April 28] M. de Belin said that if the King became Catholic, he would find the nobility of a good mind to recognize him. . . .

Thursday, April 29, the conference began at Suresne; both sides greeted and embraced each other with signs of reconciliation and friendship. Only M. de Rambouillet remained without a caress, because those of Paris thought he was one of the chief instigators of the death of [the Guises] . . . he was so hurt that he wept. As they [the conferees] left the Porte Neuve, a great crowd . . . cried, "Peace! Blessed are those who ask for it and get it! To all the devils with the others!" In the villages they went through people knelt and asked for peace with folded hands. This same day Senault said that the placards were the work of *politiques,* who blamed them on the Sixteen to bring disgrace to good Catholics. . . .

On Friday, the last day of the month, the delegates returned once more to the conference. The preachers cried out at this, the Sixteen were enraged, good men rejoiced, and the cry for peace from the people increased.

In this month of April, the [Protestant] ministers, who are no less apprehensive of the conversion than the theologians of Paris, finding themselves united on the subject, went to see His Majesty to sound him out about the great rumors that he would become Catholic. The King told them not to believe all they heard, that they could be assured of his regard, which they would always have, and that he would never change his religion, because that which he had done was always done with knowledge and with the support of his conscience. . . .

MAY

[Saturday, May 1] Rose preached in the Chapelle de Bourbon against M. de Lyons, to his face, [and] against all those who went to the conference. To those who were scandalized by this M. de Lyons said that it was permitted to a madman to say anything he wanted to anyone.

Sunday, May 2, the *curé* of St. André-des-Arts made the conference the whole subject of his sermon, which lasted two hours . . . he approved the placards, although Senault, his great friend, had condemned them as *politique.* He said that the conference signified nothing, that those of

Paris were really named by the Béarnais . . . and that the result would be a sedition in Paris in which the gates would be opened to the heretic. He said further that we must pray for M. de Mayenne, who had broken the *Semmoneux* and would break this [conspiracy] too. . . . He said he knew that it was said that he had taken doubloons, which was false, but that if he were offered any he would take them, and that although he is French it would be better to have a foreign King who was Catholic than a heretic . . . which he had said many times before, but he was repeating it so that they wouldn't forget it . . . called the King a tiger and son of a prostitute . . . a relapser who was good only for burning.

Commolet, on the contrary, condemned the placards . . . praised the conference, and said that we should pray for those engaged in this good work. De Moraines [and] the *curés* of St. Eustache, St. Sulpice, and St. Gervais . . . said that we should pray for the King's conversion . . . and condemned the placards as seditious. Among other things, the *curé* of St. Eustache said that only wicked men feared the conference . . . but what he [personally] feared was that we would get neither [peace nor the conversion] because of our sins. . . . The others mostly preached like St. André, condemning the conference and saying that they would not have the King, Catholic or Huguenot, calling him wolf, relapser, and excommunicate. . . .

Tuesday, May 4, the truce was announced for a space of ten days, during which one could go four leagues out of Paris without a passport. But the Prévost des Marchands prevented its execution, because he claimed (not without reason) that there wouldn't be a soul left in the city, and that it would give the foreign garrisons, and the mob, a chance to start some trouble. . . .

Thursday, May 6, six or seven thousand people left Paris to go to Vertus. M. de Vicq left all the gates of St. Denis open, and decreed that everyone from Paris be admitted . . . if they left their weapons at the gate.

Saturday, May 8, M. de Vicq went to service at Notre-Dame-des-Vertus, where a great crowd of Parisians saw him. He had it announced that the King was going to became Catholic, and that everyone should pray to God for him and for his conversion. He allowed women to enter St. Denis without passports, but not men.

Sunday, the 9th of the month, the King, at Mantes, was attending the Protestant service conducted by the Minister Damours. The latter, taking note of the rumors that the King was determined to become a Catholic, threatened him with the judgment of God if he did it . . . with great boldness and vehemence. Later M. le Cardinal de Bourbon and D'O . . . importuned His Majesty to punish [Damours] and not to allow it. But the King lowered his head, and said only, "What would you have me do? He told me the truth."

Wednesday, May 12, the Feast of the Holy Barricades was solemnized and celebrated in Paris, with more ceremony than ever. All the princes and lords took part in the procession. . . . Boucher preached at Notre Dame, where he exalted the day and said that it was the holiest and happiest in the history of the world. . . .

Thursday, May 13, the Duke of Feria proposed to the Council that the Infanta of Spain be made Queen of France, referred to the great merits and forces his master the King had used for thirty years to preserve the faith in France. To this Rose replied in anger (apropos for a madman they say), that the King of Spain had done nothing for religion . . . and that the fundamental laws prevented his proposal from being carried out. . . . Meanwhile the conferences continued, and the preachers cried out more than ever while the people rejoiced. . . .

[Tuesday, May 25] Today a large number of ecclesiastics went, with the Sixteen, to the Duke of Mayenne, to try to stop the peace . . . [meanwhile] the *politiques* assembled, and the next day about forty of them went to the Duke in behalf of the peace. . . . Each group came away in equal ignorance of the Duke's intentions, which were hidden, even from the most astute.

Friday, May 28, those of the Parlement assembled . . . [to discuss] the pretensions of the Duke of Feria in regard to the Infanta of Spain and the aboliton of the Salic Law . . . they resolved, briefly, that they neither could nor would [accept it]. M. Molé, Procureur-Général, among others, spoke virtuously to the Duke of Mayenne, [saying] that he and all his goods were at his service . . . but that he was a true Frenchman, had been born and would die a Frenchman, and before being anything else, he would die and sacrifice everything he had.

Sunday, the 30th, the *curé* of St. André railed against the peace, and said that the *politiques* were like frogs who go "coac, coac," with their croaking "peace, peace." . . .

231

This day the *curé* of St. Sulpice said that we should pray to God for peace and for the reconciliation of the parties, otherwise we could not receive the Holy Spirit . . . the ecclesiastics and the Sixteen went to the Duke of Mayenne, spoke to him haughtily against the peace, and demanded a King. . . . He sent them to the Estates, like the others.

In this month of May, while the King was at Mantes, the [Protestant] ministers, warned that the King had resolved to become Catholic . . . went to him to protest. . . . He spoke to them in these words . . . "When I do it you'll have no occasion to be alarmed. . . . On the contrary, I enter the house, not to live in it, but to clean it. I promise you this. And for yourselves, you'll have no worse treatment from me than you have ever had. Pray God for me, and I'll love you."

JUNE

Tuesday, June 8, the Sixteen, with the clergy, presented a request to the Estates to proceed to the selection of a King, and not to enter into any truce or conference until the Pope had been informed and had replied. . . . They were sent away without satisfaction, and their request judged so impertinent that it was said they should be sent to jail.

Wednesday, June 9, in the morning the rumor in Paris was that all was off, there would be neither truce nor peace. After dinner, quite the reverse, the news was that the truce was continued and extended. . . . Boucher thereupon went to the Duke of Mayenne anew to ask him for a King and requested that it be the Duke of Guise, and said that he had been delegated by the ecclesiastics to do so . . . to which the Duke replied that he and his companions should preach the Gospel and stop meddling in affairs of state of which they knew nothing, and that the Estates were meeting to settle things. . . .

On Friday, June 11, Master René Benoist, *curé* of St. Eustache, received a letter from the King asking for instruction, and [telling him] to bring with him two others of gentle spirit who cared for the relief of his poor subjects.

Benoist . . . went to the Duke [Mayenne], who said that he was very much pleased at the conversion, and that he personally wished no harm to the King of Navarre. . . .

June 13, which was Trinity Sunday, the *curé* of St. André said that the *politiques* were shouting about the peace . . . but that he thought our princes were too good men to make a treaty with a heretic, relapser, and excommunicate like the Béarnais, which would prejudice their honor and their sworn promises. Just the same, as they were men and could change, that if it should be true, there were many good brothers in Paris who would fight to prevent it, and that all good Catholics would die rather than endure it. . . .

Chavagnac, on the contrary, said that we should embrace the converted King, that those who asked for peace were good and holy, and those who preached the opposite were the real children of the devil.

This same day a truce was decided upon by the Council of the Duke of Mayenne, meeting at the lodgings of M. de Lyons . . . when the Legate . . . heard of this . . . he was furious, and locked himself in, with many guards . . . fearing the fury of the people. And, in fact, the butchers, of whom there are a great number in that quarter . . . said that if he tried to prevent the peace he would learn how beeves were slaughtered and disemboweled.

Monday, June 14, the Legate went to the Estates to oppose the truce . . . Boucher also preached that he and fifty thousand men with him would prevent the wicked relapser from becoming King. . . .

Wednesday, June 16, the Legate . . . went to see M. de Mayenne. The people did not salute him but turned their backs when he started to give the benediction. Only four or five *ligueurs* raised their hats. The Duke of Feria was greeted by no one at all; in fact, the majority, seeing him pass, stuck out their tongues at him. M. de Lyons was amazed at this, as he told the Council.

Friday, June 18, the Estates . . . resolved that the *politiques* should be prevented from meeting because it tended to sedition. This refreshed the Sixteen and annoyed the *politiques*. . . . In the afternoon Boucher said that it was blasphemy to say that the Béarnais could become Catholic . . . and declared that he was not worthy to become King. . . .

[June 20] Lincestre, *curé* of St. Gervais, preached in favor of peace, which sudden metamorphosis astounded many people . . . he said that one should pray to God for the conversion, and that if [the King] did so he should be received. . . . "I say to you that all those who say the contrary are wicked. . . . I am of the League . . . for the maintenance of the faith but for nothing else. . . ." Genébrard, on the other hand, vomited the maximum of injuries against the King . . . Rose, Ceuilly, Feuardant, Guarinus, and the others said the same. Those of St. Sulpice and St. Eustache [preached] like Lincestre, whom the Sixteen began to call "the new member."

This day the Estates acted on the suggestion of the Duke of Feria [that the Archduke Ernest be made King], saying that they could not reverse the fundamental laws of the kingdom. As for Ernest, he was a foreigner, and they had no authority to elect a foreign King. But if it were proposed to marry the Infanta to a French prince, they would take it under advisement. . . . When the Duke left . . . he was surrounded by a hostile crowd, and a stone was thrown at him. . . .

Monday, the 21st, the Duke of Feria proposed to the Estates . . . that the King of Spain, his master, should name within two months a French Catholic prince (understood a member of the House of Lorraine) to whom he would give the Infanta in marriage, and that they should reign jointly. These were his words. One of the deputies said [to the Estates] that "of the mantle of religion a Spanish cape was being made." . . . Du Vair, with others of the Court, voiced opposition to the idea of electing a King from any other than the House of Bourbon. . . .

Tuesday, June 22, Masparault began to speak freely for the peace, for which he was put on the list of *politiques* by the Sixteen.

Today, [June 24] a large fire was built in front of the Palais, on which were placed portraits of the King and of the Queen of England . . . because of the wind they did not burn, but fell outside the flames, and were picked up . . . at this the stupid people . . . began to shout and make a fuss, saying that it was a very bad omen, and that the Béarnais and his sister Jezebel would do them harm.

Saturday, June 26, rumors of sedition, rumors of Spaniards, assemblies of soldiers. Some said we would have a truce, others not, all trying to find out the Duke of Mayenne's game, which no one knows.

June 28, a notable declaration was made in the Court of Parlement, with all the Chambers assembled, against those who undertake to set aside the fundamental laws of the realm, and especially the Salic Law. This was printed, and is called the decision of Président Le Maistre, because he was one of the principal authors. This was a triumph for French liberty over the Spanish tyranny that was being introduced. He was bravely seconded by M. du Vair, and followed by others . . . the *ligueurs* were astounded and taken by surprise. . . .

This day there were placards placed on the Louvre, some attacking the Legate, and others the *politiques*. The Duke of Feria, frightened, reinforced his guards. The Court was threatened by the Sixteen, but they were reassured by a colonel who said that he could protect them with two thousand men whom he held in readiness. Paris is full of rumors of sedition.

Tuesday, June 29, the Court went in the morning to tell the Duke [Mayenne] about their decision of the previous day. Le Maistre was the spokesman. The Duke made a short reply . . . he seemed displeased. He changed color and dropped his hat two or three times.

The *curé* of St. Jacques preached that there were twenty-two wicked *politiques* on the Court who aroused the people to sedition, and that they should all be gotten rid of.

JULY

The Duke of Feria, pushed by the clergy and the Sixteen, proposed the marriage of the Duke of Guise with the Infanta . . . and the election of the Duke as King . . . offered to stay himself in the Bastille as a hostage until [it was done] and promised that the King [of Spain] would also supply forty thousand men and money for the prosecution of the war. M. de Mayenne, much surprised and not pleased, said that the head of the Duke of Feria was not sufficient guarantee for the Crown of France. He also said that M. de Lorraine would never consent . . . as he was the eldest of the house . . . that he would need first to see the Infanta in Paris, and the forty thousand men, and a lot of money, and then one might talk it over.

Monday, July 5, Lincestre received a letter from the King to go to him for his conversion . . . when [Lincestre] showed it to the Legate he was cursed — *Maledicat!* he said in great anger, *Maledicat! Maledicat!* Poor Lincestre replied to the contrary, *Benedicat! Benedicat!* . . . The King knew that he was a Gascon, and though people objected that he was seditious, [the King] replied that no good Gascon could ever be a Spaniard. . . .

On Sunday, July 11 . . . a tableau representing Lucifer falling from Paradise to Hell was shown; it depicted all sorts of people suffering terrible tortures . . . among others one saw the late King surrounded by devils . . . and over it was written, "The Tyrant." Brisson, Larcher, and Tardif were there . . . and others . . . called *politiques*, horribly disfigured. . . . In Paradise there were many angels with devils under their feet . . . one large black [devil] was labeled, "The Béarnais," and the angel over him, M. de Guise, "King." Another devil, M. de Montpensier; the angel over him, M. de Mayenne; still another [devil], M. de Conti, and the angel, the Duke of Mercoeur. This was called the tableau of the Sixteen of Paris.

This same day the *curé* of St. André preached furiously against the *politiques*, said that they should all be killed . . . the same hour Boucher preached against the Parlement, calling them asses and wicked men. Speaking of the election of the Duke of Guise and the Infanta, he exalted the party of the King of Spain, comparing him to Abraham for sacrificing his son. . . . He claimed that if it were not for the Court and the *politiques* we would have a King. . . . It was said that the Duke of Feria had promised Boucher the job of *ausmonier* to the new King . . . and it is known that Ceuilly, among others, gets every week from the Spanish Duke half a mutton and half a steer, and every month wheat and ten doubloons.

This day, le Doyen Séguier, threatened by the Sixteen, and fairly easily intimidated, left Paris . . . they had it in for him because he spoke freely as a *politique*, that is, as a good man.

This same day the *curé* of St. André went to see Président Le Maistre, and said that he was surprised that he, who had always been a good Catholic, had had a part in the wicked declaration of Parlement. . . . Le Maistre replied that he had indeed had a hand in it, and that he didn't feel any less Catholic for it . . . and that, on the contrary, the decision was so good, just and holy . . . that only the wicked found it otherwise. "What is more, Monsieur, there are a whole lot of men in this city, of whom you are one, who are bloodthirsty . . . and who preach nothing but blood and sedition . . . it is these sermons that keep the people stirred up. . . . You should be satisfied with having caused the death of one of the best men and Catholics in your parish [Tardif]. . . ."

Monday, the 12th of the month, the King arrived in St. Denis, and immediately wrote this letter with his own hand to the Marquise de Mousseaux:

My mistress, I arrived here at three o'clock, but have no news of the man I'm looking for. Givry is gone to fetch him. Everyone here speaks of this new royalty, my presence is vitally necessary. I shall dine and go to bed, but I pay you this tribute first, because you come first of my passions. Indeed, my dear love, you should rather fear that I love you too much than too little. This fault is pleasing to you, and therefore to me also. See how I change myself to meet your wishes, is it not worth it to be loved? I believe you do [love me] and my soul is content on that score. I close, kissing your hands a million times. This 12th of July, at St. Denis.

The Duke of Mayenne was informed today of two hundred Cordeliers arrived in Paris, furnishing arms to the Sixteen . . . who meet every day in defiance of the Duke of Mayenne and of all the world.

Today [July 13] the Abbot of Ste. Geneviève returned to this city from St. Denis, where he had begged the King to become Catholic, sooner rather than later. His Majesty promised him to do it, so he says.

[Sunday, July 18] the King went to the Protestant service for the last time. . . .

Friday, July 23, the ecclesiastics bidden to St. Denis entered into conference with the King about his conversion. The King replied so skillfully to their arguments, quoting from Scripture, that they were astonished . . . so much so that one said the next day that he had never seen a heretic so well grounded in his errors, or who could defend them so well. . . .

When they came to the prayer for the dead, he said, "Let's skip the Requiem, I'm not dead yet, and don't want to be." As for Purgatory, he said that he believed it, not as an article of faith, but as a doctrine of the Church, which he believed as a good son of the Church. He said this to please them, as it was their bread and butter. On the adoration of the sacrament, "You haven't satisfied me on this point . . . but look here: today I put my soul in your hands. I beg you take good care of it. Where I go in today I will not come out till death, I swear and protest to you." As he said this there were tears in his eyes.

After this they presented His Majesty with a paper containing an abjuration of the principal errors [he had held] . . . at this he said that he thought he had done enough, and they had better be content. Just the same he let them leave the paper so he could examine it.

He wrote that day to Madame de Mousseaux with his own hand:

I arrived early in the morning and was importuned to "Keep to God" until I went to bed. I think peace is assured. . . . Today I talk to the Bishops . . . Sunday I will take the perilous leap. At the moment I have a hundred people after me which makes me hate St. Denis as you do Mantes. . . .

The next day, which was Saturday, the 24th, he sent for Messieurs the Premiers Présidents of Paris and Rouen, and asked them if they were satisfied that he had done all he could . . . [said] that even so he had been asked to take strange oaths and to sign beliefs that he was sure most of them did not really believe, like the existence of Purgatory. "Do you," he asked, point blank, "believe in that?" They didn't reply, but returning to the original question, said that it was not reasonable to force His Majesty further. . . . [He said] "I pray you call them off, tell them I've done enough, and that if they press me further, worse may ensue." . . . Chauveau, in the presence of the assembled bishops and prelates, said that the King was not a Turk, or pagan . . . that he should be led gently from error to truth, and not treated as if he were wholly ignorant. In this he was seconded by the Bishop of Mans and others so that the oath of abjuration was softened and modified.

When the news of the conversion arrived in Paris the next day the Requiem was sung instead of the *Te Deum*. It was cried in all the quarters that no one could go to St. Denis without a passport . . . those who asked for them were refused. . . .

Sunday, July 25, the King attended Mass in St. Denis, dressed in a white satin robe, decorated in gold, with trousers to match. His coat and hat were black. . . . It was very hot. . . .

Before rising the King talked for a while, in bed, with the [Huguenot] minister La Faye, put his arm around his neck and kissed him two or three times. . . . The day before, in saying goodbye to his other ministers, he had asked them, weeping, to pray God for him, and had assured them that he would love them, remember them, and never let any harm come to them or to the [Protestant] religion.

In Paris that day excommunications were issued against all those who had gone to St. Denis to attend the conversion Mass.

The *curé* of St. André said that all those who attended . . . were damned . . . many of the preachers of Paris said that until they had further details of the form of the conversion, they could not speak fully, but would amplify their remarks later.

In the evening His Majesty took a bath. The Huguenots said of this that he was washing away the sin he had committed in hearing Mass.

Monday, the 26th of the month, a certain Thériot, bourgeois of Paris who was on guard at the Porte St. Denis, started a fight with one Thuot . . . about the conversion . . . Thériot said that the King of Navarre, now that he was Catholic, was his King; Thuot maintained the contrary.

On the same day the wife of a lawyer . . . who lives in the rue St. Antoine, who had said that [she would now recognize Henry IV], was injured by a Walloon who was passing by . . . the bystanders cried . . . that now that he was Catholic, he *was* King, and that they had no more need to deal with Walloons and Spaniards.

Wednesday, July 28, all the preachers in Paris said that the hypocrite King of Navarre had made his conversion on the day whose Gospel was that "the wolves would come in lamb's clothing" . . . that the fox had purposely chosen this day . . . so that, dressed as a lamb, he could enter the sheepfold to devour those in it . . . that he was really an old grey wolf, whom all the world should pursue to the death, instead of accepting him . . . that the ceremony was worth nothing . . . but a stinking farce.

The *curé* of St. Germain said further that the Béarnais had hastened to become Catholic to prevent the election of a brave, good, and generous King . . . that he would gain nothing by turning his coat . . . the same *curé* said later that only the angels were protecting Paris, as most of the captains and colonels were *politiques* and worth nothing, but that by the end of August the Béarnais would be confined within the walls.

Guarinus [insulted the King] . . . in the pulpit, which offended even the most devout . . . joking about the conversion, he said, "Dog, were you at Mass Sunday? Come here, my dog, let me give you the Crown!"

This day [July 30] in the Estates, the publication and observation of [the decrees of] the Council of Trent were decided upon. The deputies of Paris and of some of the provinces opposed this . . . whereupon M. de Laurens said that there was no city in the world where heretics had so much influence as Paris, but Colonel d'Aubray said that no city was as truly Catholic as Paris. . . .

. . . One of the greatest Catholics in Paris, hearing of the King's conversion . . . although he had always followed the King, nevertheless said that he was annoyed . . . saying, "Ah, Monsieur, the King is lost. Now he is vulnerable, where before he was not."

A bishop said to a friend of mine, on the same subject, "I am a Catholic by life and by profession, and a faithful servant of the King. I will live and die as such. But I think it would have been better if he had stayed in his own religion . . . in matters of conscience there is a God on high Who judges, Who should be the consideration of the consciences of men, rather than kingdoms and crowns. . . . I expect only bad luck from it."

AUGUST

Sunday, the first day of August, 1593, the *curé* of St. André preached, like all the others in Paris, against the peace, and said that the three-quarters of the city who favored it were excommunicated . . . and that the Pope himself could not absolve the Béarnais. . . .

Boucher . . . said that the King went to Mass by day and to the Protestant service by night. . . .

At six in the evening on [August 1] a general truce for three months was proclaimed in Paris . . . [it was received] with joy and applause by most of the people, except the Sixteen, the Spaniards, and the preachers, who cried out that only little children who had been paid to do it cried *Vive le Roi!* when they saw His Majesty's heralds in the street.

At the Pont St. Michel, Senault tried to start a seditious movement, using the Neapolitans . . . who beat on their drums and made a lot of noise to keep the news from being heard . . . but the outcome was quite different, as the people began to shout that if they didn't stop they would crown them with their drums . . . Colonel d'Aubray made Senault go home, saying that he had no business in [D'Aubray's] quarter, called him *coquin* in the presence of the Duke of Mayenne . . . it all passed off with mere words and the truce was finally published.

Boucher said . . . that the King was ill from too much love-making with Gabrielle. . . . Guarinus, saying the same, called him a fornicator. . . .

Belanger [when he was told that] . . . Boucher had said we should be *debourber*, said, mocking, that what we needed was to be *deboucher*.

When the King asked . . . news of Paris . . . [he was told of these sermons] which made him laugh, especially when he heard that there was one [preacher] who looked at the Cross with one bad eye. *Ventre St. Gris!** said the King, "that would be Boucher, our one-eyed master."
. . .

Tuesday, August 10, the Duke of Mayenne said to the Legate that if he couldn't restrain the preachers, who were tearing everybody apart . . . and especially him and his family, that he would be forced to throw a couple of them in the river. He also said that the King of Navarre had complained, and said that if the first gentleman of his court had injured him thus . . . he would not endure it, and would find means to stop it. After this the Legate told them to go more softly, of which they took so little account that they were worse and more seditious than they had ever been. . . .

Sunday, August 15, the Prior of Carmes said that . . . the King was a real Judas who betrayed our Savior with a kiss. He said that the month of August was not yet over, and that one could hope for a blow from the skies. The others . . . preached the same . . . like men who predict that robbers will come in the night and are themselves the robbers. . . .

In fact they had two plans for this wicked assassination: the first was by one Pierre Barrière, which was discovered, and the (would-be) assassin executed at Melun. . . . This they counted on most. The other was supposed to be through Gabrielle † and a priest of Paris who had . . . they say . . . the most subtle and potent poisons. . . . The King was told of this, but the only attention he paid it was to laugh, and in truth there was not much to be feared in that direction. . . .

Tuesday, the 17th . . . the *curé* of St. André preached that . . . the King's Mass was a stinking farce. In this he was of the same opinion as the heretics, whom he hated so.

Wednesday, August 18, Pierre Barrière, a native of Orléans, having left Lyons purposely to kill the King, arrived in Paris and went to the *curé* of St. André for advice. The *curé* embraced him, called him blessèd, and his good brother . . . and said that he did not believe that going to Mass made the Béarnais Catholic. . . . For help in the execution of his enterprise he sent him to the Jesuits.

* "Ventre St. Gris!," Henry IV's favorite oath, might be translated "by the belly of the grey saint!," referring, perhaps, to the devil.
† Gabrielle d'Estrées, favorite mistress of Henry IV.

241

Friday, the 20th . . . the Princesses [of the League] went to pay their respects to Madame, sister of the King, in Montmartre.

Sunday, August 22, a great rumor went around Paris of an enterprise to kill both the King and the Duke of Mayenne. When this had been done the Duke of Guise was to be crowned, and as men shouted, *Vive le Roi!* the throats of all *politiques* were to be cut. This was all to take place on the 24th, St. Bartholomew's Day. The King and the Duke received various warnings to this effect but they both laughed at them. . . .

Wednesday, the 25th of this month . . . a Jesuit said that it was blasphemy even to think that the Pope would accept the Béarnais, and that if an angel of God should visibly come down from the sky and say, "Accept him," the ambassador would be untrustworthy.

[Saturday, August 28] This day, news came to Paris of the arrest of Pierre Barrière, at the gate of Melun the day before . . . which angered many people in Paris, and caused others to rejoice. . . .

Tuesday, the last day of August, Pierre Barrière, sufficiently convicted of having wanted to attack the King, was executed in the great market-place of Melun . . . his right hand was burned with a knife found on him, then his arms and legs were broken . . . and [he] was left on the wheel for as long as it pleased God . . . Lugoli talked to him for a long time . . . during which he accused several others, especially the *curé* of St. André-des-Arts and Varades, a Jesuit. . . .

SEPTEMBER

Thursday, September 23, news came to Paris of barricades in Lyons on Saturday, the 18th, in which the Duke of Nemours was taken prisoner by the populace, furiously risen against him. . . . This news astounded the Duke of Mayenne [and] made Madame de Nemours weep loudly. The *politiques* laughed, the King rejoiced, and each one interpreted this stratagem according to his passion, although they really knew nothing about it.

OCTOBER

Sunday, October 17, a procession was held of the transfiguration of the devil of St. Michael . . . in which all of the Sixteen participated, and a great number of their followers, especially priests and monks.

In this procession they made a dummy, dressed in Spanish fashion, with a straw crown, a cow's tail, and a great white scarf . . . around its neck. On its face was a mask which closely resembled the King. . . . It was followed by a whole lot of children and young men who shouted, "See the devil of the Béarnais King!" When a *politique* going by called, "See the King of the Sixteen!" he barely escaped . . . such outrages are we forced to bear in these times.

October 18, there was a rumor in Paris that the truce was off . . . but all this turned out to be on account of the doubloons it was hoped to get from the Spaniard; just as soon as they had gotten all they could, these rumors, spread by the League, stopped. . . .

This month of October was cold at the beginning, the rest mild and humid, in the usual autumn way. Many little children have died in Paris of grippes and rashes.

NOVEMBER

Thursday, November 4 . . . a truce was announced to the end of the year, which gave rise to rumors that there would be no real peace but a four- or five-year truce, because the King's conversion was so sudden that the Pope wanted to see how he behaved. Thereupon all sorts of rumors from Rome: the Sixteen said that His Holiness had forbidden [Henry IV's ambassador] the Duke of Nevers to enter his lands. The *politiques*, on the contrary, said that M. de Nevers was in Rome and had been well received. . . .

Tuesday, the 16th, an assembly was held in the Salle St. Louis [Parlement], to consider a request presented by a large number of *bourgeois* and merchants, that they should not be constrained to pay their debts while the war lasted . . . the Bishop of Amiens said that this seemed reasonable, and that they should not be constrained. . . . To this Le Geay, Director of the Hôtel-Dieu, said that it was all very well for those who had a bishopric to let pass what was owed them . . . but that for others . . . there was no way to live if they couldn't collect. . . . La Bruyère said that . . . it should depend . . . that there were some who everyone knew couldn't pay, having no means whatever, and these should not be constrained, but there were others in Paris, whom he would name if necessary . . . who could pay but would not . . . and that it was reasonable that these *should* be constrained. . . . On the request . . . in a written petition that no one should have to pay until two years after a real peace was signed, the Court wrote: "Denied." . . .

Thursday, the 18th, a false rumor was spread in Paris that the Turks had taken Vienna. Another, also false and still more stupid, circulated this same day, namely that M. de Nevers was in the outskirts of Rome. . . .

November 19, one of the doctors of the Sorbonne told a friend of mine that he was leaving Paris, because it had been decided at the Sorbonne not to accept the King even if the Pope accepted him, which he [the doctor] refused to sign, as being directly counter to God's commandment and his conscience. . . .

Toward the end of the present month of November, the deputies of the Protestant churches arrived in Mantes, with the *cahiers* they had prepared for His Majesty. He spoke to them as follows:

Messieurs, I have sent for you for three reasons: first, to make you understand, from my own mouth, that my conversion means no change in my affection for you. Second, because my rebellious subjects show some signs of being open to a treaty, which I don't want to enter into without your knowing of it, so that nothing will be done to prejudice your cause, which is assured by the promises of all the princes and officers of the crown . . . that nothing will be done against the [Protestant] religion. Third, having been told of the misery of your churches in various parts of the kingdom, I want to hear the facts from you. For the rest, you know that I have nothing closer to my heart than to effect a good and peaceful union among all my subjects. . . . I am making sure that no one can prevent this, although there are some wicked ones who would like to; I hope I find a way to punish them. . . .

I am your guarantee . . . in your union with the Catholics . . . none of my subjects has trusted so much in me that I haven't trusted even more in him. I therefore receive your *cahiers* and ask you to depute four of yourselves to treat with those whom I shall choose from my council . . . but if any of you want to see me about any private matter, you are always free to come to me.

Pronounced at Mantes, by the mouth of the King, in the presence of M. de Conti, Messieurs, the Chancellor, d'O, Schomberg, de la Guische, Descars, Chasteauvieux, Bellièvre, Pontcarré, Veicour, Chandon, Beaulieu, Rusé, Dufrêne, and Forget; and of the Protestants, Messieurs de Rohan, duPlessis-Mornay, de Sancy, Rosny, Canaie. . . . Those whom the King named to the conference on the *cahiers* were the Chancellor, Schomberg, Bellièvre, Descars,

Pontcarré, Chandon, Frêne and Forget, and for the Protestants, Montulet, de Puteaux, de Montigni, Rohan, Fedeau, and de la Motte.

DECEMBER

Monday, the 6th of the month, St. Nicholas Day, my niece, Mademoiselle de Baillon, about twenty years old, died in this city of Paris, in the house of M. Lescalopier, Conseiller, where she had been confined to prevent her marriage to a gentleman for whom she had such an affection that she would use any means to see him. . . . Love, after twenty-four hours of this, killed her. Such are the crazy affections of girls.

Wednesday, the 8th of the month, Commolet preached against the nuns, who promenade with gentlemen arm in arm every day in Paris. (And in fact one sees nothing, at the Palais and everywhere, but nuns and gentlemen walking in couples, making love. . . .) [He said] that under the veils . . . were the hearts of prostitutes and courtesans . . . and that the people should throw mud and stones in their faces. . . . He got himself into such a fury, fulminating and grimacing — it seemed that he would fall out of the pulpit — (he even turned to one of the clerics and cried *Allons!*) that one wondered if he had lost his head or drunk too much. . . .

Thursday, December 9, our Master Guarinus at St. Jacques preached against the Duke of Mayenne by name, saying that he listened to and supported the *politiques* . . . and that if he didn't hang or throw in the river all those who pronounced the word "King" . . . one would be justified in saying that he had an understanding with them. . . . I was present, and I never heard such injuries and fatuous lies from any of the thieves or scoundrels of Paris. . . .

This day a *bourgeois* of Paris, at the house of the Échevin Langlois, amused himself by reading the book of the *Manant* (this is a book of the Sixteen in which the principal men of Paris who are called *politiques*, and especially the Duke of Mayenne, are torn apart). He was discovered and forced to leave the book with Langlois. . . . The latter took it to the Duke of Mayenne, who has been searching for it everywhere, and has offered 1,000 crowns to anyone who can tell him the author. He received it with great joy and hid it under his mattress with his own hands, saying he didn't want anyone to see it because he had been told that it would have a bad influence on the young.

Monday, December 13, it was commanded to find the book of the *Manant* . . . La Bruyère, Lieutenant-Civil, went to all the printers in the morning, a real way to find nothing . . . after dinner, Chaudière, Nivelle, and Rolin Thierri (who is thought to be the printer) were searched and questioned, but let go.

One [copy] was sent, still wet, by Crucé, one of the Sixteen, to Gueffier, a bookseller . . . to be rebound, and the next day about thirty were sent to him to be rebound during the night. The neighbors testified that when this lovely book appeared, about two weeks ago, Crucé went twice a day to the printing shop of Rolin Thierri.

The previous Saturday a bookseller of the rue St. Jacques sold me [a copy] for a crown. When I had read it and made an extract, I sold it to the widow Roffet for three crowns, she sold it the next day for six to a man who took it to St. Denis, where two days later it brought ten crowns from one Dubecq, who had been told by the King to get him one at any price. . . .

Sunday, December 19, Rolin Thierri and Lyon Cavelat . . . both printers to the Holy Union in Paris, and among the most zealous, were made prisoners by order of the Court, on account of the *Manant*. M. Le Maistre among others had made a great complaint about this book and brought a copy to the Parlement . . . two or three days before.

. . . Most of the preachers of Paris spoke for these two prisoners in their sermons, some more, others less. Some, in bitter terms, accused the Justices of having proceeded to their imprisonment without any legal forms . . . the Cordelier preaching at St. André said that [the arrest] wasn't surprising . . . as all the Court was no good. Guarinus . . . said that it was the most iniquitous and tyrannical procedure he had even seen, and that [the printers] were the best men and Catholics in the city . . . that God had delivered us from Henri de Valois, greatest tyrant in the world, whose name still stinks . . . but that even he had never done such a thing . . . and under the Béarnais things would be still worse. "I am not saying anything against the Catholic princes, I know that those who do will hang for it . . . I hold them to be good men, but I declare to you that their council, atheist and *politique*, is worth nothing . . . they drink with you every day . . . but they will cut your throats."

The next day he continued, "Well, Messieurs de la Justice, is it justice to imprison two good Catholics with no charge nor evidence whatever? . . . If you got what you deserve you would all hang. . . ." Coming to the Sixteen, he said, "When this good, upright, noble company had authority, religion flourished, the cities of the Union were secure, traitors were punished, everything was ordered well and reasonably. Since they have been ousted everything is in ruins, religion is trampled, as you see, the towns fall over themselves to give in to the wicked [Henry IV], traitors promenade with their heads high . . . briefly our princes have made war on God and God on them."

The Legate and the Duke of Feria spoke to [Mayenne] in behalf of the printers, but he sent them to the Parlement, saying that he did not dare or could not do anything about it.

Commolet was the preacher who spoke the most moderately on this matter, saying only that one must pray to God to move the hearts of the Court to act well and justly.

Thursday, December 23, the University, in a body, made a prayer for the printers. The Ausmonier of the Duke of Guise said that it was a shame to stir up so many people on account of a book which contained only the truth.

When the Duke of Mayenne was complaining loudly about this book, one of his council said, "You are to blame yourself, Monsieur. If you had hanged Cromé when you had him, this book would never have seen the light of day."

Friday, December 24, Christmas Eve, news came to Paris that the town of Meaux had been surrendered to the King by M. de Vitry. This so annoyed the Duke of Mayenne, they say, that he tore the letters apart with his teeth. . . .

The Échevins and principal inhabitants of Meaux went to the King at Daumartin, where something happened worthy of note. When they were presented to His Majesty they were so overcome by his presence that words failed them . . . and [they] could do nothing but prostrate themselves, frightened, on the floor. The King couldn't keep from weeping at this; he raised them, embraced them . . . saying, "My friends, I receive you not as enemies but as subjects, and embrace you as a father his children."

Sunday, the 26th of the month, all sorts of false rumors in Paris: that the Duke of Mayenne is leaving; that the Duke of Guise will remain; that the Sixteen will be reestablished; that four hundred of the leading *politiques* of the city are about to be arrested and chased out; that the Duke of Mayenne has an understanding with the King; that he agreed to the surrender of Meaux — and all sorts of idle gossip worthy of the brain of the people.

In this month of December . . . the suburbs of Paris were full of soldiers, who committed a thousand injuries and insolences, even to forcing old women and girls under ten years old. There were lots of complaints about this, but no punishment. . . .

At Christmas-time, 1593, Guarinus at St. Jacques preached in the cruelest and most bloodthirsty manner possible, inciting the people to hang and drown the *politiques*, that is, the best men in the city. He was especially violent toward the Court for not bringing to trial the wicked traitor [de Vitry] . . . who had surrendered Meaux. . . .

This morning, [December 30] when the King was still in bed in St. Denis, a *bourgeoise*, masked, was brought to him who had come from Paris the day before to tell him what was being done in the city for his service. . . . His Majesty said these words to her, which I heard from her own mouth:

Tell my good servants in Paris to do everything they can. I will stay with my forces near Paris and will not move, in order to facilitate their plans, although I don't expect that much will come of them. [Tell them] not to consult M. de Mayenne, because he will deceive them, and me, if he can. I expect no good of him, and as for the supposed intelligence between us . . . there is no more . . . than between . . . God and the devil. As for his nephew of Guise, it serves me more than it hinders . . . because of the jealousy between the uncle and the nephew which must be carefully fostered; there is nothing which is worse for their affairs, nor advances mine more. . . .

Nevertheless I desire peace, at what ever price . . . just as I gave more to Meaux than they asked, so will I do for any towns which surrender to me . . . I will do no worse for Paris than for any other, and want to make happy my servants who have worked well there. I know there are many good men and I pray them to pray to God for me . . . I only ask . . . my kingdom . . . which is in God's hands. Those who will help me I will recognize as my servants; if others betray me, God is their judge. . . .

On the last day of this year of 1593, a good *politique* of Paris, having counted his chickens and found that there were sixteen, killed one, saying there would be no sixteen in his house.

Toward the end of the year the *Banquete d'Arête*, on the pretended conversion of the King by M. d'Orléans, was printed in Paris . . . a book full of bagatelles and misstatements. As a defamatory libel it can't touch the *Catholique Anglais* by the same [author]. . . . The sermons of Boucher were also printed . . . preached in the church of St. Merry between August 1 and 9 of this year, 1593. . . . The best and most sublime [writing] of the League was the *Parables of Chicot* . . . there was also published a letter written by M. du Plessis to the King, two months after the conversion, on this subject. . . .

Toward the end of the year 1593, the League, seeing the affairs of the King prospering and their own ruin approaching, gathered all their forces for a last effort, through the Jesuits and the preachers, against the royalty of the King . . . baiting him openly, secretly, by day and by night . . . [they] incited the people to get rid of him, and take in his place the King of Spain, saying [of Henry IV's religion] that he was . . . a real atheist. . . .

THE REDUCTION OF PARIS

JANUARY

Friday, January 14 . . . a great company of *bourgeois* went to Langlois, Prévost des Marchands. La Vayer . . . was the spokesman. He told of the people's want . . . asked for permission to hold a meeting in the Salle St. Louis . . . to consult on the hardship of the people, who could bear no more. . . . [They complained] that they were always sent away and told not to precipitate things, but that they had put up with it for nearly six years, and that could not be called precipitating. They begged the Prévost to help them . . . as they were determined to sign with their blood their requests. . . .

The Prévost went to the Duke . . . and begged him to settle things as soon as possible because the people were murmuring, and there was danger of an uprising. M. de Mayenne wanted to know what the complaints were and what they demanded. The Prévost replied that the people were convinced that he was trying to make them Spaniards. . . . Then M. de Mayenne, pressing his arm, said, "Monsieur le Prévost, I know that you are my servant and a good man. Do what you can to satisfy these people until I get things arranged, which will be as soon as possible. By God's blood I swear to you, and beg you to tell them, that I am not and never will be a Spaniard, but a good Frenchman. I will show them shortly, if they will let me work things out . . . but they should take care not to infringe on my authority, which I will defend as long as I have a sword at my side."

[Saturday, January 15] the *quarteniers* of Paris, with a large troop, went to the Prévost des Marchands to assert the need to relieve the necessity of the people . . . [Upon receiving an evasive answer] Parfait, *quartenier*, said to him, "We see how it is, Monsieur, you would approve . . . if M. de Mayenne did, but you are afraid of displeasing him." "You're right," said the other, . . . but—" "No buts, Monsieur," said Parfait . . . "You are not Prévost des Marchands but Prévost of M. de Mayenne."

[The Prévost assured them that the Duke was not a Spaniard.] "He told me so, and told me to tell you. He also told me that he is working for a reconciliation of the Sixteen with you." At this they all cried out that they were honorable men and not bad ones like the Sixteen, and that they didn't want to be reconciled with them. . . .

Tuesday, the 18th, M. de Vicq . . . asked a lackey in St. Denis . . . where he was going. He replied, "To Paris." "You are mistaken," said M. de Vicq, "you are going straight to Spain, this is the frontier." . . .

In this month, to celebrate the new year, the Duke of Mayenne had coins minted in Paris, which had, on one side, his portrait, sword in hand, with the inscription: *Carolo Lothareno clavum Regni tenente*; on the other side were engraved the arms of France and Lorraine, encircled by the words: *Vacante lilio, dux me regit optimus.* I have one, which I have kept as a curiosity.

FEBRUARY

Sunday, the 6th of the month, the preachers of Paris all dealt with the subject of the raising of the siege of Ferté-Milon; Guarinus . . . said that it was one of the greatest and most extraordinary miracles . . . that a little group of men could rout the hated Béarnais at midnight. He called the King "son of a prostitute" several times, and said that his mother was so public that she was passed around to all the world, and that there were fifty or sixty ministers who regularly possessed her, one after the other. . . .

The *curé* of St. Germain, one of the wisest, said that it was rumored that there were all sorts of *politiques* who . . . favored the Béarnais. He didn't know if there were any in his parish, but if so, he would take their names off the parish rolls.

At the same time, the deputies of those of the [Protestant] religion came to the King at Mantes with a request for the Edict of January.* It was M. du Plessis who was the spokesman. But the King, joking as usual, paid them off with a word. "How come?" he asked. "Are we not in Feb-

---

* The Edict of January 1562 was the first of a series of edicts of partial toleration granted to the Huguenots under the Valois. Since the advent of the League they were constantly referring to it as a sort of *Magna Carta*.

ruary? I guess you mean the month of January that will come next, and we'll see about it." . . .

At this same time . . . the King's horses could not be fed. . . . M. d'O said, "Sire, there is no money." "My condition is indeed miserable," sighed the King . . . then, turning to his *valet-de-chambre*, asked him how many shirts he had. "A dozen, Sire, though some of them are torn." "And handkerchiefs? have I still got eight?" "At this moment, Sire, only five." Then M. d'O said that he had ordered 6,000 crowns' worth of cloth from Flanders to make him some new clothes. "That's fine," said the King, "I'll be like those scholars with furred robes who are dying of cold."

At the same time the King asked a gentleman who had always been [a Huguenot], whom he met at Mass, whether he was not still of the [Protestant] religion. "Yes, Sire," he replied. "Then why are you at mass today?" "Because you are, Sire," was the answer. "Oh," said the King, "now I understand, you have some crown you want to gain."

Sunday, the 13th, while the King was still in bed, he received the good news of the reduction of Lyons to his obedience . . . which came in letters from Captain Alphonse Corse. . . . As soon as he had read them, he got out of bed, asked for his bathrobe, and threw himself on his knees to thank God. . . . Later he [gave orders] for a *Te Deum* to be sung and fireworks set off . . . which was done in St. Denis the next day. The Paris League, when they learned of this, had the Requiem sung instead.

Sunday, the 20th, news came to Paris of the reduction of Orléans . . . which added to the sorrows of the Sixteen. . . . M. de Mayenne, much astounded, was annoyed; the Duke of Feria and the Legate still more so. They went to the Duke and said that he should immediately put four hundred *politiques* out of the town . . . and that they would pay for a garrison of 10,000 Spaniards. M. de Mayenne replied that . . . he wanted only Frenchmen devoted to his service, and that he could find 10,000 if they would pay them. As for the *politiques*, one must use caution. . . . This reply infuriated them . . . and the Sixteen . . . who said aloud that the Duke was in communication with the enemy and that he should be put in the Bastille. . . .

In this month of February the Spaniards gave all sorts of feasts and parties to the beautiful ladies of Paris and entertained them magnificently.

MARCH

Tuesday, March 1, came news of the coronation of the King at Chartres on February 27th . . . of which Guarinus said in his sermon, which I heard myself, that . . . he was no more King of France than the devil was when he offered Jesus Christ all the kingdoms of the world that he held only in imagination. He also said that there was a conspiracy in the city in which the Court shared, and that good Catholics were deprived of their liberty. "I dont dare to go and see a friend for fear of being charged with sedition."

Wednesday, March 2, the Sixteen, with permission from the Duke of Mayenne, held an assembly . . . presided over by our Master Boucher. . . . He told them that M. de Mayenne had charged him to say that he would never make peace with the heretic and [would] live and die with them in the Holy Union. Senault said the same thing. They said that there were twelve hundred of them [at the meeting] but there were actually three hundred or so.

The Court was troubled at the news of this meeting, remembering the arrest of the Court, the murder of Brisson, and other things . . . for this reason Brissac was sent by the Duke to them the next day to tell them that he had allowed the Sixteen to meet for that one time only, for special reasons, which involved no injury to them or to anyone else in the city, which he swore on his life and honor. But the Court was bitter that these good-for-nothings could meet when they could not. . . .

Sunday, the 6th of the month, the Duke of Mayenne left Paris at five in the morning. Before departing, he left the city in the hands of the captains, colonels, and the Prévost, and said that he was going to consult those of his house and do something for the welfare of the people, on whom he had pity. He didn't say goodbye to the Court. . . .

The city was displeased and full of rumors about his departure, especially the Sixteen. The *curé* of St. Cosme . . . armed himself . . . had arms taken to the Cordeliers, and marched around Paris with his satellites, armed to the teeth. That very day he baptized a child in his church . . . fully armed. A little while before he had celebrated Mass [dressed] the same way. . . .

The other preachers, although they were annoyed at [the Duke's] departure, said nothing about it, but said even more than before that all was lost and that no more help could be expected from human sources, and tried to raise a sedition against the *politiques*. Guarinus armed all the monks . . . cried as usual against the Court . . . and said that if the people didn't put their hands to the sword the *politiques* would cut their throats, though they would find two thousand monks against them. . . .

Wednesday, the 9th, at the request of the Sixteen, all the gates of the city except those of St. Antoine and St. Jacques were locked and filled with stones . . . the keys of St. Antoine were given to a monk . . . arch-*ligueur*, and those of St. Jacques to Pichonnat, the soul of the Sixteen.

Thursday, March 10, the King arrived in St. Denis. The *curés* of St. Cosme and St. Jacques at once began to collect arms in their houses . . . saying that it was for their safety and that they didn't intend to harm anyone, but that the *politiques* wanted to let the King into the city. Guarinus . . . cried in his sermon, "To arms!" . . . said that they would be lost if they didn't [arm] because the *politiques* were about to hold a massacre. . . .

Friday, the 11th, the Parlement . . . made a great complaint of the bloody sermons of Guarinus and of the insolence of the Sixteen . . . said that the houses of the preachers were full of arms, and that either they should leave the field to these gentry or assert their authority and restore order . . . they voted to appeal to the Legate to make Guarinus change his tone or be dismissed, and also decided that the Sixteen should be forbidden to assemble on pain of death. . . .

In the night . . . a great *ligueur* . . . guarding the ramparts of the Porte St. Michel . . . fell all the way to the ground . . . and died. His wife . . . complained the next day that he had paid dearly for his Spanish wages. . . . There are about four thousand of these little people in the various quarters, who are called *minotiers*, to whom a *minot* of wheat and 45 *sous* are given each week by the agents of Spain. They keep a list of the people in each street who maintain the party resolutely. . . .

The next day, which was the 13th . . . the Sixteen assembled in a mill near the Porte Neuve, but were discovered and scattered . . . then they reassembled at the Jesuits'.

Monday, the 14th, M. de Brissac left the city on private business, he said . . . but the Sixteen became alarmed. . . . When he returned he went to the Legate and prostrated himself to ask forgiveness for communicating with heretics [encounters with royalist troops]. The Legate granted him pardon, and praised his devotion (which tended in quite a different direction than Monseigneur thought) . . . the truth was that this good man was much subtler and smarter than all of them, and in the end he had the laugh on them. . . .

This same day Boucher preached that it was not in the power of the Pope, nor in that of God Himself, to absolve the Béarnais. . . .

Tuesday, the 15th . . . Boucher again preached against the Court . . . and against the King and the *politiques*. . . .

[Wednesday, March 16] the Prévost des Marchands went to see most of the Justices in their houses to assure them that the procession which was to be held next day would be controlled, and swore that he would lose his life before allowing any of them to be injured.

Thursday, March 17, a solemn procession of the chariot of Ste. Geneviève was held in Paris. There was such a crowd that a poor woman was suffocated. . . . Many of the Parlement attended, [except that] Neuilly was the only Président. . . .

Saturday, March 19, there was a rumor that the Bastille had been surrendered to the enemy; some took this to mean the King, others the Spaniard. . . . Sunday, the 20th, all the preachers talked about this and about the chariot of Ste. Geneviève . . . all the rumors were spread about by those who were secretly preparing the reduction of the city to the King's obedience.

Late on the eve of the reduction [March 21] the Spaniards and the Sixteen . . . warned that something was afoot to ruin them, went to M. de Brissac to ask him to put things in order. He told them . . . that if they let things alone, and trusted him, he would see to everything . . . they saw the results next morning, though quite different from what they expected. Thus God laughs at the vanity of the plans of men. . . .

Tuesday, March 22, at seven in the morning, the King entered Paris by the same gate by which the late King had left. The city was reduced to its obedience without sack or bloodshed, except for a few lancers and two or three *bourgeois* of the city. The King has since said that he wished he could buy back their lives for 50,000 crowns to leave as a remarkable witness to posterity that the King had taken Paris without the death of a single man.

When he came to the rue St. Honoré . . . he asked Marshal Mattignon (as if he were surprised to find himself in such a city amid so many people) if the gate was under control, and to see to it. Seeing a soldier who was taking bread from a baker by force, he set upon him himself, as if to kill him.

Passing by the Innocents', stopping with his men, he saw a man in a window with his head covered, who looked for a long time at His Majesty and made no sign of saluting him. Finally he closed the window and retired . . . the King laughed, and said that no one should go into the house to annoy or molest anyone.

When he arrived at the Pont Notre Dame and heard the people joyous-ly crying, *Vive le Roi*! he said, "I can see that these people have been tyrannized over." When he set foot on the ground in front of Notre Dame, the people pressed in on him and the captains of the guards tried to push them back, but he wouldn't let them, and said he would rather . . . have them at their ease, as "they are famished for the sight of a King."

As soon as he arrived at the Louvre he wanted to talk to Captain St. Quentin of the Walloons, prisoner of the Spaniards, about the service he would have rendered, if he could, in the reduction. When [St. Quentin] came, His Majesty said that he wanted the foreigners to leave the city within two hours of noon. The other . . . thanked His Majesty for his life and liberty (he was scheduled to hang that afternoon) and offered him his services. The King accepted and kept him, because, he said, he was no Spaniard but a Frenchman, and [said] that he should remain near him and fear no more.

In the morning early he had sent the Count of St. Paul to the Duke of Feria to say that although His Majesty held their [the foreigners'] lives and goods in his hand, he wanted neither the one nor the other. He gave them to them freely, provided that they would leave Paris promptly, with no delay nor excuses. The Duke promised this quickly; he had not thought to get off so cheap. He said two or three times, "Great King, great King."

His Majesty had published throughout the city a declaration made at Senlis on the 20th, pardoning everyone, even the Sixteen. He sent greetings to Mesdames de Nemours and Montpensier, with his assurance that no harm would come to their persons, goods, or houses, which he had taken under his protection. These ladies, though discomfited, thanked His Majesty humbly. . . .

At the first word Madame de Montpensier received of the news that the King was in Paris she was so despairing and cast down that she asked if there were not someone who would run her through with a dagger. Later she regained her spirits a little, and turned her anger against M. de Brissac, called him "wicked traitor." She said that she had known he was a coward for a long time, but not till this hour had she known him for a traitor.

At three in the afternoon the Duke of Feria, with the foreign garrisons, left Paris by the Porte St. Denis. Above it was a great window where the King sat to see them pass. The Duke greeted him *à l'éspagnole*, that is, very seriously and formally. The King made fun of this, lifted his hat half-way and returned the salute, pleasantly.

The wife of one of the Spaniards, passing with the troops, asked to be shown the King, and said loudly that France was lucky to have a King so great, so good, so gentle and kind as to have pardoned them all. . . . When the King was pointed out to her she cried aloud, "I pray to God, good King, that God will grant you prosperity. When I am in my country, or wherever I am, I will always bless you, and glorify your goodness, your greatness, and your clemency." The Neapolitans also said in leaving, "You have a good prince today, in place of the wicked one you used to have."

. . .

The King sent for the Secretary Nicholas, during his dinner, to have a little fun with him. When he asked him whom he had followed during the troubled times, the said Nicholas replied that he had in truth left the sun to follow the moon. . . . "But what do you say to seeing me in Paris thus?" "I say, Sire," replied Nicholas, "that what belongs to Caesar has been rendered to Caesar, as what is God's should be rendered to God." *Ventre St. Gris!* cried the King, "I haven't been treated like Caesar; it was not given to me [*rendu*] but sold to me [*vendu*]!" He said this in the presence of M. de Brissac, the Prévost, and others of the *vendeurs*.

At the insistence of the English ambassador the picture of the so-called cruelties of the Queen of England against the English Catholics — which the League had installed in Notre Dame — was removed, by express command of His Majesty.

When two important matters were mentioned to him . . . the King said, "I must confess that I am so happy to be where I am that I don't know what you are saying, nor what I should say myself."

[The officials of the city] brought him sweet wine, *dragées*, and torches, begging him to excuse the poverty of their gifts. He thanked them for having given him their hearts the day before, and now their goods. [He said] that he accepted them with all his heart, and would show them that he would stay with them, in their care, and wanted no other protection but that . . . .

Wednesday and Thursday [March 24 and 25] at St. André and certain other parishes the priests wouldn't hear confession until they heard how those who had come felt about the King's entry. Those who said they were pleased were sent away without being confessed. No sermons were preached either. . . . When this was reported to the King he said that they should be forgiven because they were still annoyed.

A simple girl said that two *bourgeois,* one a mason and the other a baker, had said that they were resolved to die, but that before they did, they would kill the King.

Thursday, March 24, the *curé* of St. Jacques gave communion to sixteen persons in the Church of Ave Maria . . . (he has received a *billet,** which he well deserves, and worse), and told them to give thanks that the reduction had gone so smoothly, that the King had shown himself marvelously kind . . . although he [personally] had to leave, wherever he was he would always praise and glorify His Majesty's generosity. . . .

This day the King went to see Madame de Nemours and Madame de Montpensier. He asked them if they were surprised to see him in Paris, and especially [to see] that no one was robbed or sacked, nor harm done to anyone. . . . Turning to Madame de Montpensier, he said, "What do you say to that, Cousin?" "Sire," she answered, "we cannot say anything but what a kind, great and generous King you are." The King smiled a little at this and said, "I don't know whether you are saying what you really think. One thing I do know, you are very angry with Brissac, aren't you?" . . . [She replied] "There is only one thing I would have changed in the reduction, and that is, that my brother [Mayenne] was not here to let down the bridge to let you in." *Ventre St. Gris*! said the King. "He might have made me wait a long time, I wouldn't have been here so soon."

The same day when His Majesty went to the Louvre he said to the

* Royal command to leave Paris. Henry IV's magnanimous policy resulted in the issuance of very few. The recipients were those who would have been in danger from their neighbors.

Chancellor, "M. le Chancelier, in your opinion, should I believe that I am where I am?" "Sire, I don't see how you can doubt it." "I don't know," said the King, "the more I think about it the more amazed I am, for surely there is nothing human in this, it is one of the most extraordinary works of God." And in truth it is a miraculous thing that such an enterprise, known to so many beforehand, could succeed, because it is a rare thing to have a secret kept by my countrymen.

Friday, March 25 . . . the *curé* of St. Germain l'Auxerrois preached against the King, in spite of the pardon he had received the day before, on condition of being wiser and more restrained in his sermons. When he left the pulpit he was seized by Lugoli . . . [and] questioned. He maintained that the King was excommunicated. For these words he was dismissed, but the King would allow no other punishment. . . .

Many *ligueurs* left Paris today, some because of *billets*, and others without waiting for them, fearing worse.

Master Pierre Senault, told by Colonel d'Aubray to recognize the King, said that he would do what his *curé* did, and that he would always follow him as his leader. His *curé* [St. André] said that no good Catholic could recognize him until the Pope absolved him. . . .

Saturday, March 26, the King promised the Parlement to re-establish them, in spite of opposition by those who importuned him to wait for the Parlement of Tours. His reply to them was short but most apropos, "Those of Tours took care of their own affairs, those of Paris took care of mine."

Sunday, March 27, the King heard Mass at Ste. Geneviève, where there were so many people shouting, *Vive le Roi*! that the King said he would be deafened. The day before, he was at St. Eustache, where the same thing happened.

This day Du Bourg surrendered the Bastille and left, wearing a black scarf. He would accept no money for it, showing his worth. Being solicited to recognize the King and told that he was a good prince, he said that he was sure of it, but that he was the servant of M. de Mayenne, to whom he had given his allegiance . . . he said that Brissac was a traitor . . . and that the first thing he would do would be to challenge him to a duel. . . .

This day the *curé* of the Madeleine did not speak for the King in his sermon, but for the Catholic princes, as if the League still held the city . . . his impudence was punished by the imposition of a simple silence.
. . .

259

Monday, March 28, M. le Chancelier came to the Court and the Parlement assembled. . . . The Chambre des Comptes was also re-established.

The declaration of the King about the reduction of Paris was published today, in which one can see . . . that the crowns of France work as well as the doubloons of Spain.

The *curé* of St. André . . . and other *zelés* left Paris by the Porte Bussi . . . he asked pardon of his parishioners and asked them to pray for him as he would for them.

Cardinal Pellevé, good Spaniard and bad Frenchman, aged eighty, died this day in Paris. Two days before, when he heard that the Bastille hadn't surrendered yet, he said, "That's good." In spite of all the wrongs he had done to the King and the Crown, the King wanted him to die in peace.

Tuesday, March 29, a general procession was held in Paris, and the King stayed the whole time, in spite of the rain and foul weather. All the [monastic] orders were there except the Jacobins, who were forbidden to attend. There were fireworks, and cries of *Vive le Roi*! (melody not pleasing to the ears of some). Madame de Montpensier, hearing this music, said that Brissac did better than his wife. In fifteen years she had only made one cuckoo sing, but in a week he had made more than twenty thousand parrots sing in Paris. . . .

Wednesday, March 30, Président Le Maistre took his oath as seventh Président in the Court. . . . His Majesty called him his good Président, for the services he had rendered, which he wished to recognize by giving him that office . . . as he did also by giving the office of Maître des Requêtes to Langlois, who took his oath at the same time. He did good work the day of the reduction, entertaining the Spaniards cleverly with romances, awaiting the King's arrival.

Two women of the League died today in Paris . . . of annoyance at seeing the King . . . one lost her tongue at the news, and later her life. . . .

Thursday, March 31, the lawyers and *procureurs* of the Court took their oaths of fidelity to the King.

Today the power of the Duke of Mayenne was broken by order of the Court, and news was brought of the reduction of Rouen, which caused bonfires to be lighted throughout the city.

APRIL

The books of D'Orléans and Boucher, which speak against the King, together with others of the League, were burned today . . . [April 2] in the Place Maubert. The printer, Guillaume Bichon, was banished from Paris by a *billet*.

[April 4] Those of the Sorbonne went to salute the King today. He greeted them pleasantly, called them "Messieurs our masters," and swore to them that he would live and die in the Roman, Catholic, and Apostolic faith, with never a departure from the Church which he had embraced. He said that he knew the word "relapser" had held them back for a long time, but that he had never been one, for his "conversion" at the time of St. Bartholomew had been forced if ever anything was. He knew that they had preached against him and treated him most unworthily in their pulpits, but that he wished to forgive and forget . . . all of them, even his own *curé*, but not Boucher, who preached such lies and libels against His Majesty and the state (from Beauvais) that he could not be pardoned. Even so, he wouldn't take his life, though he certainly deserved to lose it as a public example, but that if he would be quiet, [the King] would forgive him. The King said that he wanted a peaceful reconciliation with all his subjects and especially those of the Church, and most particularly their Faculty, which he would love and honor always. "Messieurs our masters" went away very much pleased, saying as much good of His Majesty as they had formerly said bad.

Commolet and Lincestre, those *grands ligueurs* turned royalist, or at least pretending to be, recommended the King strongly in their sermons, especially Lincestre, who held forth at such length in praising His Majesty that one thought he would never finish. The day of the reduction, as His Majesty was dining, he threw himself at his feet and asked pardon, which was granted. All the same, when he approached the King said, "Watch for a knife." M. de Sancy didn't want to let him in, but the King ordered it when he understood that it was Lincestre. . . .

Sunday, the 3rd, Palm Sunday, the King took communion at St. Germain l'Auxerrois, his parish, and like a good member, watched the whole procession on his feet, holding his palm in his hand like everyone else.

Holy Wednesday, April 6, at eleven in the morning, the King returned from St. Germain-en-Laye to Paris on purpose to go to confession at Notre

Dame. M. de Bourges heard his confession. . . . As he left the church a poor woman cried, "God give you long life and good, Sire." The King bowed his head in thanks. Then, redoubling her enthusiasm, she said, "Good King, may God help you always with His Holy Spirit and may your enemies be dissipated and confounded!" The King answered her aloud, "Amen, God have mercy on me and on you too."

Maundy Thursday, the 7th of the month, the King performed the customary ceremony of washing the feet of the poor, at the Louvre . . . he went to the Hôtel-Dieu to visit the sick, and gave each one alms with his own hand, without overlooking one. He exhorted them to the love of God and their neighbors, and to patience, a beautiful thing in a King.

The next day, which was Good Friday, he went to the prisons, had himself conducted to the cells by torchlight; he pardoned one criminal condemned to death . . . and freed from the Conciergerie a great number of pitiful prisoners of the League, who shouted *Vive le Roi*! as they came out. . . . He gave eighty crowns to the Filles-Dieu, fifty to the Repenties and the same to those of L'Ave Marie. These were all gestures of piety which cost the King little but served him well in the opinion of the people.

The King said to those who spoke of the imminent return of the Parlement of Tours, "I want to put an end to this division of those of Paris and those of Tours, that they should call it quits and be good friends."

Wednesday, April 13, Madame, sister of the King, arrived in Paris accompanied by eight carriages and wagons. The people of Paris, watching the train, seeing gentlemen . . . said to each other, "Those are the [Protestant] ministers."

Thursday, April 14, the Parlement of Tours arrived . . . there were about two hundred in their retinue . . . it had been said that they had so much money they could hardly carry it, but their poor mounts and equipment could hardly carry them, much less any treasure. The people were lined up along the streets as if it were a royal entry, women were at the windows . . . all saluted them joyfully and prayed God that they would never leave again and see that justice was done to the League.

As soon as they arrived they went to salute the King, who received them well, but he said that his will was that the past should be forgotten, and on both sides all should be forgiven, that if he had been able to forgive injuries to himself they should be able to do the same. . . .

Tuesday, April 26, three sergeants and the Vicar of St. Cosme were made prisoners for their part in the death of the late Président Brisson.

Wednesday, April 27, a solemn funeral for the late Président, which had been decreed by the Court the day before, was postponed until the arrival of those of Châlons . . . and finally omitted. . . .

MAY

Poictevin, doctor of Navarre, received a *billet* today [May 2] which he wished to disobey, but menaced with prison, or worse, he packed up and left the next day.

La Place, conseiller . . . also received one. He pulled all sorts of strings to get it revoked, but finally it was proved that he had said . . . that the King couldn't escape being killed before Easter, even if he had to do it himself. Words deserving the rope and not a mere *billet*.

Master René Chopin, lawyer in the Court, got one too. He was a learned man but a great *ligueur*, as he showed in his writings. All the same . . . through the influence of M. de Châstre's son-in-law, he was allowed to stay. . . .

Sunday, May 8, came news of the reduction of Toulouse, for which bonfires were held and a solemn *Te Deum* sung.

This day [May 8] M. d'O, as Governor of Paris, received the oaths of the captains of the city in the Church of the Augustinians. Most of them were appointees of the late King, deposed by the League, whom the King wished to reinstate, as seemed reasonable. . . . Some, who were notoriously of the League, kept their charges through influence or money, among others one LaCroix, who had a hand in the imprisonment of the Court, and an apothecary who lives near the Madeleine, who bought off his *billet*, being a very rich man, though seditious and a desperate *ligueur*.

The King, on the other hand, pardoned the whole world, and prosecuted no one, however active a *ligueur* he might be . . . saying that he didn't want to hear about *billets* or chasing people out, because *ligueurs* were as much his subjects as others. When one remonstrated with him for too great clemency to his enemies, which annoyed his good and faithful servants, he replied in these words, worthy of a King and a true Christian prince:

If you, and all those who talk this way, said your Pater Noster every day sincerely, you wouldn't say what you do of me. I know that all my victories come from God, who extends all sorts of mercy to me, although I am unworthy, and as He pardons me, so will I pardon, and, forgetting the faults of my people, be even more merciful and forgiving to them than I have ever been. If there are some who are forgotten, it is enough for me that they are forgiven, and I wish to hear no more of it.

PARIS UNDER HENRY IV

MAY 1594 — JANUARY 1599

1594

THE REDUCTION OF PARIS

MAY

Thursday, the 12th, the Rector [of the University] came to the Court of Parlement to beg it, in the name of the University, to chase the Jesuits out of France. There was no lack of people in Paris to support this request, even in the Parlement. . . .

JUNE

In this month there appeared the League of Poor Men [*Crocants*], which was immediately dissipated, like the old Jacqueries which it resembled, having no leaders nor organization. They had it in for the governors and treasurers especially, which made the King say, joking in his usual way, and using his *Ventre St. Gris*, that if he weren't who he was, and had a bit more free time, he would gladly volunteer to become a member. . . .

JULY

Tuesday, the 12th, the case [of the Jesuits] was heard behind closed doors, as had been decided, and when a number of people, moved by curiosity, tried to sneak in, the King's lawyer Séguier demanded that the decision be enforced and that they be put out, which they were. Then M. Antoine Arnauld began his prosecution, which was violent throughout . . . he called them "thieves, corrupters of youth, assassins of Kings, conspirators against the state, public pests and disturbers of the peace." In short he treated them not only like people who should be driven out of Paris, the court and the kingdom, but also exterminated on the whole face of the earth. . . . If he had used a bit more moderation and less passion (as he usually does) he would have found more favor even with those who don't like the Jesuits and wish them all in the Indies converting the heathen. . . .

Monday, the 25th, news came to Paris of the negotiations for the reduction of Laon to the King. . . .

Saturday, July 30, at two o'clock in the afternoon, M. le Cardinal de Bourbon died in his *hôtel* in the faubourg St. Germain, in the prime of life . . . a good prince . . . if he had not been badly advised, as is often the case with princes. A few days before his death the King jokingly said that nothing would cure him unless he was promised to become King soon. . . .

AUGUST

Friday, the 5th, I saw a letter from the King in which he said that he had entered Laon on the 2nd, and that on the same day the citizens of Amiens had driven out the Duke of Mayenne and sent deputies to treat with His Majesty.

The day before M. le Chancelier had the news . . . ordered a *Te Deum* sung, which was solemnly attended by the officers of [Paris], the Court and all the companies. . . .

Saturday, the 27th, Aubin, priest of St. Germain-le-Vieux (who said that he was dying for his religion), Jean Roseau, hangman of the city, and one Danès, sergeant . . . were hanged and strangled in the Place de Grève for the murder of the late Président Brisson. . . .

SEPTEMBER

Friday, September 2, Mesdames de Nemours, de Guise, and de Montpensier, who had taken an oath of fidelity to the King, arrived in Paris. When Madame de Montpensier, passing through Compiègne . . . wished to find accommodations, the inhabitants refused to oblige her, saying that they knew well that it was she who instigated the murder of the late King, and that if she tried to stay there they would set fire to the house.

Thursday, September 15, the King made his grand entry into Paris, between seven and eight in the evening, by torchlight. He was mounted on a great grey horse . . . dressed in grey velvet embroidered in gold, with a grey hat and white feather. The garrisons of Mantes and St. Denis marched ahead, with the officials of the city. Messieurs of Parlement, in their red robes, waited for him at Notre Dame, where a *Te Deum* was sung. . . .

It was eight o'clock when the King crossed the Pont Notre Dame, accompanied by much cavalry and surrounded by magnificent nobility. He was smiling, and so happy to hear the people shouting, *Vive le Roi*! that his hat was in his hand most of the time, especially as he saluted all the ladies in the windows. . . . Here I must tell of an episode I witnessed, that is . . . Mesdames de Nemours and de Montpensier, in their carriages on the bridge . . . had to stop because of the great crowd . . . of which only two or three saluted them, although they were very conspicuous. Others looked off their noses, pretending not to know them, which I don't doubt hurt them, especially the one who was called "the Queen Mother" before the reduction. Many, like me (right opposite where they were forced to stop) took pleasure in looking at them and in considering the vanity of the world and its turnings, which God manages, and turns this way and that, as it pleases Him.

Friday, the 16th, the King played tennis all afternoon . . . and dice all evening with M. d'O. . . .

Toward the end of this month, Messieurs de Hère and Bordeaux, conseillers, returned to Paris, from which they had been chased as *ligueurs* by royal command. Various others returned at the same time, and it was said that they had bought their way out of the commands. . . . There was no question of recalling the workmen and humbler members of the League, because there was no money in it — so goes the world.

OCTOBER

Saturday, October 1, the Court assembled for the reception of the Duke of Bouillon as Marshal of France, to which there was much objection because of his [Protestantism]. Opinons were divided . . . M. le Président de Thou said that it was not a question of theology, but of a Marshal of France, and that religion was beside the point. He said further that M. de Bouillon had a good sword to offer His Majesty in this capacity . . . that we didn't have enough good captains in France . . . and that if ever there were a gentleman worthy of the honor it was this one. . . .

Sunday, the 16th, M. le Cardinal de Gondi, accompanied by other members of the clergy, complained to the King of the [Protestant] preachers of Madame, his sister . . . saying that it was thought strange that this should be allowed in Paris, and even in the Louvre. The King replied that he found it even more strange that anyone should dare to speak to him thus, in his own house, and especially about his sister, but . . . that he would speak to her about it. . . .

Tuesday, the 25th [after the death of D'O] the King sent a memorandum to the officials of the city that he did not intend to appoint anyone to the now-vacant office of governor of Paris; he wished to honor his good capital by being himself its governor. This resolution was applauded by everyone. . . .

NOVEMBER

In this month of November, the Edict of Pacification of the year 1577,* accorded to those of the Religion by the late King, was renewed by the King, in the presence of his council. The King said aloud, "that he knew there were those who had called the late King a heretic on this account, but the next person who said so would be hanged."

He had previously firmly and brusquely (as well as wisely) refused [the Protestants] the renewal of the Edict of January, mixed chambers, and a Protector, saying "that he didn't wish anything in the way of innovations . . . that the Edict of 1577 was enough, if not too much. As for a Protector, he wanted them to understand clearly that there would be no other protector of anybody in France but himself, and that he would personally take care of anyone who dared to assume that title. . . ."

DECEMBER

Monday, the 5th, a certain Chupin, printer, newly arrived from Geneva, told me of going to the Louvre on business, where he met Madame de Liancourt [Gabrielle d'Estrées] magnificently dressed, with her retinue, at the door. Since he didn't know her, but saw that everyone was treating her with great honor, he asked who she was. He was taken aback when one of the archers of the guard said aloud, "That's no one who counts, friend, it's only the King's whore." . . .

Tuesday, the 27th of the month, the King, having returned from his trip to Picardy, entered the apartment of Madame de Liancourt, still booted . . . [and] received the salutations of [various seigneurs]. While he was greeting them, a young man named Jean Chastel, about nineteen years

* "Peace of *Monsieur*," 1576. See above, p. 50.

old, son of a clothier of Paris who lives near the Palais, slid into the room unseen, approached close to the King, and tried to cut his throat with a knife. But because the King was leaning over to raise up the seigneurs, the blow hit his upper lip instead of his throat (by a secret and admirable providence of God). Immediately the King felt the wound, looking about him he saw his fool and cried, "To the Devil with her! She has wounded me!" She denied it and ran away to close the door so that the assassin would not escape. He was seized and beaten, threw his bloody knife to the floor, and confessed all.

Then the King said to let him go, that he would pardon him. On being told that he was a disciple of the Jesuits, he said, "Must they then be convinced by my mouth?"

As soon as this prodigious attack was known in Paris there was a great murmuring, especially against those of the League. . . . [Officers of the King] were sent to the Jesuits to place a guard about them. The whole family of Chastel was imprisoned. . . .

When Madame de Montpensier heard this news she fainted, either from her great affection for His Majesty, or, according to others, from her great regret that the blow had failed.

As for Madame, the King's sister, she was deeply moved . . . and held at once long and well-attended prayers to thank God for her brother's escape. . . . The King, with his usual clemency, saved the *ligueurs* of Paris from a bad turn that was brewing against them. . . .

The next day Chastel was interrogated, and blamed everything on the Jesuits . . . [said] that only his zeal for religion had made him obey them. [He also said that] Henri de Bourbon, as he called the King, was the enemy of the Church until he was absolved by the Pope, and it was good to kill kings who lacked papal approval. . . .

Thursday, the 29th . . . Chastel . . . had his hand cut off, holding the knife . . . then was drawn into four quarters in the Place de Grève, his body burned, and the ashes thrown to the winds.

Those of the League made of this little assassin a martyr. . . . This year ended with as much sorrow to Parisians as the springtime of the reduction had given them joy, for this blow caused apprehension . . . so that the merchants had less business . . . and six hundred newly returned scholars fled the University . . . whence they had just commenced their studies. . . .

JESUITS AND HUGUENOTS

JANUARY

Saturday, the 5th, a general procession was held in Paris, attended by the Court and all the companies. . . . The King attended in person, with great numbers of the nobility. He was dressed entirely in black, his face was sad and melancholy, with a small bandage over his wound. . . . The people cried so joyfully, *Vive le Roi*! that the air rang, and such enthusiasm was never seen. . . . One of the lords near the King, commenting on this, said, "Sire, see how your people rejoice to see you!" But the King shook his head and said, "These are the people — if my greatest enemy were in my place they'd shout even louder."

Nevertheless, by the time they reached Notre Dame, he was joking as usual. Seeing the Parlement in their red robes, and that Pontcarré wasn't wearing his, he said to M. de Longueville, "There's Pontcarré, he's forgotten his red robe, but his beautiful red nose, he's not left that behind!" . . .

On this same day Messieurs of the Hôtel de Ville, in a body, begged the King to allow them to chase the remaining *ligueurs* out of the city. . . . But he replied firmly that he would not give his approval to drive anyone out, that he recognized them all as his subjects, and that he would treat them all equally. But he did command them to keep an eye out [to see] that the wicked men did not do any harm to the good ones.

The Jesuits, meanwhile, were blamed and attacked on all sides, even worse than the Huguenots used to be. Their beautiful library was sacked. . . .

Sunday, the 8th, after dinner, the Jesuits obeyed the order . . . to leave the city of Paris. They were conducted by an usher of the Court. Thus, was accomplished today, by a simple usher, something which many battles couldn't bring about.

Tuesday, the 17th of January, the Declaration of the King opening the war against Spain was published in Paris. The horrible attempt on his life hastened this action. . . .

Tuesday, the last day of the present month of January, the Edict of Pacification of 1577 was finally verified by the Court, with all chambers assembled, after twelve days of discussion. . . .

Opinions had been sharply divided, especially on the matter of having Protestants in the sovereign courts.

M. Fleury . . . advocated the verification without qualifications, on the ground that to do otherwise was to limit the royal power. . . . M. Brisart, on the contrary, advocated that the Edict stand as it had in the time of the late King, without any Protestants in office. . . . M. du Drac maintained that all true Frenchmen should be treated alike and that to make distinctions on the specious basis of religion . . . was to open the door to Spain. M. La Voix said that if they verified the Edict he feared people would say, in reference to the King's conversion, "The dog returns to his vomit" . . . and said that he doubted . . . that the King would take the Prince of Condé from the Huguenots to be instructed in the true faith . . . or that the Huguenots would let him. . . . M. Rancher spoke violently against it . . . saying, first, that it would antagonize the Pope . . . that one mustn't deceive oneself that the Prince could be released . . . that if [Condé] were taken by force then one wouldn't have to bother conciliating the heretics with Edicts. . . .

M. de Landes . . . said that one heretic judge could do more harm than an entire army. . . . On the other hand, M. Coquelay . . . said that there was no worse disservice one could do to the country than to set up further divisions between Catholics and Protestants . . . that to unite was the only way to have peace in the kingdom. . . . M. Veau rejected the Edict entirely, saying that such edicts had been the cause of the late troubles. . . . Messieurs Poisle and Maréschal seemed, indirectly, to be justifying the rebellion of the League . . . which was censured by the Premier Président. . . . M. Ripault held an individual opinion which was a bit confused: that is, to verify the Edict with thirty conditions which would keep the Court busy till Easter. M. du Four, good man, voted for everything, verification, modifications, remonstrances, and all.

Thus was the Court divided on this Edict. But finally those who were for verification pure and simple won by six votes. Out of 112, there were 59 for, 53 against. . . .

On this last day of the month the Venetian ambassadors arrived in Paris. . . .

Most of the diseases of this season are unknown to the doctors, caused by the weather, humid and warm after a long, hard freeze, which always causes a lot of sickness.

FEBRUARY

Friday, February 3, the ambassadors of the Signory of Venice were given a warm reception by the King at the Louvre. Their speech was short because they had been warned that His Majesty didn't like long speeches.

Sunday, the 5th, many ballets, masquerades, and feasts were held in Paris. At the court the most beautiful women of the town were there at His Majesty's command to entertain the ambassadors. They were richly dressed . . . and so covered with pearls they could hardly move. . . .

Friday, the 17th, came news of the fall of the garrison of Soissons to the King . . . in which at least fifty of the most desperate *ligueurs* in France died. This is a new blow for the League, which is more and more feeble.

MARCH

This day [the 18th] the King, hearing that . . . many Parisians say [of his plan to spend Easter in Fontainebleau] that he was doing it so that he could celebrate it *à la Huguenote*, replied, "The people is a beast which allows itself to be led around by the nose, especially the people of Paris. It is not they, but a few wicked among them, who are responsible. But to show them how wrong they are, I shan't budge from this spot." All the same he celebrated Easter in the Bois de Vincennes. . . .

Easter Day, the 26th, it snowed all day long. There was such a crowd to hear the preaching of the Protestants, in the apartments of Madame, that no one could sit down.

This month of March was very wet, with snow, rain, and wind. Great floods on the rivers, which raised the cost of living. These, with the war, afflicted the people sorely.

APRIL

At the beginning of April the King was very sick with a cold which disfigured his face. There are a lot of these colds in Paris, due to the terrible cold, unsuited to the season, which end in strange and sudden deaths. There is also the plague in some quarters. All of these are the flails of God, but one doesn't see any mending of their ways by either the great or the small.

MAY

Saturday, the 20th, a bushel of wheat cost twenty-four or twenty-five francs in Paris; the necessity mounts visibly from hour to hour . . . and it was decided to hold an assembly in the Salle St. Louis to do something about it. The changing weather, cold, windy, freezing, threatens worse. It is said that the King keeps to himself and prays, weeping over the misery of his people. I have proof of this from one of his household, a good man, who told me that the King said to him, "I pity my poor people, I know that they are badly off. But if I try to do anything about it, they'll treat me even worse."

Monday, the 22nd, a *Te Deum* was sung in Paris to celebrate the fall of Autun to the King, the inhabitants having cut the throats of the League garrison. . . .

Tuesday, the 30th, a drive for alms for the poor was begun in Paris, in which each one was supposed to give in proportion to the size of his house. By the report of those who keep track of the beggars from outside the city, the number entering in the last fortnight is more than fourteen thousand persons.

In this month Sanguin . . . was allowed to return to Paris and to resume all his goods and offices . . . although he was one of the worst of the Sixteen and it was in his house . . . that the murder of the late Président Brisson was planned. . . .

JULY

Thursday, the 27th, came news of the defeat of the French at Dourlans in Picardy, followed by the sack of this poor town by the Spaniard, who committed all sorts of excesses and cruelties. . . . I lost there my eldest son, Louis de l'Estoile, who was killed among the first. . . .

AUGUST

Saturday, the 12th, a wolf, having swum across the river, ate a child in the Place de Grève, a monstrous thing and a bad omen.

News came today of a siege laid to Cambrai by the Duke of Fuentes, the Spaniard, and that M. de Nevers has sent the Duke of Retelois his son . . . to help the prudence and valor of M. de Vicq . . . [in defense of the town].

Tuesday, the 22nd, came news of the death of the Duke of Nemours, by poison, according to the rumors . . . happy in this respect, that God touched his heart at the end of his days to make him regret his rebellion. He died recognizing God and the King and exhorting all men to their duty. . . . Thus does God give us a mirror of His mercy, in the end of this prince, one of the most dangerous of the leaders of the League.

In this month died Don Antonio, King of Portugal, at least in theory; his means had reduced him to the rank of a simple gentleman.

SEPTEMBER

Monday, the 4th of September, the King made his entry into Lyons. . . .

Friday, September 23, the very day the King granted a truce to M. de Mayenne, the good news came to Paris of the absolution granted in Rome by the Pope on the 18th of this month, which caused great rejoicing of the people. . . .

Messieurs d'Ossat and du Perron were most helpful in bringing the Pope to this action. For his services D'Ossat got the red hat. Du Perron, son of a minister of Berne, was given a hope of a cardinal's hat, provided that he continued to oppose the Huguenots firmly, and get as many as possible to follow his example in revolting from them, combatting them in his sermons and writings. He was most careful in carrying out this injunction, knowing that the Pope's eye was on him. . . .

DECEMBER

The 6th of December, day of St. Nicholas, a general procession was held in Paris to thank God for the absolution given by the Pope to the King. Fireworks were set off all over the city.

The King, carrying out his promise to the Pope, sent for Henri de Bourbon, Prince of Condé, aged seven, first prince of the blood, to have him instructed in the Roman, Catholic, and Apostolic religion . . . and put him in the charge of the Marquis of Pisani, as gifted a man as there is in France. . . .

1596

CAPITULATION OF MAYENNE

JANUARY

Wednesday, the 24th, the little prince [Condé], who was at St. Germain-en-Laye at the express command of His Majesty, changed his religion, and was instructed by M. Pierre de Gondi, Cardinal-Bishop of Paris, who catechized him as much as his age would permit. He changed his religion and went to Mass.

Wednesday, the last day of this month, the Duke of Mayenne, accompanied by only six gentlemen, went to the King at Mousseaux to yield to him. Madame la Marquise [Gabrielle] did the honors of the house. She met him at the door of the Château, where, after receiving him with as much graciousness and as many caresses as possible, [she] conducted him by the hand to the King, herself. His Majesty awaited the Duke seated on a dais.

The Duke of Mayenne, entering the room, bowed deeply three times. At the third, as he knelt to kiss His Majesty's hand, the King, smiling, raised him and kissed him, saying, "My cousin, is it you? or am I having a dream?" To this the Duke replied with great submission and reverence. The King said a few words which nobody else could hear, then took him by the arm, and, after a few turns around the room, led him to his study where they spent some time together. Afterward they dined, the King with the Marquise at his side, the Duke at a table adjoining, with Mademoiselle Diane d'Estrées, sister of the Marquise. The two sisters did the honors, and the King drank to the Duke. . . .

[Meanwhile] processions of the poor took place in Paris, in such numbers as were never seen; they cried for hunger while in their mansions the rich gorged themselves with banquets and luxuries, an abominable affront to God, whatever excuse is given. . . .

FEBRUARY

The King, in this month, was constrained by need of money to reestablish the intendants of finances whom he had abolished the month before, and he said to one of them . . . that neither he nor any of his fellows had a tooth in his head that hadn't cost [the King] ten thousand crowns.

MARCH

Friday, the first day of March, a woman was burned in Paris, in front of St. Nicholas-des-Champs, for having killed two of her children with her own hands. She said that she had done it because she had nothing to give them to eat.

Saturday, the 2nd, a *Te Deum* was sung in Paris for the reduction of the city of Marseilles to the King's obedience, by the valor of the Duke of Guise. The said Duke did a signal service to the King in this, because if His Majesty had lost the city, the Spaniards could have made themselves masters of Provence and Languedoc.

Friday, the 8th, there was hanged in the Place de Grève one La Ramée, a young man of twenty-three or twenty-four who claimed to be the natural son of King Charles IX, and demanded to be crowned King . . . in another time he would be locked up in some monastery, which would seem about right for such a poor fool — if the royalties of the League weren't so fresh [in people's minds]. Thus one saw, this day, a "son of France" in the Place de Grève.

Saturday, the 16th, the number of poor in Paris rose by two-thirds, six or seven thousand having arrived in recent days.

APRIL

Monday, the 21st, came to Paris the sad news of the taking of Calais by the Cardinal of Austria . . . by the same stratagem that the [former] Duke of Guise used to take it from the English. . . . Two days later came a false rumor that it had been retaken. . . . The people, who by themselves are an animal volatile, inconstant, and stupid, began to speak ill of the King . . . making an excuse that he spent too much time with Madame la Marquise. . . .

The managers of the Hôtel-Dieu report that more than six hundred persons died in the hospital in this month.

MAY

Monday, the 6th, one hour after midnight, Madame de Montpensier died in her house in the rue des Bourbonnais, of a terrible hemorrhage in all parts of her body. This was a fitting end to her life, as were the thunder and lightning of the night appropriate to her evil, seditious, and tempestuous spirit, which was the cause — admitted even by those of the League — of the death of her brothers. . . .

JULY

Sunday, the 21st, at six in the evening, M. le Cardinal de Florence, Alexander de Medici, made his entrance into Paris, having been sent as Legate by the Pope . . . there was never a better nor more peacefully inclined Legate than this one. In the ceremonies to honor him, the little prince [Condé] took part, then fell ill. . . .

Three hundred and five persons are ill with this disease in the Hôtel-Dieu. . . . Many of the best houses in the city are infected. In the parishes of St. Nicholas, Montmartre, St. Denis, and St. Martin . . . where because of poverty the people are dirty and herded in together (where disease is usually rampant), there is little . . . the faubourg St. Germain is very badly afflicted . . . which is worthy of note. . . .

AUGUST

Friday, the 23rd, Pierre de La Rue, tailor, died of the current sickness . . . former governor of the city of Paris under the League. He died in a rage, out of his mind . . . regretted by all the drunks like himself, and disappointing many who hoped to see him hang and not die in bed.

In this month the sickness spread into the villages . . . two hundred were released from the Hôtel-Dieu as cured, but they weren't and so spread the contagion further. . . . Another sort of sickness, robbery, reigned in Paris also . . . especially of deserted houses. . . . One hears of nothing else. . . .

NOVEMBER

Monday, November 4, news came to Paris of the death of M. Pithou . . . a good man and learned, one of the lights of the Palais.

In this month of November the King, entering the Estates at Rouen, made a fine speech, but brusque and short, in keeping with his humor, which is very military at the moment. He wanted the opinion of the Marquise, his mistress, who heard it all, hidden behind a tapestry. When he asked her what she thought, she said that she had never heard him speak better, but she was surprised to hear him speak of putting himself into their [the Estates'] hands. *Ventre St. Gris!* he replied, "I'll listen to them with my sword handy."

DECEMBER

Thursday, December 12, the King arrived in Paris. The next day he went to the Hôtel de Ville and spoke in a royal manner . . . about taking the income of the municipal bonds. He threatened with the Bastille anyone who resisted, because he had been warned that the people were murmuring aloud. . . .

Sunday, December 22, at a quarter past six in the evening, the Pont-aux-Musniers fell, causing a tremendous ruin of houses, goods, and men. Eight times twenty people perished. . . . It was remarked that the majority of those who died were rich and comfortable, but that they had gotten that way by the usury and looting of St. Bartholomew and the League.

1597

THE SIEGE OF AMIENS

JANUARY

Friday, the 17th, a Cordelier was taken to the Conciergerie for having preached . . . that the King was a real excommunicate, and that it was not in the power of all the Popes to absolve him.

FEBRUARY

Monday, the 10th of February, the Duke of Nemours and the Count d'Auvergne were at the Fair, where they committed a thousand injuries. A lawyer of Paris lost his hat and was beaten by them. . . .

MARCH

This night [March 1st] Madame was very sick and the King was with her until midnight.

The next day, after dinner, His Majesty returned to see her. There he found Vaumesnil, who was playing the lute and singing the 78th Psalm to console her. The King began to sing also . . . but Madame de Mousseaux, who was near, laid her hand on his lips . . . and he stopped. Some of the [Protestants] at hand were indignant at this, and [said] . . . "See how this wicked woman keeps the King from singing the praises of God."

That night the King played dice with M. de Lesdiguières, and gained 5,000 crowns, and from Sancy a string of pearls valued at 8,000. . . .

Wednesday, the 5th, the son of the Constable [Montmorency] was baptized . . . the King held him, and the Legate performed the ceremony. Madame la Marquise was there, beautifully dressed in green. The King amused himself by playing with her hair, but complained that there were not enough brilliants in her coiffure. There were only twelve, and he said that there should be fifteen.

Ballets, masquerades, music of all sorts, and all that could stimulate voluptuousness (of which there was already plenty) followed this occasion . . . symbols of the wrath of God which fell on us soon afterward, for on Wednesday, the 12th of the month, in mid-Lent, while these amusements were going on, came the piteous news of the surprise of the town of Amiens by the Spaniards, who used our ballets as batons to beat us with. This news greatly troubled the city of Paris and the court. Even the King, whose equanimity is not easily upset, turned to God (as he always does in adversity rather than in prosperity), and said, "This is a blow from the skies. Those poor people, after refusing a little garrison I offered them, are lost." Then, after thinking a bit, he said, "Enough of the King of France! It is time for the King of Navarre!" Turning to the Marquise, who was crying, he said, "My mistress, I must leave these arms for others, mount my horse and fight another war!"

This he did, the very same day, marching at the head of his men to show them that fear . . . could find no place in his heart. . . . This served to hearten the people and inspire the nobility to fight well and firmly under the leadership of so brave and generous a King. He could have avoided this inconvenience long before, if he had taken the advice of the Duke of Mayenne to leave the ballets of Paris for Amiens. . . . But God, who wished to humble him and rouse him, and also to chastise the people, who deserve this flail — especially the great — would not permit this good advice to be followed. . . .

APRIL

Thursday, April 10, one Charpentier, son of the late Master Jacques Charpentier, Reader in the University of Paris, a learned man . . . but great massacrer, who killed the great Ramus on St. Bartholomew, was broken on the wheel in the Place de Grève . . . for carrying messages which involved a conspiracy against the King and the state. . . .

Wednesday, the 23rd, Messieurs of Parlement, from whom the King demanded money and the verification of certain financial Edicts, went to call on His Majesty, who was still in bed. M. le Premier Président was the spokesman. The King was so angry that he seemed almost demented. He compared them to the fools of Amiens, who had refused him 2,000 crowns and then had to give a million to the enemy. As for him, he

283

would go to Flanders, and if a bullet found him they would learn, at their own expense, what it was to lose a King.

When the Premier Président said that "God had put justice in their hands and they were responsible for it," he retorted, "On the contrary, it was to him, the King, that God had given it, and *he* to them." To this the Premier Président said nothing, outraged, it is said, by anger and frustration, so that he fell ill and had to be bled. When the King heard this he asked if with the blood the arrogance had been drawn from him. . . .

MAY

In this month Sancy abjured the [Protestant] religion, which he had always professed. He made a solemn public conversion in the Jesuits' Chapel in the rue St. Antoine, receiving absolution from the Legate. . . . Because he wept a lot (or, according to some, pretended to do so) the Legate said aloud, "See how this poor gentleman weeps for his errors, with a heart so full he can't speak." The King made fun of this emotion, saying that all Sancy needed was a turban — as if a Turk were being converted.

Toward the end of the month the King sent for some of the leading members of Parlement whom he knew to be among the most comfortable men in Paris, and asked them for money in such a way that they could not refuse, though they were most reluctant. Meanwhile he spent most of his time playing tennis where Madame la Marquise [and other ladies] watched him. He caressed and kissed the Marquise before all the world. But in spite of this, His Majesty did not fail to take care of affairs . . . in Amiens, and in the following month he said goodbye to love and gambling, did the job of a King, captain, and soldier all in one, thus putting as much fear in the hearts of his enemies as ardor to emulate him in the hearts of his followers.

JULY

In this month M. de Lesdiguières fortunately defeated the troops of the Duke of Savoy, and the Chevalier Du Pescher . . . the garrisons of Cambrai. These tidings were welcome to the King and gave him a bit of cheer to offset his anxiety over Amiens. . . .

In this month of July the King bought the Duchy of Beaufort for Madame la Marquise, his mistress, and she became a Duchess on Thursday, the 10th of the month. Since that day she has been called the Duchess of Beaufort, or, by others, the Duchess of Excrement.

He also made his little Caesar a Peer of France, for whom some said that Alexander the Great would be a better name. . . .

AUGUST

In this month of August fifty or sixty women, called devout, ran about the town complaining of the Protestant preaching in the apartments of Madame, and saying that this was the cause of all our ills. . . . M. le Premier Président . . . gave them a most appropriate answer, to wit, that he would . . . tell their husbands to lock them in their houses . . . they are said to have the support of certain ecclesiastics. . . .

Toward the end of the month came news of the defeat of some Spaniards trying to rescue Amiens . . . which, without relief . . . will fall of its own weight. All Europe hangs on the outcome of this siege, on which depends the servitude of France, or its liberty.

SEPTEMBER

Thursday, the 25th of the month, Amiens fell to the King, who took it not by guile but by the greatest feat of arms known to the world.

Thursday, the 30th, the Parlement rendered a decision against the adherents of the Spanish faction, and the Duke of Mercoeur . . . and other little would-be royalties, whose kingdom expired with the fall of Amiens, because their estates were based on the ruin of France and their revenues came from the coffers of Spain. . . .

NOVEMBER

In this month M. du Plessis-Mornay, Governor of Saumur, was traitorously attacked . . . by one St. Phalle, right in the street . . . in Angers. He beat him so that he was left for dead. . . .

Whereupon M. du Plessis, turning to all his friends . . . wrote to the King to ask for justice. The King wrote him the following letter:

M. du Plessis, I am extremely displeased at the outrage upon your person, in which I share, both as King and as your friend. In the first capacity, I shall see that you get justice, and I too. If I had only the second title, there would be no sword readier, nor any who would risk life more gaily than I. Believe this, I will do you the offices of King, master, and friend. On this truth I close, praying God to keep you. From Fontainebleau, this . . . November.

DECEMBER

In this month a rumor circulated in Paris and throughout all France of the death of M. Beza, who is supposed to have died in Geneva a good Roman Catholic, having abjured the religion he had preached all his life. This lie was fabricated by the Jesuits. . . .

Toward the end of this year the sacred word, peace, came to be heard, which is the great desire of all the people, the pillar of law and the source of order on earth. It was said that it would be brought about by the Pope between the two kings [of France and Spain] through the mediation of the Legate.

And thus ended the year 1597, with as much glory at the end as the beginning was shameful and unhappy for France. In which we see the great goodness and bounty of God, who alone can bring great good from great evils.

1598

END OF THE LEAGUE AND
PEACE WITH SPAIN

JANUARY

At the beginning of January in the year 1598, the King, desiring to put the finishing touches to the great work of restoring the monarchy, took the road for Brittany, for the reduction of that great and beautiful province, which King Charles VIII preferred to all the Low Countries and the County of Burgundy. Of all the League chiefs, there remains only the Duke of Mercoeur, whom the King was sworn to bring to justice, by force or by persuasion, before the end of March.

The 22nd of this month of January, died in the city of Lyons, Henri Estienne, a great man, gifted with a fine mind, and very learned, as he proved by his studies of Greek and Latin authors — but bizarre and aloof, who was kept in Geneva more by the legacy of his father than by [concern for] religion. . . .

MARCH

In this month Brittany, and the Duke of Mercoeur, were reduced to the King's obedience, and the treaty was published in the Parlement de Paris on the 26th. . . . The composition was advantageous and honorable. . . . The final clause of the treaty was the marriage of young Caesar with the Duke's daughter. This involved an exchange between the King and Madame [de Mercoeur], who found His Majesty fixing little Caesar's hair. . . . She asked him, laughing, if it was possible that a great King could be a good barber. To which he replied in a flash, "Why not, Cousin? I'm barber to the whole world. Didn't you see how good a job I did, a few days back, on M. de Mercoeur, your husband?" . . .

287

MAY

Saturday, the 2nd of this month, peace was concluded between the two Kings at Vervins, contrary to expectation. His Majesty embraced the peace . . . to show that he knew how to finish as well as begin wars. . . .

In this same month a conspiracy was discovered (in Leyden) of the Jesuits at Douai to assassinate Count Maurice, by means of the knife of one Pierre Panne, who was put to death. . . .

M. de Serres, author of the *Inventory of the History of France*, a learned man, passionate for the reunion of the churches, died in this month in Orange. His zeal was misinterpreted and his actions libeled, as is common with good men. The rumor was even spread that he had died a Roman Catholic, which was false, as his will proves.

JUNE

Friday, the 12th of this month, the proclamation of peace between the King and the King of Spain and the Duke of Savoy was published and placed on the marble table in the court of the Palais with great solemnity and public rejoicing. Fireworks were set off, and the bell of the Palais rang all day long. Messieurs of the Court attended a *Te Deum* at Notre Dame, in their black robes . . . and ten thousand loaves of bread were distributed to the poor in front of the Hôtel de Ville . . . and wine was given to all comers. . . .

Tuesday, the 16th, the Legate arrived in Paris . . . all the people blessed him, as the chief agent of the peace . . . and he was escorted to his house by a crowd of more than three thousand persons. . . .

Thursday, the 18th, the Duke of Ascot and the other Spanish ambassadors arrived in Paris by the Porte St. Denis. The Count of St. Paul . . . accompanied by a large number of the French nobility . . . escorted them . . . who, to speak objectively, presented quite a contrast to the Spaniards in their showy garb.

Friday, the 19th, the [Spanish] Duke, with a great company, went to pay his respects to His Majesty at the Louvre, who . . . seated on a great dais . . . received them more humanly than royally, as they say, being dressed entirely in black. . . .

Later the King . . . went to play tennis . . . the foreigners were there watching . . . and the ladies, including the Duchess of Beaufort, whom the King asked to remove her mask so that the Spaniards could see her clearly. . . . Under the gallery . . . was the little prince, whom His Majesty . . . sent for to introduce to the guests. . . . His tutor, the Marquis of Pisani, talked to them a long while, responding for the prince to their questions, in French, Italian, and Spanish. . . .

Saturday, the 20th, the King took the Duke and his company hunting . . . taking more pleasure in exercising them than in supporting them . . . which comes to 2,000 crowns a day, for the seven hundred mouths that they had. . . .

Sunday, the 21st, in a ceremony at Notre Dame, the peace was sworn . . . His Majesty all dressed in black. . . . Later he tendered a magnificent dinner in the Palace of the Bishopric to the Legate and the Spanish ambassadors, where he drank twice to the health of the King of Spain, smiling and seeming marvellously happy.

A Spanish gentleman . . . said to His Majesty that he found Paris, where he had been during the League, so changed that he almost didn't recognize it. "I can believe that," said the King, "for it was then in the hands of the valet, but now is in the hands of the master."

Tuesday, the 28th, the King set fire, with his own hand . . . to the effigy of war . . . which was burned in the Place de Grève. . . .

A magnificent collation [followed] at the Hôtel de Ville . . . at which the Duchess of Beaufort . . . chose what she wished to eat with one hand . . . and with the other . . . caressed the King. . . .

In this month the King gave the entire administration of his finances to Rosni,* who is Protestant, removing them from Sancy, new convert . . . to understand this, without paying any attention to the court gossip . . . we must look to God, who laughs at the great plans of men and often brings very different results from what they expect.

A pleasant tale was told in Paris at this time, reputed to be a fable at first, but finally accepted as the truth, of a poor man whom the King met in the woods . . . who was leading a cow to sell it in order to meet the *taille*. Seeing that the man didn't know who he was, the King took pleasure in talking to him, and pulled out of him the gist of the complaints of the people . . . because of the constantly increasing taxes. . . . To take full advantage [of the situation] His Majesty said that no doubt they must have a very bad king. . . . "He's not so bad," the good man is sup-

* Who later became the Duke of Sully.

posed to have replied, "but there is a beautiful Gabrielle who scratches him, and spoils everything for us." The King took to laughing at his naïveté, and gave him 12 crowns so he would not have to sell the cow. The next day he told the tale to his mistress, saying that he had given 12 crowns for love of her.

Toward the end of the month, satisfied with the King but worn out with all the exercise he made them take . . . the Spaniards asked leave of the King and departed for their own country, where he had wished them a long time since. The fattest of them, very tired . . . said that "France was a wicked country where a man could get no sleep."

JULY

In this month of July appeared in Paris a book of our Master Boucher, against the King, printed in octavo in Brussels. Three were brought to this city in the baggage of Jeremy Périer, bookseller in the rue St. Jacques: one went to the Premier Président, another to the conseiller Rivière, and the third was put into the hands of Servin, Lawyer of the King, who gave it to M. de Bouillon to show to the King. I borrowed this latter one evening and made in haste the following extracts of this fine book, worthy of the fire, with its author. Its title: *Apology for Jean Chastel, Parisian, put to death; and for the Fathers and Scholars of the Society of Jesus, banished from the realm of France. Against the decision of the Parlement condemning them in Paris, the 29th of December, 1594. Divided into five parts.*

The five parts of this beautiful book are: first, the sources of error; second, that the act of Chastel was a good one; third, that the act of Chastel was heroic; fourth, the vices and impertinences of the decision against Chastel; fifth, the vices and impertinences of the decisions against the Jesuits. . . . His conclusion . . . is one long and violent exhortation to exterminate the King, whom he calls the enemy of God and His Church. The very end is a plea to all good Catholics to rally to the King of Spain, as the flag-bearer of the Faith. . . .

AUGUST

In this month the book of M. du Plessis-Mornay, printed in La Rochelle, in quarto, dealing with the question of the Eucharist versus the

Mass, began to be sold in Paris, in spite of the efforts to stop it . . . which increased the demand, as is usual in our France.

All the Sorbonne and the clergy were scandalized and much disturbed by this book, and they realized that it required an answer. One was attempted by a certain Jules Boulanger, Doctor of Theology, which, although he was well versed in Hebrew . . . didn't amount to much because it was done too hastily . . . it was followed by another by one Du Pui . . . while waiting for the great battery that was produced by the Bishop of Evreux [Du Perron] who is thought here to be the Atlas of the Roman, Catholic, and Apostolic Church in this kingdom.

SEPTEMBER

Monday, the 28th of this month, Messieurs of the clergy, through M. François de Guesle, Archbishop of Tours, made a remonstrance to the King . . . the gist of which was [to urge] the maintenance of the Roman Church . . . and publication of the degrees of the Council of Trent. To which the King replied summarily as follows:

"You have urged me to do my duty, I urge you to do yours. Let us do well, both of us. You go your way, I'll go mine, if they meet things will work out well. My predecessors gave you fancy words, but I, in my old grey coat, give you action. I am grey outside but solid gold within. I will write to my council about your *cahier*, and will put it in as favorable light as possible."

This same day [September 28] came news of the death of the King of Spain, who died on Sunday, the 13th of the present month. It was not at first believed, because now people don't care, whereas during the war the desire for it was so great that we had him dead and then resurrected three or four times a year.

In this month the King named M. de Villiers Séguier, Président in the Parlement, to be his ambassador to Venice, though he didn't want to go, and used [every means possible, including an appeal to Gabrielle] to get out of it. . . . It is said (and I think it's true) that it was those of the [Protestant] Religion who pressed the King to this appointment, because of their Edict which is coming up, to which they know the said Séguier to be very much opposed . . . and the King appreciates their arguments . . . desiring the Edict to be enacted.

The ecclesiastics, knowing this, murmured about it, saying that bit by bit good Catholics were being done away with.

The Palais bade him goodbye with great regret, as he is one of the best, a good judge, learned and incorruptible, and very efficient, especially in criminal cases. . . .

OCTOBER

Friday, the 30th of this month, while the court was at Mousseaux, the city of Paris was much troubled by the news of the seriousness of the King's illness . . . a severe retention of urine which threatened to send him to the other world, an event as much feared by good men as desired by wicked. The best doctors in Paris were sent for . . . and many leading [seigneurs] left Paris to go to the King, while all the governors retired to their provinces.

The alarm was great in Paris (where they had him already dead) until late that evening when M. de Montpensier arrived and reassured the city that his condition was much improved, though for two days at the worst of it he had not spoken nor moved. . . .

When Marescot [one of the doctors] took leave of His Majesty [the King] said "that he knew that many were building beautiful castles based on his death, but to tell them firmly to go build them in Spain, because he wasn't dead yet and had no intention of dying." He said also "that he heard they were murmuring in Paris because he had sent for Casauban,* because he was a Huguenot, but that his only motive in this was to make the University flourish." . . .

DECEMBER

Sunday, the 13th, the baptism of the son of Madame la Duchesse de Beaufort took place at St. Germain-en-Laye with all the accustomed ceremonies. . . . Afterward there was a magnificent feast, and a ballet was performed for the King called the Ballet of the Five Nations. . . . There was also a young man . . . one of the most supple seen in our time, who delighted the King and all the court by dancing on a rope, jumping, turning somersaults, and all sorts of tricks. . . .

* Isaac Casauban was a leading Hellenist and scholar, formerly of Geneva.

At this time all the preachers railed against the Edict, giving the people to understand that it provided for the erection of temples in Paris . . . thereby rousing the people who . . . libeled the King. There was much talk of a new St. Bartholomew . . . all this to stop the publication and execution of the Edict, against which opposition grows more fierce each day, in all parts of France. . . .

Finally His Majesty sent the Edict itself to the Sorbonne to show them that it was nothing but the Edict of 1577 . . . (which they already knew, but they feared its enforcement this time). . . .

Wednesday, the 23rd, the King and all the court returned from St. Germain to this city, where Madame held her services the next day with such a crowd that there were more outside than in . . . also [this occurred] on Christmas Day with the doors open, to show the preachers of Paris that they were not bothered by their cries. . . . The preachers kept silent in the pulpits, because of the presence of Their Majesties . . . but nevertheless continued their offensive *sub rosa*, using the Christmas confessions . . . to ask people if they hadn't gone to the services out of curiosity, or if they associated with those who did, or if they had forbidden books like M. du Plessis' . . . if anyone confessed anything he was sent away without absolution.

They even went further . . . in some parishes trying to renew the League . . . asking those who came to confession to take an oath to join with all good Catholics to oppose the Edict before they would give them absolution . . . they sent to the Duke of Mayenne to ask him to lead such a group, but he sent them away promptly and virtuously.

They even tried to use Madame la Duchesse in this cause . . . but she replied . . . [to Séguier] that she knew well the King's mind in this matter . . . and that she saw no reason to prevent those of the Religion, who were good servants of the King, from holding offices, when he had allowed *ligueurs* who had borne arms against him to do so. M. de Bouillon thanked her for this.

Thursday, the last day of the month and year, the King, in person, heard the opinions of his council on the Edict. They agreed to accept it without reservations, Schomberg, among others, saying that those of the Religion were good servants of the King and that the holding of offices should not be denied them.

No fruit worth mentioning this year, and little wine. Everything in

Paris very expensive, especially bread. The weather very humid and rainy, even this last day of the year, when it never stopped raining. This caused colds and grippe to be widespread. Many ballets in Paris lighted with candles, as though they were chapels, but these signified prayers to saints not in the calendar.

1599

THE EDICT OF NANTES

JANUARY

Sunday, the 3rd of the month, the first banns of the marriage between Madame, sister of the King, and the Marquis of Pont, eldest son of M. de Lorraine, were published. Madame had them announced at the start of the services in her house. For the Prince of Lorraine [they were announced] in his parish, St. Germain-l'Auxerrois.

Thursday, the 7th of the month, the King sent for the members of the Parlement to come to the Louvre to verify the Edict for those of the Religion, and spoke to them in choice and exquisite terms. . . .

You see me in my cabinet, not in royal costume with sword and cape like my predecessors, nor like a prince parleying with foreign ambassadors, but dressed as a father of the family, in everyday clothes, who comes to talk frankly to his children.

What I have to say is that I want you to verify the Edict which I have granted to those of the Religion. I have done it to bring about peace. I have made it abroad; I want it at home. You should obey me even if there were no other consideration but my station and the obligation of subjects, but you, of my Parlement, have a special obligation. I restored their houses to some, who had been exiled, their faith to others, who had lost it. If obedience was due to my predecessors it is due still more to me, as I have re-established the state, God having chosen me to come into this heritage. The members of my Parlement wouldn't be in office without me. . . . I know the road to sedition which led to the Barricades and the assassination of the late King. I'll take care that it doesn't happen again. I will root out all factions, discipline all seditious teaching . . . I have jumped over the walls of cities . . . barricades are not so high.

Don't throw the Catholic religion in my face. I love it more than you do; I am more Catholic than you are. I am the eldest son of the Church. You are mistaken if you think you have the Pope on your side. He is with me instead. I know all that you do and all that you say.

Those who don't want the Edict to pass want war . . . you are ungrateful to cause me this worry . . . I call as witnesses those of my council who have found it good and necessary, M. le Connétable, M. le Chancelier, Messieurs de Bellièvre, Sancy, and Sillery . . . who have advised me to do it. . . .

I am the sole conserver of religion . . . I am King now, I speak as King and I will be obeyed. Indeed justice is my right hand, but if gangrene sets in in it, the left will have to cut it off. When my armies do not serve me, I break them up. . . .

[Interruption to warn Sillery that his brother, a preacher, must stop preaching against the Edict], then, returning to the Parlement,

There is not one of you who doesn't find me willing when you ask me for something. Yet to me, though I'm good to you, you return evil. The other Parlements, by their refusals, have caused those of the Religion to raise their demands. I don't want still more [demands] because of your refusal. . . . There's not one of these great devout Catholics who, if I gave to this one a 2,000-crown benefice and to that one 4,000 in income . . . wouldn't shut his mouth. . . . Some wrongdoers hate sin and avoid it because of the fear of punishment, others for the love of virtue. . . . I can't say that I know those of you who hate sin from love of virtue, but I know well how to deal with those who hate it because of fear of punishment . . . you'll thank me later, as a son does his father. . . .

The last word you'll have from me is to follow the example of M. de Mayenne. Some have tried to incite him to defy my will, but he replied that he was too much obliged to me. All my subjects are similarly under obligation because I have saved France in spite of those who wanted to ruin her. . . . And if the chief of the League speaks thus, how much more should you, whom I restored to your offices, both those who were faithful and those whom I had to win back — what should they do, at that price!

Give to my prayers what you would not give to threats. You will have none from me. Do as I command, or rather, as I entreat. You will be doing it not only for me but also for yourselves and for the sake of peace.

The opposition was sufficiently overawed by this masterful speech for the Edict to pass, thus bringing to an end thirty-six years of civil war in France. Henry IV had eleven years of his reign still ahead, in which he restored and increased the royal power, and, with the aid of Sully, brought about the economic reconstruction of the kingdom.

With the Edict, however, France entered a new era. The later years of Henry IV's reign constitute the beginning of the absolute monarchy in its final form, which reached its height under his grandson, Louis XIV, and continued until the Revolution of 1789 destroyed it.

CHRONOLOGICAL OUTLINE
OF EVENTS

GLOSSARY OF TERMS

INDEX

APPENDIX A

CHRONOLOGICAL OUTLINE OF EVENTS

(Asterisks indicate events which occurred before the beginning of the *Mémoires-Journaux* of Pierre de l'Estoile.)

*1562–70   First three religious "wars" between Huguenots and Catholic nobles. A series of skirmishes and truces in which the Protestants gain conditional freedom of worship and the possession of certain fortified cities.

        Catherine de Medici pursues opportunistic policy of opposing whichever group is stronger at a given moment in attempt to hold kingdom together. Her ineffectual son, Charles IX, occupies the throne.

*1572   Massacre of St. Bartholomew in Paris and other cities of France on the occasion of the marriage of Marguerite de Valois, daughter of Henry II and Catherine de Medici, to Henry of Navarre, leader of the Huguenot party and heir to the throne after the Valois.

*1572–73   Fourth War of Religion, the first siege of La Rochelle by Catholic nobles and a royal army commanded by Henry, Duke of Anjou, brother of Charles IX, later Henry III.

        Offer of the Polish throne to this prince before the military issue was clarified results in truce and further Huguenot gains.

1574   At the death of Charles IX, Henry of Anjou, King of Poland, succeeds to the throne of France as Henry III.

        L'Estoile begins the *Journal de Henri III*.

1576   Peace of *Monsieur* concludes fifth War of Religion: Henry III makes greatest concessions yet to Huguenots. Holy League set in motion to defend the Catholic religion, really a device by which the House of Lorraine-Guise hopes to take over the crown. (*Monsieur* is Duke of Alençon, Henry III's younger brother, temporarily on Huguenot side.)

1576–84   Henry III antagonizes the nation, especially Paris, by constant financial demands and by his personal behavior and that of his favorites, the *mignons*. The King and Catherine de Medici attempt to use the League for their own purposes and it is not well received.

1578–84   Duke of Alençon recruits French troops and interferes in the

301

war in the Low Countries between Spain and her rebellious provinces. He also courts Queen Elizabeth.

1584   Assassination of William of Orange.

Death of Alençon. Henry of Navarre becomes heir apparent. Duke Henry of Guise revives the League, aimed not only against the Huguenots but also against Henry III who is accused of being a "tyrant" because of concessions to the Huguenots.

1585–88   Organization of the Paris League in the Corporations and in the Sixteen quarters. Leaders called "the Sixteen."

1586   Temporary truce between Henry III and Henry of Guise.

1587   Henry III and Guise win a victory over German Protestant forces at Auneau in Lorraine. Paris preachers give Guise all the credit, and antagonism between the King and the Duke greatly increases; Madame de Montpensier, sister of the Duke of Guise, takes charge of Paris propaganda and subsidizes leading *prédicateurs* (preachers).

The League plans an uprising on the pretext that the *prédicateurs* are to be arrested (*Journée de St. Séverin*). This fails because royal officials are warned by Nicholas Poulain who is playing the role of double spy.

Mary Stuart executed by Elizabeth in England.

REBELLION OF THE PARIS LEAGUE
AGAINST THE CROWN, 1588–1594

1588   *January–April.* The Paris League, impatient for action, importunes the Duke of Guise to come to Paris. Henry III forbids him to do so and takes some measures for the defense of the city.

May 9. The Duke of Guise comes to Paris against the King's express command. He confers with the Sixteen and solidifies plans for revolt.

May 12. The Day of the Barricades. Henry III is forced to flee.

May 13. Guise is king of Paris.

May–July. The League takes over the police, the Bastille, the Hôtel de Ville, and other offices. It negotiates with Henry III, who is in Chartres, through the agency of Catherine de Medici and Villeroy, Secretary of State. A treaty called the Edict of Union is drawn up embodying all the demands of the League.

August. Defeat of the Spanish Armada greatly weakens the Guise party.

September. Henry III dismisses his advisers and turns from his mother's guidance.

October. Estates-General, called by Henry III, meeting in Blois, is dominated by the League.

December 23–24. Assassination of the Duke and Cardinal of Guise in the château at Blois at the King's orders.

Paris revolt is strengthened by the murders and the Duke of Mayenne takes his brother's place as head of the League.

1589 *January–March*. Paris League organizes for war: raises armies, imposes taxes, and undertakes diplomatic offensive by writing letters to the leading princes and cities of France and to the Pope, rallying them to the cause.

The clergy sponsors excessive mourning for the Guise martyrs. Madame de Montpensier and the *prédicateurs* call for revenge on the tyrant, Henry III.

The Parlement de Paris is purged by Bussi-LeClerc, governor of the Bastille. Barnabé Brisson, moderate *ligueur*, becomes Premier Président.

April. Henry III acknowledges Henry of Navarre as his successor. They join forces and march on Paris.

August 1. Assassination of Henry III in St. Cloud by Jacques Clément, Jacobin monk and tool of the League.

Henry of Navarre recognized as King in the royal armies. Paris celebrates murder of Henry III, the tyrant, and determines to resist heretic King.

1590 *March*. Henry IV wins the battle of Ivry against League armies led by the Duke of Mayenne.

May–August. Henry IV lays siege to Paris, and the people suffer severe hardship. The clergy and Madame de Montpensier, with the aid of the Spanish ambassador Mendoza, maintain morale. Siege lifted by Spanish troops under the command of the Duke of Parma, August 30.

1591 *January*. Spanish and Neapolitan troops brought into Paris.

April. Brigard, courier of the League, is accused of treason but acquitted by the Parlement. The extremists demand another purge of the Parlement in revenge.

November 1–15. Secret meeting of the extreme faction, in which attack on the Parlement is planned.

November 15. Arrest and murder by the extremists of Brisson, Premier Président, and Larcher and Tardif, leading royalists.

December. The Duke of Mayenne returns to Paris to restore his authority. Four members of the Sixteen hanged as punishment for the murders.

Many defections from the League, which is henceforth openly split between moderates (*Mayennistes*) and the extremists (*éspagnolizés*), of whom the majority are members of the clergy.

1592   Throughout the year many demands for truce with Henry IV, or at least for an agreement to permit trade between Paris and the royalist suburbs. Mayenne loses ground between the Spanish faction and the growing number of royalists, called *politiques*.

1593   *January–June.* Meeting of the Estates-General of the League, whose purpose is to "elect" a Catholic King. Very little action taken because of the unpopularity of the Spaniards who attempt to bring about an abolition of the Salic Law and place on the throne of France the Spanish Infanta, daughter of Philip II and Elizabeth de Valois.

April. Conferences held in Suresne between Catholics adhering to Henry IV and moderate *ligueurs*, preparatory to his abjuration of Protestantism.

June. The Parlement de Paris, under the leadership of Jean Le Maistre and Guillaume du Vair, declares the Spanish proposition to set aside the Salic Law invalid, thus solidifying nationalist sentiment, and dealing a blow to the League.

Henry IV asks instruction in Catholic dogma from leading ecclesiastics.

July 25. Henry IV announces his conversion, attends Mass in St. Denis. *Prédicateurs* of Paris denounce it as invalid, and fight a rear-guard action in a Paris increasingly royalist.

August. Adjournment of the Estates of the League, signaling their failure to produce a "Catholic" King.

December. Publication of the *Dialogue d'entre le Maheustre et le Manant,* probably by Cromé, member of the Sixteen, and of the *Satyre Menipée,* satire by a group of leading royalists, including the lawyer Pierre Pithou.

Ridicule poured on the League in latter pamphlet proves of major importance in discrediting the League.

1594   *January–February.* The Duke of Mayenne has increasing difficulty in controlling the city. *Politiques* make secret preparations for the King's entry.

February. Henry IV crowned in Chartres.

March 3. Last meeting of the Sixteen, attended by 300 people.

March 6. The Duke of Mayenne leaves Paris to its fate.

March 22. Reduction of Paris by Henry IV with almost no resistance, amid great rejoicing. Departure of Spaniards.

April–December. Order restored in the city, the Hôtel de Ville and the Parlement. Clemency and magnanimity of Henry IV to all but a handful of League partisans heals wounds of civil war.

EVENTS OF THE REIGN OF HENRY IV
AFTER THE REDUCTION OF PARIS

1595 Pope Clement VIII gives absolution to Henry IV and recognizes him as King.

1595–98 Gradual reduction of other cities of the League.

1598 *March.* Duke of Mercoeur, last of League nobles, surrenders Brittany to the King.

May. Henry IV wins final victory over the Spaniards and concludes the Peace of Vervins with Philip II.

June. Maximilien de Béthune, Marquis of Rosni (later Duke of Sully), becomes Minister of Finance, later also Grand Voyeur and Grand Master of the Artillery of France. Beginning of reconstruction of the kingdom after nearly forty years of civil war.

September. Death of Philip II of Spain.

December–January 1599. Edict of Nantes grants to Huguenots religious freedom (except within five miles of Paris), political equality, and a large number of fortified towns, which they had gained in the course of the wars.

APPENDIX B

GLOSSARY OF TERMS RELATING TO SIXTEENTH-CENTURY FRANCE AND THE WARS OF RELIGION

Bureau de la Ville. Paris was governed partly by a royal official, *Prévost du Roi,* and partly by a *Prévost des Marchands* (mayor) and four *Échevins* (aldermen) and twenty-four *conseillers* who were known collectively as the "Bureau." They had jurisdiction over all affairs relating to business, trade, prices, and the *rentes,* or public bonds, of the city. For details of their election, term of office, etc., see Doucet, *Les Institutions de la France au seizième siécle,* Paris, 1948, vol. I, pp. 360–380. The Bureau was under the general jurisdiction of the Parlement de Paris.

Chambres des Comptes. Sovereign courts with no appeal, established to hear, judge, and verify the accounts of the royal officers of finance (Paris, Dijon, Aix-en-Provence, Grenoble, Nantes, Montpellier, Blois, Rouen, Pau, and Dôle).

Concordat. In the *Mémoires-Journaux* reference is to the Concordat of Bologna, 1516, an arrangement between Francis I and Pope Clement VII by which the French Kings gained still greater powers over the appointment of church offices in France, with the right to control their revenues. This arrangement supplanted the Pragmatic Sanction of Bourges, 1438, under which the French Church was largely self-governing.

Conseiller. See Parlement.

Estates. France under the *ancien régime* was considered to consist of three Estates of the realm, clergy, nobility, and third estate, or commons, which included the bourgeoisie and the peasants.

Estates-General. Sessions called by the King, in which each estate held its own meeting. Dating from the early fourteenth century (Philip IV, the Fair), they played quite a role during the Hundred Years' War. Since they met only when the King called them, were dismissed at will by him, and never acquired the power of the purse, they did not become a check on the monarchy. They were indeed a tool of the kings, who tended to call them when they needed money, which they usually voted to give, at least in part, in return for certain "reforms" of abuses which were listed in the *cahiers* prepared beforehand.

Members of the first and second estates were called by royal writ, by name, e.g., Bishop of Chartres, Count of Soissons. The third estate elected

306

its members. (For details see Doucet, *Les Institutions*, vol. I, pp. 312–337.)

The domination of the Estates of 1577, 1588, and 1593 by the League discredited the institution in the eyes of loyal Frenchmen. Henry IV never called them into being. The last regular session was that of 1614, called by the regent Marie de Medici.

Fundamental Laws. Traditional, unwritten laws which served France as a constitution under the *ancien régime* in the minds of political theorists at least. The Parlement considered themselves the "guardians" of these laws and were quick to protest any action or theory which seemed inconsistent with them. In the late medieval period the two most important ones were: that the royal domain could not be alienated from the crown; and the Salic Law, forbidding the French crown to a woman or to a man whose claim derived from his mother. The most important example was the denial of the claim of Edward III of England to the throne of France through his mother, daughter of Philip IV, 1328.

During the Wars of Religion a third "fundamental law" was asserted, i.e. that the King of France, whose titles included "Most Christian King" and "Eldest Son of the Church," must belong to the Roman Catholic Church.

A conflict developed in the 1590's between those who gave precedence to this third law, namely the extremists of the League, and those who supported the Salic Law, the royalists and *politiques*. The former group wished to set aside the Salic Law and give the throne of France to the Infanta Isabella of Spain, daughter of Philip II, whose claim derived from her mother, Elizabeth Valois, daughter of Henry II, rather than recognize the heretic Henry IV. The *politiques*, on the other hand, supported the Salic Law and defended the claim of Henry IV despite his Calvinist religion. The resolution of this conflict was essential if civil war was to be ended. When Henry IV became a Catholic in July 1593, the conflict was resolved for the great majority of Frenchmen and both laws were thus upheld.

Gallican, Gallicanism. In general a nationalist point of view of the Catholic Church in France:

Ecclesiastical Gallicanism is the point of view that the bishops were established no less than the Pope — which makes for a theoretical decentralization in the church.

Political Gallicanism in France refers to the belief that the Pope has no temporal power, and spiritual power over the church only with the King's consent.

The Pragmatic Sanction of Bourges, 1438, marks the high point of

Ecclesiastical Gallicanism; the Concordat of Bologna, 1516, of Political Gallicanism. For full detail see article of Georges Weill, *Encyclopedia of Social Sciences*, New York, 1937.

Ligueurs. Partisans of the Duke of Guise, adherents to the Holy League, formed in the 1570's to oppose the power of the Huguenots, and later extended to oppose Henry III. Supporters of the rebellion against him in 1588 which continued under Henry IV to 1598.

There were factions in the League, notably the extremists, described as *éspagnolizés* by L'Estoile because they were either in the pay of Spain or followed those who were, and the French *ligueurs*, sometimes called moderates, or *Mayennistes*, because they followed the Duke of Mayenne rather than the clergy and the Spaniards.

Lit de justice. A formal session of the Parlement de Paris, held in the presence of the King, usually in order to force the Parlement to register a royal Edict against their will. Although many theorists of the Parlement throughout the *ancien régime* tried to claim that they had the right to refuse to register if the Edict seemed contrary to "the fundamental laws of the realm," of which they considered themselves the guardians, they never succeeded in establishing their independence in the face of a personal command of the King in a *lit de justice*.

Manant. Parisian slang for ordinary Parisian, of the *petite bourgeoisie*. During the League it came to mean *ligueur*.

Money. In Pierre de l'Estoile's time, Frenchmen had two distinct kinds of "money." One was precious metal, coined by the crown to conform to known weight and purity; the other was simply an artificial system used for accounting. There was seldom any definite relation between these two kinds of money.

In the period 1574–99 there were several types of coins, some gold, some silver. All these coins were believed to have "intrinsic" value — that is, they contained their value within them — so there was no need for a reserve or guarantee on the part of the government. Among the major types of coins were (in gold) *écus de la couronne*, and *écus au soleil*, translated as crowns; (in silver) *francs, testons, quarts d'écu*, and smaller ones.

All accounts, banking, and business transactions were recorded in the fictitious monies of account, which were not coined. Most common was the *livre tournois*, which was divided into 20 *sous*, or 240 *deniers*. Another system, less common but important, was the *livre parisi*. Since the thirteenth century one *livre parisi* had always equaled one and one-fourth *livres tournois*.

There was also an *écu* in the money of account, which equaled *exactly* three *livres tournois*, which is not to be confused with the coined *écu*. Pierre does not indicate in most entries which he means, and it is to be assumed that he means the *écu* of account except when he speaks of *écus de la couronne* specifically.

In November 1577, Henry III attempted to establish a fixed ratio between the two kinds of money — coin and fictitious — but this was contrary to established habit and it never was accepted. In view of the role of financial policy in general in fostering the League Rebellion against him, this is interesting to the reader of the *Mémoires-Journaux*.

The usual procedure of the crown was to define these monies of account by decree, in terms of silver, as France and all European countries were on a "silver standard" at the time; gold was merely a commodity.

In attempting to measure sixteenth-century French money in terms of our money today, there are two elements to be considered: changes in the metallic equivalent of the money, and changes in the price of goods and services.

In terms of metallic weight the modern equivalent of the coined *écu* is about $2.50 (as of January 1958), that of the *livre tournois* about $0.85, and of the *livre parisi* about $1.10. These represent averages for the yearly variations between 1573 and 1600.

Comparing prices is a much more complex problem because it involves changes in the standard of living as well as changes in the price of individual commodities. One estimate is that the cost of living is about seven times as great today, that is, what one ounce of precious metal would buy in 1600 would be worth seven ounces today.

If a pound of butter during the siege of 1590 cost one *écu*, as Pierre reports, that is $2.50, but it would take $17.50 to equal its purchasing power today. If an office in the Parlement cost 7,000 *écus* or 21,000 *livres tournois*, it would correspond to about $17,500 in terms of metallic weight, but in purchasing power nearer $122,000.

The editor is deeply obliged for this information to Mr. Donald Wiedner who generously simplified the relevant material from elaborate tables in his doctoral thesis, "Coins and Accounts in Western European and Colonial History, 1250–1936," Harvard University, 1958.

Palais. In the writings of Pierre de l'Estoile, the Palais de Justice in Paris, seat of the Parlement.

Parlement. There were eight high courts, or Parlements, in France, located in Paris, Bordeaux, Aix-en-Provence, Grenoble, Toulouse, Dijon, Rouen, and Nantes. The Parlement de Paris was not only the oldest, dating from the thirteenth century, but it also outranked all the others. Certain matters of

high importance, such as the registration of treaties and the trials of
Dukes and Peers, were in its exclusive domain, and the area under its
jurisdiction included most of central France, Picardy, and Champagne,
totaling 33 *Baillages* and 17 *seneschausées*.

When no city is named, "Parlement," in the writings of the period,
refers to the Parlement de Paris.

In 1594 there were 188 members, seven *présidents*, the rest *conseillers*,
about evenly split between clergy and laymen.

The *Premier Président* was a member of the King's council, an office
of great power and prestige.

There were two chambers of *Enquêtes*, one of *Requêtes*. For matters
of major importance, such as the registration of Edicts, all the chambers
met in full session, Grand' Chambre.

All royal cases, ecclesiastical matters (including heresy) and cases
"evoked" by the King came to the Parlement de Paris directly, and cases
from other Parlements and all matters of conflicting jurisdiction could be
appealed to it. Doucet says *competence illimité*, but never clearly defined.

The theory was that the King had delegated his judicial powers to the
Parlement, but when he appeared for a *lit de justice* they reverted to him.

The Chancellor was the royal official in most constant contact with the
Parlement. He was usually an *ancien parlementaire* himself. Some of the
resentment against the Italian Biragues, Chancellor of Henry III, stemmed
from his lack of this background, and the fact that he was instead a royal
favorite.

For full detail see Doucet, *Les Institutions*, vol. I, pp. 167–187.

Politique. A royalist partisan, opposite of *ligueur*. The *politiques* as a party
were Catholic in a nationalist rather than in a Counter-Reformation sense.
They remained loyal to Henry III despite great disapproval of his policies,
and supported Henry IV before his conversion. The gradual realization
that the League was a tool of Spain, which threatened the dissolution of
the kingdom, made most Frenchmen *politiques* by 1593. *Maheustre* was
a slang synonym for *politique*, as in the *Dialogue of the Maheustre and
the Manant*, which might be rendered, "Dialogue between a royalist and
a *ligueur*."

Président. See Parlement.

Procureurs. Agents with legal training, licensed to represent litigants in the
Parlements. Office became hereditary under Henry III. Ordinances regu-
lated persons entitled to their services and circumstances in which one
might avail oneself of a *procureur*.

Procureur-Général, somewhat like Attorney General in the United

States, represented the Crown in cases before the Parlement de Paris.

Salic Law. See Fundamental Laws.

Satyre, Satyre Menipée. *Politique* satire on the League by a group of leading royalists. Its appearance in December 1593 was one of the causes of the collapse of the League. Witty and well written, it is a very effective example of the force of ridicule as a political weapon.

Sixteen. The Paris League was organized by occupations in the corporations, and in the sixteen quarters of the city. Actually there were far more than sixteen leaders, but this word came to apply to the extreme League faction as such. L'Estoile speaks, for instance, of Senault as "the leading Sixteen of our quarter," on another occasion he concedes that someone is "quite bright, for a Sixteen." Again, he refers to "a meeting of 300 of the Sixteen."

Trent, Council of, 1545–63. Meeting of leaders of Catholic Church (Bishops, Heads of Orders) in which the Society of Jesus played a leading part. It reaffirmed all major tenets of dogma challenged by the reformers, and organized the Church to combat heresy. Its decrees, reasserting papal power, were very controversial in France. In general they were supported by the League, but not by the Gallicans, which included the Parlements and most of the leading bishops.

INDEX

Reference is made only to the text of the *Mémoires-Journaux*. Many place names and those of obscure persons are omitted. Titled persons will be found under the principal surname, e.g. Guise, (3rd) Duke of, (Henri de Lorraine). Other names will be found under surname, not particle, e.g. Thou, Christophe de, except where the particle forms part of the name, e.g. Du Moulin. Principal alternate spellings and other titles are also given.

Acarie, Pierre, 205, 212, 220
Alençon, Duke d' (François de Valois), Monsieur, brother of Henry III, heir apparent, d. 1584; 32, 33, 34, 37, 44, 85, 92, 103; and Elizabeth, 71, 78, 79, 84; and Henry III, 42, 44, 49, 63, 68, 70, 79, 81, 99; and Catherine de Medici, 45, 49; and Henry of Navarre, 47; and Flanders, 61, 65, 66, 84, 92, 95; illness and death of, 100–102; and League, 102, 105; and Huguenots, 105
Alexander, Colonel of the Neapolitans, 202, 209, 211, 227. *See also* Spaniards in France
Ameline, *ligueur*, 205, 212, 213, 216
America, 122
Amiens, Siege of, 283–285 *passim*
Amyot, Jacques, Bishop of Auxerre, 33
Anroux, *ligueur*, 213, 214
Antwerp, 54–55, 84, 92
Armada, 157–158
Arnauld, Antoine, 267
Arques. *See* Joyeuse
Arques, battle of, 184
Aubray, Claude d', Colonel, 239, 240, 259
Aubry, Christophe, *Curé* of St. André-des-Arts, 138, 185, 193, 194, 199, 201, 203–204, 210, 211, 217, 218, 227, 229, 230, 231, 233, 235, 236, 239, 240, 241, 258, 259, 260
Augustinians, 93, 186, 263
Aumale, Duke d' (Charles of Lorraine), 65, 88, 111, 140, 141, 165, 168, 171, 172
Auneau, 135
Aussonne, 110, 115
Austria, Cardinal of, 279

Baïf, Lazare, 81
Baillon, Jean de, 52
Balafré, Le. *See* Guise, (3rd) Duke of
Barricades, Day of, 146–151, 178, 231
Barrière, Pierre, 241–242
Béarnais, Le. *See* Henry of Navarre

Beaune, Renault de, Archbishop of Bourges, 102, 159, 262
Beauvais-La Nocle, Jean, 48
Beauvais-Nangis, 65
Belin, Count of (Jean-François de Faudoas), Governor of Paris, 212, 216, 219, 227, 229
Bellemanière (pseud. Pierre de l'Estoile 1592), 220
Bellièvre, Pomponne de, Chancellor and diplomat, 76, 81, 95, 122, 124–125, 145, 150, 159, 244
Benoist, René, *Curé* of St. Eustache, 139, 174, 192, 230, 232
Bernard, Brother, Little Feuillant, 132–133, 169
Bernardines. *See* Feuillants
Beza, Theodore, 158, 195, 286
Biragues, René de, Cardinal and chancellor, 43, 64, 66, 80, 97
Biron, Baron and Marshal (Armand de Gontaut), 148, 150, 184
Bodin, Jean, 57
Bouchage, Sieur de, (Brother Angel, Henri de Joyeuse), 153
Boucher, Jean, *Curé* of St. Benedict, 131, 133, 136, 138, 180, 189, 193, 198, 200, 203, 204, 216, 221, 231, 236, 240, 249, 253, 255, 261, 290
Bouillon, Duke of (d. 1588), 109
Bouillon, Duke of, Marshal (Henri de la Tour-d'Auvergne), Vicomte de Turenne, 269, 290, 293
Bourbon, (1st) Cardinal of (Charles de Bourbon), Archbishop of Rouen, proclaimed King by League 1589, d. 1590, 52, 67, 68, 81, 112, 134, 140, 155, 157, 168, 182, 188, 214
Bourbon, (2nd) Cardinal of (Charles de Bourbon), Cardinal of Vendôme, inherited uncle's titles 1590; d. 1594, 225, 231, 268
Bourbon, Catherine de. *See* Catherine de Bourbon

INDEX

Bourbon, House of, 109, 188, 234

Brigard, Jean, 145, 152, 199, 204, 205, 206

Brissac, Charles, Marshal, Governor of Paris, 148, 150, 254, 255, 257, 258, 259, 260

Brisson, Barnabé, Président, 76, 78, 88, 170–171, 191, 204–212, 214, 224, 236, 262, 263, 268, 275

Brulart (Brulard), Pierre, Secretary of State, 150, 159

Bureau de la Ville. See Paris, Bureau de la Ville

Bussi-LeClerc, Jean, 151–152, 156, 158, 169–170, 197, 199, 205, 206, 209, 212, 213, 214, 218

Bussy d'Amboise, 58–59, 62, 63, 66, 71–72

Caesar, Duke of Vendôme, son of Henry IV and Gabrielle d'Estrées, 205, 287

Cajetan, Cardinal (Henri), Papal Legate, 186, 187, 193, 194, 195

Calendar, reformation of, 90

Canaie, Philippe, Sieur de Fresnes, 244

Capet, Hugh, 109

Capet, House of, 54

Capuchins, 119, 126, 153, 187, 219

Casauban, Isaac, 292

Casimir, Duke of, John, 216

Catherine de Bourbon, Madame, sister of Henry IV, 228, 242, 262, 269–270, 271, 274, 282, 285, 293, 295

Catherine de Medici, Queen of France, Queen Mother; wife of Henry II, 59, 61, 77, 82; regency of, 31–32; reputation of, 36, 41, 42, 44, 53, 113, 156, 228; and Cardinal of Lorraine, 39; and Henry III, 41; reconciliation of children, 45, 63, 67, 99; policy of, 79, 87, 135; and Bourbons, 113, 168; and Guises, 113, 145, 150, 152, 156, 161, 168; on Coutras, 134; and Day of Barricades, 150, 152; death of, 167–168

Ceuilly, Jacques, Curé of St. Germain-l'Auxerrois, 131, 199, 200, 204, 218, 219, 234, 236, 239, 251, 259

Châlons, Parlement of, 203, 204

Charlemagne, 109

Charles IX, 1560–1574, 31, 32, 33, 127, 216, 279

Charles, Grand Prior of France, Monsieur, 132

Chartier, Mathieu, 88, 213

Chartres, Siege of, 198–200

Chastel, Jean, 270–271, 290

Châtillon, Sieur de (François de Coligny), 178, 184, 215

Chavagnac, Curé of St. Sulpice, 192, 200, 232, 233

Cheverny, Count of (Philippe de Hurault), Garde des Sceaux, 88, 94, 158

Chicot, Court fool, 217, 249

Cimier, Jean de, 63, 66

Civil War, 31, 36, 38, 40, 42, 46, 49, 51, 57, 59, 60, 65, 67, 73, 94, 111, 115–116, 118, 124, 141, 178, 194, 230, 242, 248

Claude de France, Duchess of Lorraine, 113

Clément, Jacques, 180–184, 186, 204

Clergy, 57 and passim; divisions of, 53, 118, 192, 233; and Mayenne, 199, 201, 232, 245. See also Clerical offensive; Gallicanism; Henry III, and clergy; League, and clergy

Clerical offensive, 129, 130, 131, 132, 133–134, 136, 138, 150, 167, 172, 177, 179, 183, 186, 188, 190, 193, 198–201, 203, 216, 217, 218, 226, 227, 230, 233–235, 236, 238–240, 244, 246, 248, 251, 253, 254, 255, 258, 259, 282, 293

Clothes, regulation of, 96, 107

Coconas, 32

Coligny, Gaspard, Admiral of France, d. 1572; 44, 48, 51, 178

Collège de Forteret, 127

Commolet, Jacques, Jesuit prédicateur, 199, 200, 204, 218, 229, 230, 245, 247, 261

Compans, Jean, Échevin, 152, 156

Condé, Princess of, 41

Condé, Prince of (Henry I de Bourbon), d. 1588, 35, 37, 47, 56, 59, 83, 114, 140

Condé, Prince of (Henri II de Bourbon), heir-apparent to crown until 1601, 273, 277, 278, 280, 289

Conti, Marquis and Prince of (François de Bourbon), Prince of the Blood, son of Louis I de Bourbon, Prince of Condé, 78, 83, 225, 236, 244

Cordeliers, 77, 179, 183, 190, 213, 237

Corse, Alphonse. See Ornano

Cossé, Marshal, 32, 45, 62, 78

Cost of living, 41, 91, 120, 129, 132, 275, 293

Cotteblanche, François, 152, 156

Cotton, André-Gerard, 193, 205, 211

Counter Reformation, 86, 108, 291. See also Clerical offensive; Council of Trent; Papacy; Society of Jesus

314

Court festivities, 59, 61, 69, 80–83, 89, 108, 274, 283, 288–289, 292

Coutras, Battle of, 134

Crime, 57, 74, 100, 140, 217

Crocants, League of, 267

Cromé (Marin-Cromé), Louis, 205, 206, 209, 212, 214, 224, 247. See also *Manant*

Crucé, Oudin, 209, 212, 246

Cujas, Jacques, 195

Damville, Count of. *See* Montmorency, Marshal (Henri)

David, Jean, 54

Davy, Jacques. *See* Du Perron

De Moraines, Claude, *Curé* of St. Merry, 230

Denmark, 58, 119

Des Près, Robert, Échevin, 152, 224

Dijon, 110

Disease, 74, 75, 196, 216, 225, 274–275, 280, 294

D'O, François, Governor of Paris, 148, 150, 161, 231, 244, 252, 263, 270

Domont (Aumont), Jean, Marshal, 148, 163

Don Antonio, King of Portugal, 86, 276

Don Juan of Austria, 54, 68

D'Orléans, Louis, 210, 214, 220–221, 249, 261

Dormans, battle of, 45

D'Ossat, Cardinal (Arnaud), 276

Drake, Sir Francis, 122

Du Bourg, Governor of Bastille, 213, 216, 259

Du Cerceau, Baptiste Androuet, 65, 116–117

Du Perron, Cardinal (Jacques Davy), Bishop of Evreux, 97, 276, 291

Du Vair, Guillaume, 234, 235

Economic conditions, 75, 120, 122, 190–193, 227–228, 243–244, 271, 274, 275, 278, 279

Edict of January, 1562; 251, 270

Edict of Nantes, 1598–99, 291, 293, 295–296

Edict of Pacification. *See* Edict of January; Edict of Nantes; Edict of Union; Peace of Monsieur

Edict of 1577. *See* Peace of Monsieur

Edict of Union, 1588, 154, 156, 160

Elbeoeuf, Marquis and Duke d' (Charles of Lorraine), 65, 85, 162

Elizabeth of Austria (Isabella), Queen of France, wife of Charles IX, 31, 216

Elizabeth, Queen of England, 58, 104, 122, 127–128, 131, 234; and Alençon, 71, 78, 79, 84; and Henry III, 107–108, 122–123, 124–125; and Mary Stuart, 124–125

Emmonot, *ligueur*, 185, 213–214

England, 107, 122, 157–158; ambassadors from, 151–152, 257

Entragues, Seigneur de (Charles de Balsac), 64, 110

Épernay, treaty of, 111

Épernon, Duke d' (Bernard de Nogaret), Seigneur de la Valette, 78, 83, 85, 88, 101, 113, 129, 133, 140, 141, 154, 156

Ernest, Archduke of Hapsburg, 234

Espinac (Épinac) Archbishop of Lyons (Louis d'), M. de Lyons, highest ranking member of clergy to join League, turned *politique* 1593, 57, 146, 147, 156, 163–164, 192, 226, 229, 233

Estates General: of 1577, 56–57, 73; of 1588, 159–162; of 1593 (of the League), 202, 222, 223, 224–234

Este, Alphonse d', Duke of Ferrara, 80

Estienne, Henri d', 112, 287

Estrées, Diane d', 278

Estrées, Gabrielle d'. *See* Gabrielle

Faye, Jacques, 76, 118, 150

Feria, Duke of, Spaniard, special envoy of Philip II to League, 226–227, 228, 231, 233, 234, 235, 236, 247, 252, 257. *See also* Spaniards in France

Ferrières, Jean de, *Curé* of St. Nicholas des Champs, 159

Feuardant, League *prédicateur*, 218, 226, 234

Feuillants, 132, 187

Filles-Dieu, 262

Flanders, 61, 65, 66, 75, 79, 81, 84, 92, 95, 107, 108. *See also* Henry III, foreign policy, Flanders

Forty-five, Gascons (bodyguard of Henry III), 141, 163

Four, Guy du, Sieur de Pybrac, Président, 67, 106, 273

François II, 1559–1560, 128

Fundamental laws, 231

Funerals, 33, 56, 74, 88, 97–98, 102

Gabrielle d'Estrées, Countess of Liancourt and La Roche-Guyon, Marquise of Mousseaux, Duchess of Beaufort, Mistress of Henry IV, 194, 237, 238, 240, 270, 278,

INDEX

279, 282, 284, 285, 288, 289, 290, 291, 292, 293

Gallicanism, 114–115, 118, 203. *See also* Clergy, divisions of; L'Estoile, *politique*, on religion; *Politiques*

Gelosi, I, Italian players, 58–60

Genébrard, Gilbert, 212, 226, 234

Germanies, 58, 123

Gohorri, Secretary of Henry IV, 190

Gondi, Albert de, Marshal, Count and Duke of Retz, 33, 85, 139

Gondi, Alphonse de, 38

Gondi, Hièrome de, 100

Gondi, Pierre de, Cardinal, Bishop of Paris, 33, 53, 168, 192, 269, 278

Gregory XIII, Pope, 110

Gregory XIV, Pope, 196, 198

Guarinus, Jean, Cordelier, 204, 218, 224, 234, 239, 240, 245, 246–247, 248, 251, 253, 254

Guesle, Charles de la, Procureur General, 91, 153

Guesle, François de, Archbishop of Tours, 291

Guesle, Jean de la, Procureur General and Président, 91, 153, 180

Guische, Philibert de la, Grand Master of Artillery, 244

Guise, (1st) Cardinal of (Louis de Lorraine), d. 1578, 64

Guise, (2nd) Cardinal of (Louis de Guise) Archbishop of Rheims, brother of 3rd Duke, assassinated 1588, 64, 65, 93, 159, 160, 163–164

Guise, (2nd) Duke of (François de Guise), d. 1563, 163, 279

Guise, (3rd) Duke of (Henri de Lorraine, Henri de Guise), leader of League Rebellion, assassinated 1588; 45, 48 and *passim*, leadership of, 53, 145, 155, 157; and *mignons*, 67, 85; and Henry III, 118–119, 136–137, 145, 157, 160, 161–164; reputation of, 119, 135, 136, 146–148, 167, 172, 173; Day of Barricades, 145–152; assassination of, 162–164

Guise, House of, 112, 268 and *passim. See also* Guise-Lorraine

Guise-Lorraine, 54, 56, 57, 65, 77, 94, 109, 128

Hamilton, Jean (Scot), *Curé* of St. Cosme, 131, 188, 205, 206, 209, 212, 253, 254

Harlay, Achille de, Seigneur de Beaumont,

Premier Président, 88, 91, 167, 169, 283–284, 285, 290

Henry III, King of France, 1574–1589, (Henri de Valois), return to France, 34–35; foreign policy, Germanies, 35, 123, Flanders, 61, 65, 79, 107, Denmark, 119, Swiss Cantons, 84, 85, 89, Ottoman Empire, 83, Venice, 111; and nobility, 35; religion of, 35, 45, 53, 67, 93, 96, 97, 100, 105–106, 119, 120, 126, 138, 141, 153; and Roman Catholic Church, 35, 56; financial policy, 38, 39, 41, 46, 49, 50–51, 53, 60, 68, 79, 85, 87, 90, 91, 93, 115, 120, 121, 126, 130, 131; and clergy, 39, 67, 92, 118; coronation, 40; marriage, 40; and Henry of Navarre, 42, 68, 95–96, 101, 105, 120, 176–177; diversions of, 45, 47, 58, 73, 77, 78, 92, 99, 109, 113, 126, 133, 139; weakness of, 46, 57, 59, 65, 69, 79, 92, 94, 107, 109, 119, 120, 121, 126, 129, 130, 138, 139, 159; reputation of, 54, 65, 106, 112, 121, 135, 136; extravagance of, 58, 59, 80–81, 85, 133; patron of arts, 58, 70, 80–82, 116; government of, 62, 86, 99, 112, 118, 158–159; and *mignons*, 62, 64–65, 66–67; health of, 66, 72; humor of, 68, 105, 136, 156, 157, 173; character of, 93, 105, 110, 133, 134, 135, 141, 156; Day of Barricades, 146–151, 153, 160; assassination of, 180–182. *See also* Alençon; Catherine de Medici; Elizabeth; Huguenots; League; Parlement

Henry of Navarre, King of France and Navarre, Henry IV, 1589–1610 (Henri de Bourbon), 32, 37, 41, and *passim*; escape from Paris, 47–48; religion of, 47, 101, 105, 123, 161, 217, 232, 237, 249, 274; humor of, 48, 68, 96, 141, 187, 190, 210, 224, 252, 257, 272, 284, 287, 289; and Marguerite de Valois, 95–96; claim to throne, 101, 114–115, 156, 161, 177, 186; excommunication of, 114–115, 130; leadership of, 134, 184, 185, 187, 189, 248, 270, 272, 281, 283, 287, 291, 292, 295–296; character of, 176, 196, 272, 275, 285–286; magnanimity of, 179–180, 189, 193, 247, 255–264, 271; accession to throne, 181–182; *amours*, 194, 237, 279, 284; conversion of, 199, 221, 229–230, 232, 235, 237–240, 241; and Mayenne, 232, 248, 278; poverty of, 252, 279; coronation, 253; and Paris, 255–264,

268–269; and Parlement, 259, 281, 283–284; health of, 274, 292; absolution of, 276; foreign policy, Netherlands, 288; legend of, 289–290. *See also* Alençon; Guise; Henry III; Huguenots; League; Spain

Hieronimites, 96, 141

Holy League. *See* League

Hotel-Dieu, 262, 279, 280

Huguenots, 40, 109, 262 and *passim*; persecution of, 32, 42, 74, 77, 100, 116, 126, 129, 139, 155, 197, 228, 269–270, 285, 293; and Henry III, 35, 48–49, 50, 74, 112, 126, 129; propaganda of, 37, 39, 98, 116; forces of, 38, 51, 56, 58, 140; concessions to, 50, 112, 274, 295–296; fears of, 52, 54, 69, 72, 244; conversions of, 116–117, 284; and Henry of Navarre, 229, 231, 238–239, 244–245, 269, 282, 293; demands of, 251, 270, 291, 293, 295–296. *See also* Edicts; League, and Huguenots; Parlement, and Huguenots

Inquisition, 86

Isabella of France, 31

Isabella, Infanta of Spain, daughter of Philip II, granddaughter of Henry II of France through her mother, Elizabeth Valois, 231, 234, 235, 236

Italians, 43–44, 58, 58–60, 93, 197

Ivry, battle of, 187

Jacobins, 179, 180–184, 186, 204, 260

Journée de Pain, 190–192

Joyeuse, Duke of (Anne, Seigneur d'Arques), 78, 80–83, 85, 86, 88, 113, 129, 134

Joyeuse family, 94, 153

La Bruyère, *ligueur*, 205, 206, 209, 212, 243, 246

La Chapelle-Marteau (Michel Marteau), Prévost des Marchands, 153, 156, 159, 189, 222

La Faye, Huguenot minister, 238

La Mersilière, Secretary of Henry of Navarre, 120

La Motte-Fenelon, 78, 245

Langlois, Martin, Prévost des Marchands, 205, 206, 212, 214, 227, 245, 250, 255, 260

La Noue, François, Seigneur de, *Bras-de-Fer*, 75, 178, 194, 223

Lanssac, Seigneur de (Guy de St. Gelais), 78, 124

La Ramée (natural son of Charles IX), 279

Larcher, Claude, 208, 209, 236

La Rue, Pierre, 165, 209, 214, 224, 280

Launay (Launoy), Mathieu de, 205–206, 212, 214

La Valette family, 78, 85. *See also* Épernon

Law, customary, 73

League: origin of, 51, 53, 109; and Parlement, 53, 57–58, 155, 167, 169, 175, 191, 199, 204, 206, 216, 253, 255; propaganda of, 54, 57, 65, 69, 77, 93, 94, 102, 105–106, 119, 121, 123, 128, 132, 133–134, 138, 140, 171, 177, 186, 261, 290; and clergy, 56; and Henry of Navarre, 56, 123, 161–162, 198, 214, 226, 228, 271; organization of, 57, 152, 154, 174–175; opposition to, 58, 201; and Henry III, 58, 68, 92, 109–110, 111–112, 116, 123, 129, 131, 135, 138, 145–151, 153–154, 156–157, 160, 165, 171, 175; and Huguenots, 77; growth of, 109–110, 111, 112, 116, 120, 121, 123; resources of, 154, 168–169, 188; printers of, 174, 246, 261; divisions of, 201, 204, 206, 210, 212, 214, 218, 220, 221, 228, 229, 231, 234, 236, 237, 239, 246; decline of, 209, 228, 233, 234, 240, 242, 244, 252, 253, 259, 261, 268, 274. *See also* Clerical offensive; Papacy; *Politiques*; Spain

Legate, Papal, 186, 193, 233, 235, 241, 253. *See also* Cajetan; Medici

Le Maistre, Jean, Président, 210, 211, 213, 226, 234, 235, 236, 246, 260

Lenoncourt, Cardinal, Philippe de, 150, 202

Les Belles Figures et Drolleries de la Ligue, 177

Lesdiguières, Duke and Marshal (François de Bonne), 282, 284

L'Estoile, Pierre de, on religion, 34, 66, 97, 111, 132, 156, 245; on League, 53, 77, 92, 94, 108–109, 112, 131; on the people, 54, 56, 156, 174–175, 279; *moraliste*, 60, 62, 71, 72, 73, 78, 89, 101, 106, 113, 119–120, 128, 133, 139, 140, 158, 164, 177, 181–184, 187, 194, 195–196, 223, 259, 269, 275–276, 279, 280, 283, 289, 294; curiosity of, 61, 90, 118, 119–120, 222; on sale of offices, 64, 76; on Henry III, 72, 92, 106, 119, 151, 156, 162, 164–165, 181–182; skepticism of, 76, 106, 127, 201; on war, 92, 115; *politique*, 104–105, 109, 116, 121, 125, 147, 156, 185; author of reply to papal bull, 114–115; gallicanism, 114–115; objectivity of, 135, 193; on Day of Barricades, 147–151; predicament in *ligueur* Paris, 165, 180, 210–211, 220; collection of, 177; on Henry of Navarre, 283, 284, 286 and *passim*

L'Estoile family, 115, 185, 192, 195, 245, 275

L'Huillier (L'Huilier), Jean, Prévost des Marchands, 220

Liancourt, Madame de. *See* Gabrielle d'Estrées

Lincestre, Jean, *Curé* of St. Gervais, 138, 159, 165, 167, 204, 233, 235, 261

Longueville, Duke of (Henri I d'Orléans), 178

Lorraine, (2nd) Cardinal of (Charles de Guise), d. 1574, 39, 109

Lorraine, (3rd) Cardinal of (Charles de Lorraine), d. 1607, 63

Lorraine, Duke of (Charles III), 42, 65, 94, 235, 295

Lorraine, Henri de. *See* Guise, (3rd) Duke of

Lorraine, House of, 113, 140. *See also* Guise, House of; Guise-Lorraine

Lorraine, Marguerite de, Duchess of Joyeuse, 80

Lothair, 109

Louchard, Anselme, 170, 205, 209, 212, 213, 216

Louise de Vaudemont (Lorraine), Queen of France, wife of Henry III, 40, 60, 76, 86, 134

Lugoli, Pierre, *Échevin*, 152, 242, 259

Lyons, M. de. *See* Espinac

Lyons, 36, 242, 252, 276

Macon, 110

Madame. *See* Catherine de Bourbon

Malmédy, physician, 75, 100–101

Manant, Dialogue d'entre le Maheustre et le Manant, 1593, 245–247

Marcel, Claude, 61

Marchaumont, Sieur de (Clause), 152–153

Marguerite de France, Duchess of Savoy, 34, 36

Marguerite de Valois, Queen of Navarre, sister of Henry III, wife of Henry IV, 67, 95, 111, 115

Marseilles, 110, 279

Martin, Blasius, League *prédicateur*, 204, 212, 218, 223

Mary Stuart, 122–123, 124–125, 127–128

Mattignon, Marshal of, 115, 255

Maurevert, 51, 71

Maurice, Count of Nassau, 288

Maximilian of Hapsburg, Holy Roman Emperor, 56, 216

Mayenne, Duke of (Charles de Lorraine), leader of League after 1588, brother of 3rd Duke Henri de Guise, 53, 65, 67, 93, 120, 214, 222, 253, 293 and *passim*; leadership of, 174, 175, 179, 185, 189, 190, 194, 212, 222, 232, 234, 236, 250, 251; and Spain, 196, 235, 250, 252; and Sixteen, 210, 212, 214, 220, 224, 245–247, 250, 253

Medici, Alexander de, Cardinal of Florence, 280

Medici, Catherine de. *See* Catherine de Medici

Medici family, 168

Medicine, 74, 76

Memoires of State and Religion under Charles IX, 37

Mendoza, Don Bernadino, Spanish ambassador to League, 188, 193

Mercenaries: German, 37, 40, 74; Swiss, 135, 141, 146, 148

Mercoeur, Duke of (Philippe Emmanuel of Lorraine), 236, 285, 287

Mercoeur, Madame de, 236, 287

Méru, Seigneur de (Charles de Montmorency), 149

Metz, Marshal, 163

Mignons, 52, 60, 62, 63–67, 69, 70, 78, 80, 82, 85, 86, 92, 93, 99, 126, 139

Miron, François, 113

Miron, Marc, 161

Molé, Edouard, Président, 191, 231

Monsieur. *See* Alençon; Charles, Grand Prior of France

Mont-Saint-Michel, 60

Monthelon, François de, *Garde des Sceaux*, 159, 195

Monthelon family, 211

Montmorency (1st) Marshal and Duke (François), d. 1579, 32, 45, 66, 70

Montmorency, (2nd) Marshal and Duke of (Henri), Count of Damville, 38, 40, 56, 59, 94, 282

Montpensier, (1st) Duke of (Louis II de Bourbon), Prince of the Blood, d. 1582, 49, 67, 87

Montpensier, (2nd) Duke of (François de Bourbon), d. 1592; 110, 150, 218

Montpensier, (3rd) Duke of (Henri de Bourbon), d. 1608; 225, 236, 292

Montpensier, Duchess of, Madame de (Catherine de Lorraine), sister of 3rd Duke (Henri) de Guise, and Mayenne, 131, 134, 138, 152, 159, 171, 177, 182, 190, 192, 256, 258, 260, 268, 271, 280

Montsoreau, Seigneur de, 71

Mousseaux, Marquise de. *See* Gabrielle d'Estrées

Natural phenomena, 44, 61, 85

Neapolitans. *See* Spaniards in France

Nemours (Nemoux), (1st) Duke of (Jacques), Duke of Savoy, d. 1585, 53, 88

Nemours, (2nd) Duke of (Charles Emanuel), Duke of Savoy, Governor of Lyons, d. 1595, 160–161, 173, 191, 193, 196, 242, 276, 282, 284

Nemours, Duchess of, Madame de, (Anne d'Este) wife of (2nd) Duke François de Guise, mother of (3rd) Duke of Guise and Mayenne, later wife of Jacques, Duke of Savoy and Nemours, 183, 211, 217, 242, 258, 268

Neuilly, Jean, Président, 50, 153, 213, 255

Nevers, Duke of (Louis de Gonzague), Governor of Normandy, Picardy and Champagne, 88, 202, 243, 244, 276

Nobility, 56, 57

Offices, sale of, 64, 76, 86, 104

Orange, Prince of (William I), 84, 103

Order of the Garter, 108

Order of the Holy Spirit, 69, 119, 126

Order of St. John of Jerusalem, 132

Order of St. Michael, 33

Orléans, 110, 252

Ornano, Marshal (Alphonse Corse), 146, 148, 252

Palais de Justice, 116 and *passim*

Palissy, Bernard, 197

Panigarole, Francois, Bishop of Ast, 197

Papacy, 51, 63, 86, 90, 104, 108, 114, 158, 194–195, 196; and League, 110, 136–137, 198, 201–202; and Henry of Navarre, 114, 243–244, 276. *See also* Clerical offensive; Counter-Reformation; Sixtus V

Paré, Ambrose, 196

Paris, Bureau de la Ville, 35, 75, 88, 89 and *passim*; and Henry III, 46, 51, 91, 149–153 and *passim*; Day of Barricades, 149, 152–153, 154; and Mayenne, 222; and Henry of Navarre, 257–258

Paris, *passim*; rumors in, 37, 41, 192, 201, 202, 218, 220, 227, 232, 234, 247–248, 255; religious atmosphere of, 49, 90, 159, 174, 200, 291; religious processions in, 93, 96, 100, 153, 172, 173–174, 200; defense of, 109–110, 119, 126, 135, 146–147, 154–155, 179, 254–255; leadership of, 121; Siege of 1590, 187–193; population of, 1590, 188; reputation of, 202; reduction of, 255–264

Parlement de Paris, *passim*; and Henry III, 49, 50, 51, 60, 79–80, 93, 120–121, 126, 130, 131, 165, 171, 180; and Huguenots, 51, 269, 273, 295–296; nepotism of, 76–77; and Roman Catholic Church, 114, 254; and fundamental laws, 234–235; and Henry of Navarre, 283–284. *See also* Brisson; De Thou; Edicts; Harlay; League; Offices, sale of

Parma, Duke of, 95, 103, 107, 137, 196, 217, 222

Parma, Prince of, 194, 217

Peace of Monsieur, 49–53, 56, 270, 272–273, 293

Pelletier, Julien, *Curé* of St. Jacques, 131, 188, 209, 218, 224, 225, 235, 254, 258

Pellevé, Cardinal (Nicolas de), Bishop of Amiens and Sens, 124, 224, 225, 228, 260

Penitents, 93, 100, 119

Perreuse, Seigneur de (Hector de Marle), Prévost des Marchands, 152

Philip II, King of Spain, 51, 75, 79, 86, 87, 89, 95, 107, 111, 122, 201, 211, 225, 231, 234, 235, 236, 288, 291

Pigenat, François, *Curé* of St. Michael, 138, 159, 172

Pilon, Germain, 116

Pinart (Pinard), Charles, Seigneur de Cremailles, Secretary of State, 38, 78, 150, 159

Pisani, Marquis of (Jean de Vivonne), 277, 289

Pithou, Pierre, 280

Plague, 74, 75, 77, 105, 196, 216

Plessis-Mornay, Philippe du, 105, 244, 249, 251, 285, 290–291, 293

Politique, position, 57, 131, 154, 165, 172, 175, 178, 180, 183, 191, 192, 200, 204, 206, 209, 252 and *passim*. *See also* L'Estoile, *Politique*; Clergy, divisions of; League, divisions of

Politiques, 126, 140, 152, 154, 165, 172, 180, 191, 198, 200, 204, 206, 209, 210–211, 219, 228, 254

Poncet, Maurice, *Curé* of St. Pierre-des-Arts, 94, 121, 123
Pont, Marquis of (Henri de Lorraine), Duke of Bar, 295
Pont-Aux-Musniers, 281
Pont Neuf, 65
Pontcarré, Camus de, 244, 272
Portugal, 74, 87
Poussemouthe family, 207
Prévost, Jean, *Curé* of St. Severin, 88, 131, 133, 138, 139, 192, 207–208
Prévost des Marchands. *See* La Chapelle-Marteau; Langlois; L'Huillier; Neuilly; Paris, Bureau de la Ville; Perreuse
Procureurs, 120–121
Public Good, League of, 44, 87
Pybrac. *See* Four

Queen Louise. *See* Louise de Vaudemont
Queen Mother. *See* Catherine de Medici
Queen Mother of League. *See* Nemours
Queen of Navarre. *See* Marguerite de Valois
Quélus, Seigneur, 63, 64, 66

Rainssant, *ligueur*, 205, 212, 224
Ramus, Pierre, 283
Rancher, Pierre du, 76, 273
Rapin, Nicholas, 133, 176
Regicide, 103, 104, 122, 241, 242, 271, 288. *See also* Clément; Clerical offensive; Society of Jesus
Religious toleration, 77. *See also* Edicts; Huguenots, demands
Rentes, 50–51, 91, 130, 281
Retelois, Duke of (Charles de Gonzague), 276
Retz, Duke of. *See* Gondi
Réveille-Matin, 37
Rivière (La Rivière), 149, 290
Rohan, Duke of, Henry, 244
Rolland (Roland) brothers, 130, 210
Ronsard, Pierre de, 81, 117
Rose, Guillaume, Bishop of Senlis, 92–93, 131, 187, 200, 204, 218, 229, 231, 234
Rosières, François de, Archdeacon of Toul, 94
Rosny (Rosni), Marquis of (Maxmilien de Bethune), 244, 289

St. André-des-Arts, church of, 88; *curé* and parish. *See* Aubry
Sainte Chapelle, 70
St. Cloud, 180–184 *passim*

St. Denis, 189, 202, 218, 220, 230, 236, 237
Ste.-Geneviève, chariot of, 90, 131, 175, 255
St. Germain, fair of, 48, 69, 99, 139, 282
St. Séverin, day of, 133–134
Salic Law, 231, 234
Salignac, Baron of (Jean de Gontaut-Biron), 77
Saluces, Marquisate of, 160
Sancy, Baron of (Nicolas de Harlay), Superintendent of Finances, 244, 261, 282, 284, 289
Sanguin, *ligueur*, 206, 212, 228, 275
Savoy, Duke of (Charles-Emmanuel). *See* Nemours
Savoy, Duke of (Henry), 288
Savoy, Duchess of. *See* Marguerite de France
Schomberg (Chomberg), Marshal, Gaspard, 244
Scotland, 116
Sebastian, King of Portugal, 74
Séguier, M. le Doyen, 227, 236
Séguier, Pierre, Président, 50, 76
Séguier (Villiers-Séguier), Antoine, 147, 267, 291, 293
Séguier family, 76
Semmoneux, 220, 221, 222, 223, 230
Senault, Pierre, 160, 165, 170, 174–175, 183, 192, 211, 212, 218, 228, 229, 240, 253, 259
Seneçay, Baron of (Claude de Bauffremont), 57, 159
Serres, Jean de, 288
Sillery, Sieur de (Nicolas Brulart), 296
Sixteen, Council of, 165, 168, 170, 174–175, 180, 185, 192, 203, 204, 209–214, 216, 218, 226, 232, 236, 240–241, 242, 245, 246, 249, 251, 253, 254
Sixtus V, Pope, 111, 114
Society of Jesus (Jesuits), 103, 104, 116, 191, 241, 242, 249, 254, 267, 271, 272, 286, 288, 290
Sorbonne, (Faculty of Theology, University of Paris), 131, 135, 171, 183, 186, 193, 214, 226, 244, 247, 261, 267, 291, 293
Sorcery, 127
Spain: and League, 54, 86, 108, 122, 157, 211; war with, 272, 275, 279, 284, 285; peace with, 286, 288–289
Spaniards in France, 103, 115, 191, 195, 198, 199–200, 202, 211, 217, 219, 222, 225, 226–227, 231, 233, 234–236, 243, 251, 252, 254, 255, 257, 285, 288–290. *See also* Feria

INDEX

Stemmatum Lotharingiae, 94

Strozzi, Philip, 62, 75, 86–87

Students, 43, 69–70, 149, 150, 174, 271

Sully, Duke of. *See* Rosny

Suresne, Conference of, 228, 229, 231, 232

Sweden, 58

Swiss Cantons, 58, 84, 89. *See also* Henry III, foreign policy, Swiss Cantons

Tardif, Jean, 204, 208, 209, 210, 236

Tavannes, Vicomte de (Guillaume de Saux), 115

Third Party, 225

Thou, Augustin II de, lawyer, d. 1595; 50, 89

Thou, Christophe de, Premier Président, d. 1582; 50, 57, 65, 73, 88–89

Thou, Jacques-Auguste de, Président, historian, 169, 203, 269

Thou, Nicolas de, Bishop of Chartres, 89

Tours, Parlement of, 204, 259, 262

Trent, Council of, 86, 118, 239, 291

Turks, 41, 83, 244

Union, oath of, 186–187

Urban VII, Pope, 195

Vallée, Geoffrey, 33

Valois: family relations, 37, 62, 70, 95, 99, 102–103, 111; House of, 109, 124, 182. *See also* Catherine de Medici, reconciliation of children

Vendôme, Cardinal of. *See* Bourbon

Venice, 34, 111, 273, 274, 291

Versoris, Pierre, 57

Vervins, Peace of, 288

Vicq, Dominique de, Governor of St. Denis, 202, 230, 250, 276

Vienna, 34, 244

Villeroy, Sieur de (Nicolas de Neufville), Secretary of State and diplomat, 113, 150, 154, 159, 185, 225

Vitry, Marquis of, Louis de l'Hospital, Governor of Meaux, 201, 212, 217, 247, 248, 251

Warwick, Earl of, 107

Weather, 41, 47, 70, 78, 89, 91, 93, 98, 106, 130, 138, 203, 216, 217, 225, 226, 243, 274, 294